Civil RICO
A Definitive Guide

Second Edition

Gregory P. Joseph

Section of Litigation

Defending Liberty
Pursuing Justice

Cover design by ABA Publishing.

The materials contained herein represent the opinions and views of the authors and/or the editors, and should not be construed to be the views or opinions of the law firms or companies with whom such persons are in partnership with, associated with, or employed by, nor of the American Bar Association or the Section of Litigation unless adopted pursuant to the bylaws of the Association.

Nothing contained in this book is to be considered as the rendering of legal advice, either generally or in connection with any specific issue or case. Nor do these materials purport to explain or interpret any specific bond or policy, or any provisions thereof, issued by any particular insurance company, or to render insurance or other professional advice. Readers are responsible for obtaining advice from their own lawyer or other professional. This book and any forms and agreements herein are intended for educational and informational purposes only.

Printed in the United States of America.

04 03 02 01 00 5 4 3 2 1

Joseph, Gregory P., 1951-
Civil RICO : a definitive guide / Gregory P. Joseph.--2nd ed.
p. cm.
Includes index.
ISBN 1-57073-765-7
1. Civil RICO actions. I. Title.

KF9375 .J67 1999
347.73'53--dc21

99-056268

Discounts are available for books ordered in bulk. Special consideration is given to state bars, CLE programs, and other bar-related organizations. Inquire at Book Publishing, ABA Publishing, American Bar Association, 750 North Lake Shore Drive, Chicago, Illinois 60611.

www.ababooks.org

Summary of Contents

Contents

For Barbara

Foreword to the Second Edition

This edition updates the text to include developments since 1992. The Supreme Court has delivered several RICO opinions in the interim, and the courts of appeals have rendered scores more. Congress has amended both the RICO act and significant predicate act statutes.

The goal of this edition is to refresh the focus in light of these developments. While there has been some clarification of the law in the eight years since the first edition of this book was published, it is probably more accurate to say that many issues have simply shifted in focus rather than been resolved.

Judge Jed S. Rakoff, a noted RICO scholar before assuming the bench, once observed that, until 1992, "the Supreme Court's attitude toward RICO was that of a scolding aunt toward an unruly nephew: 'Rico's an ugly little beast but it's up to his father [Congress] to discipline him.'" Rakoff, *The Supreme Court Scolds RICO,* 15 RICO L. REP. 668 (1992). Since 1992, however, the Supreme Court and Congress have been distinctly more active in refining the scope of the statute's civil remedy, and this edition takes these developments into account.

The courts daily wrestle with one fundamental problem: "When a statute [specifically, RICO] is broadly worded in order to prevent loopholes from being drilled in it by ingenious lawyers, there is a danger of its being applied to situations absurdly remote from the concerns of the statute's framers." *Fitzgerald v. Chrysler Corp,* 116 F.3d 225, 226 (7th Cir. 1997) (Posner, Ch.J.). Virtually every issue discussed in this book manifests this concern—and the parallel concern that too stinting a civil reading could restrict intended criminal applications. The goal of this book is to identify the salient issues to facilitate clarity in the analysis and resolution of RICO disputes.

G.P.J.

Preface

This book is designed to provide a concise and readable analysis of the major legal issues arising in civil actions litigated under the Racketeer Influenced and Corrupt Organizations Act, 18 U.S.C. § 1961–68. Principal attention is focused on opinions of the United States Supreme Court and federal courts of appeals. Whether the law is clear or the circuits are in conflict (a commonplace occurrence), the primary authorities are reported and analyzed with minimal editorial comment. To the limited extent that any suggestions are offered toward resolving open issues, they are clearly indicated to be just that.

Justice Scalia has observed that, with Supreme Court guidance, one discrete aspect of RICO law (the pattern requirement) "produced the widest and most persistent Circuit split on an issue of federal law in recent memory." *H. J. Inc. v. Northwestern Bell Tel. Co.*, 492 U.S. 229, 251 (1989) (Scalia, J., concurring). As this book reflects, a good number of RICO issues (including the pattern requirement) are still competing for this distinction. The purpose of this book is to assist lawyers practicing in such an environment by identifying those issues that are settled, segregating those that are not, and addressing practical problems posed by the lingering uncertainty of outcome-determinative legal standards.

G.P.J.

CHAPTER 1

Introduction

§ 1. Four Causes of Action

The civil RICO cause of action is created by 18 U.S.C. § 1964(c): "Any person injured in his business or property by reason of a violation of section 1962 of this chapter may sue therefor in any appropriate United States district court and shall recover threefold the damages he sustains and the cost of the suit, including a reasonable attorney's fee. . . ." This single sentence has generated an avalanche of litigation. The reference to section 1962 incorporates four separate causes of action arising out of various aspects of racketeering activity (statutorily labeled "prohibited activities").

- **Investment.** Under section 1962(a), it is unlawful to invest any income derived from a pattern of racketeering activity (or through collection of an unlawful debt)[1] to acquire any interest in, or to establish or operate, any enterprise that is engaged in or affects interstate or foreign commerce.[2]
- **Acquisition.** Under section 1962(b), it is unlawful to acquire or maintain any interest in, or control of, any enterprise that is engaged in or affects interstate or foreign commerce through a pattern of racketeering activity or collection of an unlawful debt.[3]
- **Participation.** Under section 1962(c), it is unlawful for any person to conduct or participate in the conduct of the affairs of an enterprise that is engaged in or affects interstate or

---

1. Allegations of the "collection of unlawful debt" are extremely rare in civil RICO cases. Throughout this book, although it is separately discussed (*see, e.g.*, § 11(E), *infra*), the emphasis is placed on the "pattern of racketeering activity" jurisprudence.

2. *See* §§ 6–7, *infra*, for a discussion of standing to sue under § 1962(a), and § 12, *infra*, for the elements of a cause of action under that provision.

3. *See* §§ 6 and 8, *infra*, for a discussion of standing to sue under § 1962(b), and § 13, *infra*, for the elements of a cause of action under that provision.

foreign commerce through a pattern of racketeering activity or collection of an unlawful debt.[4]

- **Conspiracy.** Under section 1962(d), it is unlawful for any person to conspire to violate any of the provisions of section 1962(a)–(c).[5]

An extensive body of law has grown up around the questions of standing,[6] injury and damages,[7] equitable relief,[8] causation,[9] and a variety of pleading and practice issues.[10] The question of constitutionality is not yet definitively resolved,[11] and there exist complicated questions involving aider and abettor liability and vicarious liability.[12]

§ 2. History and Purpose

The Racketeer Influenced and Corrupt Organizations Act (RICO) was enacted as Title IX of the Organized Crime Control Act of 1970, Pub. L. No. 91-452, 84 Stat. 922, 941 (1970). Originally, the Senate bill (S. 30, 91st Cong., 2d Sess. (1970) limited civil remedies to injunctive actions brought by the United States, but the House added a treble-damages remedy modeled on section 4 of the Clayton Act. H. R. 1549, 91st Cong., 2d Sess., 116 Cong. Rec. 35,363-64 (1970).[13] The Senate acquiesced in this amendment. 116 Cong. Rec. 36,296 (1970). Due to this Clayton Act pedigree, the courts frequently turn to Clayton Act case law for guidance in construing RICO.[14]

---

4. *See* §§ 6 and 9, *infra,* for a discussion of standing to sue under § 1962(c), and § 14, *infra,* for the elements of a cause of action under that provision.

5. *See* §§ 6 and 10, *infra,* for a discussion of standing to sue under § 1962(d), and § 15, *infra,* for the elements of a cause of action under that provision.

6. *See* chapter 3 for a general discussion of standing under § 1964.

7. *See* §§ 6(A)(2)–(3) and 18–19, *infra.*

8. *See* § 20, *infra.*

9. *See* § 6(A)(4), *infra.*

10. *See generally* chapter 7, *infra.*

11. *See* chapter 10, *infra.*

12. *See* chapter 5, *infra.*

13. *See* Dickerson, *Curtailing Civil RICO's Long Reach: Establishing New Boundaries for Venue and Personal Jurisdiction Under 18 U.S.C. § 1965,* 75 Neb. L. Rev. 476, 484 (1996) (citing first edition of this **Treatise** [hereinafter "**Treatise**"]).

14. *See, e.g.,* Agency Holding Corp. v. Malley-Duff & Assocs., Inc., 483 U.S. 143 (1987); Shearson/American Express, Inc. v. McMahon, 482 U.S. 220 (1987); Comment, *Holmes v. Securities Investor Protection Corp.,* 18 Del. J. Corp. L. 923, 927 (1993) (citing **Treatise**).

As the title of the statute suggests, the Organized Crime Control Act of 1970 sought "the eradication of organized crime in the United States" by providing enhanced and novel legal tools, including RICO.[15] Apart from governmental applications, civil RICO cases rarely have anything to do with these ends. The eleventh-hour addition of a civil remedy not confined to governmental plaintiffs may help to explain the volume of issues that Congress never expected or considered.[16] While RICO is designed to combat the infiltration into and corruption of America's legitimate business community by organized crime, Pub. L. No. 91-452, 84 Stat. at 943 (1970), it is only occasionally put to these ends in civil cases today.

§ 3. Liberal Construction

Section 904(a) of the Organized Crime Control Act of 1970 expressly provided that "[t]he provisions of this title [RICO] shall be liberally construed to effectuate its remedial purposes." 1990 U.S. Code Cong. & Admin. News 1104. This admonition has been taken to heart by the courts, including the Supreme Court. *See, e.g., Sedima, S.P.R.L. v. Imrex Co., Inc.*, 473 U.S. 479 (1985) ("if Congress' liberal-construction mandate is to be applied anywhere, it is in § 1964, where RICO's remedial purposes are most evident"; rejecting attempts to engraft certain procedural limitations on civil RICO actions); *Tafflin v. Levitt*, 493 U.S. 455 (1990) (applying a liberal construction in endorsing concurrent state court jurisdiction over civil RICO claims).

There is always a tension between a liberal construction of a statute and a tendency to overextend it to accomplish ends that the statute was never designed to achieve. *Compare*, for example, *Grider v. Texas Oil & Gas Corp.*, 868 F.2d 1147 (10th Cir. 1989) and *Ouaknine v. McFarlane*, 897 F.2d 75 (2d Cir. 1990) (both rejecting the argument that the legislatively mandated liberal construction requires expansion of section 1962(a) beyond the "investment use" doctrine (discussed in § 7, *infra*) with *Busby v. Crown Supply, Inc.*, 896 F.2d 833 (4th Cir. 1990) (accepting the same argument). Few courts would disagree with the proposition that "the general principle that RICO is to be accorded a liberal interpretation cannot

---

15. *Statement of Findings and Purpose*, Pub. L. No. 91-452, 84 Stat. 922 (1970), *reprinted in* 1970 U.S. CODE CONG. & ADMIN. NEWS 1073.

16. *See* Kurzweil, *Criminal & Civil RICO: Traditional Canons of Statutory Interpretation and the Liberal Construction Clause*, 30 COLUM. J.L. & SOC. PROBS. 41, 60 (1996) (quoting **Treatise**); Note, *RICO*, 17 U. Ark. Little Rock L.J. 343, 353 (1995) (citing **Treatise**).

justify expanding [the statute] beyond the limits of [its] own language," *Grider,* 868 F.2d at 1150, or that to do so would sometimes "permit abrogation of the explicit words of the statute," *Ouaknine,* 897 F.2d at 83. The problem is always determining when the expansion is undue and at what point the explicit words of the statute are effectively abrogated. As the Supreme Court observed in *Reves v. Ernst & Young,* 507 U.S. 170, 183–184 (1993): "RICO's 'liberal construction' clause . . . seeks to ensure that Congress' intent is not frustrated by an overly narrow reading of the statute, but it is not an invitation to apply RICO to new purposes that Congress never intended. Nor does the clause help us to determine what purposes Congress had in mind."

In this respect, courts have not always sufficiently heeded the fact that the liberal construction called for in section 904(a) is one that will "effectuate [RICO's] remedial purposes." Strictly speaking, these purposes—as set forth in the statement of findings of the statute—are primarily "the eradication of organized crime" because of the serious threat that it poses to American society. 1970 U.S. Code Cong. & Admin. News 1073. Often, it is considered necessary to construe the statute liberally in cases not involving organized crime in order to effectuate the intended remedial purpose, since any stinting construction may also apply in organized crime prosecutions. However, not every civil case has criminal implications or requires a liberal construction to effectuate the statutory intent.[17]

There is, moreover, a salient statutory distinction between civil and criminal RICO actions—namely, section 1964(c). Section 1962 describes behavior that is considered dangerous to society in and of itself. For that reason, criminal penalties automatically attach. Section 1964(c), however, interposes a four-factor standing test before civil liability accrues for the same conduct.[18] The distinguishing function of section 1964(c)—and its injury and causation components—underlay numerous civil standing requirements unparalleled in the criminal law, such as the investment-injury requirement of section 1962(a);[19] the acquisition-injury requirement of section 1962(b);[20] the proximate cause jurisprudence of section 1962(c);[21] and the requirement of injury from a predicate

17. *See, e.g.,* Shapiro, *Attorney Liability under RICO § 1962(c) after Reves v. Ernst & Young,* 61 U. CHI. L. REV. 1153, 1155 (citing **Treatise**).

18. *See* § 6, *infra.*

19. *See* § 7, *infra.*

20. *See* § 8, *infra.*

21. *See* § 6(A)(4), *infra.*

(overt) act under section 1962(d).[22] The significance of section 1964(c) for statutory construction purposes is not always considered as fully as it ought to be. *See, e.g.*, *Beck v. Prupris*, 162 F.3d 1090 (11th Cir. 1998) (Tjoflat, J.) ("for a criminal conspiracy charge, there is no need to prove that the conspiracy led to an injury-causing criminal activity. In a civil context, however, the purpose of a conspiracy claim is to impute liability—to make X jointly liable with D for what D did to P. . . . Those courts that have recognized a [section 1962(d) conspiracy] claim [where the injury was not the product of a predicate act] usually rely on criminal RICO cases, thus demonstrating a possible confusion about the separate functions of civil and criminal conspiracy claims"), *cert. granted*, 119 S. Ct. 2046 (1999).

---

22. *See* § 10, *infra*.

CHAPTER 2

Jurisdiction and Venue

§ 4. Jurisdiction

A. Federal

1. Generally Federal subject matter jurisdiction is conferred by section 1964(c), which creates the civil RICO cause of action.[1] Personal jurisdiction is conferred by section 1965,[2] which authorizes nationwide service of process. *Stauffacher v. Bennett*, 969 F.2d 455 (7th Cir.), *cert. denied*, 506 U.S. 1034 (1992) ("The RICO statute authorizes nationwide service of process"); *accord Lisak v. Mercantile Bancorp, Inc.*, 834 F.2d 668 (7th Cir. 1987), *cert. denied*, 485 U.S. 1007 (1988); *Butcher's Union Local No. 498 v. SDC Inv., Inc.*, 788 F.2d 535 (9th Cir. 1986).

Section 1965(a), the principal venue provision, permits a party to institute a civil RICO action in any district in which a defendant "resides, is found, has an agent, or transacts his affairs."[3] Section

---

1. § 1964(c) provides that "[a]ny person injured in his business or property by reason of a violation of section 1962 of this chapter may sue therefor in any appropriate United States district court and shall recover threefold the damages he sustains and the cost of the suit, including a reasonable attorney's fee. . . ."

2. § 1965(a)–(b) and (d) provide that

   (a) Any civil action or proceeding under this chapter against any person may be instituted in the district court of the United States for any district in which such person resides, is found, has an agent, or transacts his affairs.

   (b) In any action under section 1964 of this chapter in any district court of the United States in which it is shown that the ends of justice require that other parties residing in any other district be brought before the court, the court may cause such parties to be summoned, and process for that purpose may be served in any judicial district of the United States by the marshal thereof.

   . . .

   (d) All other process in any action or proceeding under this chapter may be served on any person in any judicial district in which such person resides, is found, has an agent, or transacts his affairs.

3. See § 5(A), *infra*, for a discussion of these criteria.

1965(b) provides that, as long as one defendant is subject to service in a district, additional parties residing in other districts may be brought before the forum court, in the court's discretion, to the extent that "the ends of justice require." Section 1965(c) governs subpoenas. Section 1965(d) provides that "all other process" may be served in any judicial district in which the target resides, is found, has an agent, or transacts affairs.

There is a split in the circuits as to the proper interpretation of section 1965. The Second, Fifth, and Ninth Circuits hold that personal jurisdiction attaches only if at least one defendant "resides, is found, has an agent, or transacts his affairs" in the district within section 1965(a) (or, presumably, is appropriately before the court pursuant to a state long-arm statute or the general federal venue provision).[4] *See, e.g., PT United Can Co. v. Crown Cork & Seal Co.,* 138 F.3d 65 (2d Cir. 1998) ("a civil RICO action can only be brought in a district court where personal jurisdiction based on minimum contacts is established as to at least one defendant"); *Caldwell v. Palmetto State Sav. Bank,* 811 F.2d 916 (5th Cir. 1987) (at least one defendant must be subject to jurisdiction within the strictures of section 1965(a) before the nationwide service provision of section 1965(b) may be triggered); *Butcher's Union Local No. 498 v. SDC Inv., Inc.,* 788 F.2d at 539 ("For nationwide service to be imposed under section 1965(b), the court must have personal jurisdiction over at least one of the participants in the alleged multidistrict conspiracy and the plaintiff must show that there is no other district in which a court will have personal jurisdiction over all of the alleged co-conspirators"). The Eleventh Circuit, in contrast, holds that section 1965(d) "provides for service [of a summons] in any judicial district in which [any] defendant is found" and thereby "becomes the statutory basis for personal jurisdiction" nationwide. *Republic of Panama v. BCCI Holdings (Luxembourg) S.A.,* 119 F.3d 935, 942 (11th Cir. 1997). The Seventh Circuit view is that personal jurisdiction is conferred exclusively by section 1965(b), which authorizes nationwide service of process without regard to section 1965(a), which is viewed as purely a venue provision. *Lisak v. Mercantile Bancorp, Inc.,* 834 F.2d 668 (7th Cir. 1987), *cert. denied,* 485 U.S. 1007 (1988) ("§ 1965(b) creates personal jurisdiction by authorizing service").

This issue warrants Supreme Court review. The majority approach accords a plain meaning to all subsections of section 1965, reading subsection (a) as focused on commencement of the action against the initial defendant; subsection (b) as dealing with

---

4. See §§ 4(A)(2) and 5(A), *infra.*

commencement as to other (nonresident) defendants; subsection (c) as essentially superfluous to the analysis, since it concerns subpoenas only; and subsection (d) as addressing process "other" than the summons (which is covered in subsections (a) and (b)) and subpoenas (the subject of subsection (c)). The Eleventh Circuit's is not a labored reading—it simply construes subsection (d) as referring to process "other" than subpoenas, the topic of subsection (c), and subsections (a) and (b) as venue provisions. One problem: the Eleventh Circuit analysis appears to render subsection (b) nugatory (effectively superseded by subsection (d)). The Seventh Circuit's construction is tenable and leads to much the same result as the majority approach: dismissal will result under either analysis if section 1965(a) (or a state law counterpart) is not satisfied.

Whether the defect is viewed as creating a lack of proper venue or jurisdiction matters: the objection must be timely and accurately asserted or will be waived by operation of rule 12(h)(1).[5] *See, e.g., Omni Video Games, Inc. v. Wing Co., Ltd.,* 754 F. Supp. 261 (D.R.I. 1991) (venue objection waived where dismissal motion—predicated on alleged lack of personal jurisdiction—failed to raise it).

2. Service of Process Because of the close linkage between personal jurisdiction and service of process,[6] it is important to bear in mind that section 1965 does not provide the sole source of authority for effecting service. Service may also be effected in accordance with state law, pursuant to Fed. R. Civ. P. 4(f). *See, e.g., Combs v. Bakker,* 886 F.2d 673 (4th Cir. 1989) ("Personal jurisdiction . . . may be grounded in state long-arm (or other) jurisdiction statutes in civil RICO cases as in federal question cases generally"); *Brink's Mat Ltd. v. Diamond,* 906 F.2d 1519 (11th Cir. 1990) ("The RICO service of process provision is permissive, not restrictive").

---

5. FED. R. CIV. P. 12(h)(1) provides that "[a] defense of lack of jurisdiction over the person [or] improper venue . . . is waived (A) if omitted from a motion in the circumstances described in subdivision (g), or (B) if it is neither made by motion under this rule nor included in a responsive pleading or an amendment thereof permitted by Rule 15(a) to be made as a matter of course." Rule 12(g) provides that, if a party makes a rule 12 motion "but omits therefrom any defense or objection then available to the party which this rule permits to be raised by motion, the party shall not thereafter make a motion based on the defense or objection so omitted," with certain irrelevant exceptions (e.g., failure to state a claim).

6. Butcher's Union Local No. 498, 788 F.2d 535 (9th Cir. 1986) ("A federal court obtains personal jurisdiction over a defendant if it is able to serve process on him"); *see also* Omni Capital Int'l, Ltd. v. Rudolf Wolff & Co., Ltd., 484 U.S. 97 (1987) (that "a defendant is amenable to service [is] a prerequisite to [a federal court's] exercise of personal jurisdiction" over that defendant).

This state law alternative is significant because section 1965 does not permit service beyond the borders of the United States. State law provisions authorizing service abroad fill this gap. *See, e.g., Stauffacher v. Bennett,* 969 F.2d 455 (7th Cir.), *cert. denied,* 506 U.S. 1034 (1992) ("The RICO statute authorizes nationwide service of process, but not international service. For that the RICO plaintiff must rely on the long-arm statute of the state in which he files his suit") (citations omitted); *Brink's Mat Ltd. v. Diamond,* 906 F.2d at 1523 ("In light of Congress's evident interest to broaden the scope of amenability to service of process through [section 1965(b)], we decline to interpret it as restricting state law authority . . . to effect service . . . abroad").

3. Due Process Under section 1964(c), RICO defendants are subject to federal question jurisdiction. Section 1965 in turn authorizes nationwide service of process. In light of these provisions, due process requirements are satisfied if the defendant's contacts with the United States as a whole—not with the forum—satisfy the "minimum contacts" test of *International Shoe Co. v. Washington,* 326 U.S. 310 (1945). This is sometimes described as a "national contacts" test. *See generally United Rope Distrib., Inc. v. Seatriumph Marine Corp.,* 930 F.2d 532 (7th Cir. 1991); *Herbstein v. Bruetman,* 768 F. Supp. 79 (S.D.N.Y. 1991); *American Trade Partners, L.P. v. A-1 Int'l Importing Enters., Ltd.,* 755 F. Supp. 1292 (E.D. Pa. 1990); *Federal Sav. & Loan Ins. Corp. v. Provo Excelsior Ltd.,* 664 F. Supp. 1405 (D. Utah 1987).

4. Extraterritorial Application The phrase "extraterritorial application" has at least three meanings when used in connection with a federal statute. First, extraterritorial application may refer to the ability to effect service of process beyond the borders of the United States. As discussed above,[7] extraterritorial service of process may be effected in RICO actions in accordance with state law, under Fed. R. Civ. P. 4(f).

Second, extraterritorial application may refer to the amenability of foreign defendants—that is, noncitizens of the United States—located abroad to lawsuits under the statute in the United States courts. A foreign defendant who can effectively be served is subject to the personal jurisdiction of the federal courts if there exists a constitutionally sufficient nexus between the

7. See § 4(A)(2), *supra.*

defendant and the forum. *Brink's Mat Ltd. v. Diamond,* 906 F.2d 1519 (11th Cir. 1990).[8]

Apart from reliance on state long-arm statutes and the criteria stated in section 1965,[9] additional theories for securing personal jurisdiction over foreign defendants in RICO actions include (1) the absent co-conspirator doctrine, effectively a common law analog to section 1965(b), under which a court may assert jurisdiction over an absent party based on a co-conspirator's presence before the court, *see, e.g., Soltex Polymer Corp. v. Fortex Indus., Inc.,* 590 F. Supp. 1453 (E.D.N.Y. 1984), *aff'd,* 832 F.2d 1325 (2d Cir. 1987) (factual basis lacking); and (2) perhaps an "effects doctrine" under which personal jurisdiction might be established by demonstrating that a foreign defendant's acts had a foreseeable impact within the United States. *See generally North South Fin. Corp. v. Al-Turki,* 100 F.3d 1046 (2d Cir. 1996) (declining to specify whether a "conduct," "effects," or other test should be used to determine RICO jurisdiction but suggesting that: "It may be that the effects-oriented approach borrowed from antitrust cases is an . . . appropriate test, especially since 'the civil action provision of RICO was patterned after the Clayton Act'") (citation omitted); *Kauthar SDN BHD v. Sternberg,* 149 F.3d 659 (7th Cir. 1998), *cert. denied,* 119 S.Ct. 890 (1999) (like *North South,* declining to specify test; citing *North South* for the probable inappropriateness of a "conduct" test); Goldsmith & Rinne, *Civil RICO, Foreign Defendants and "ET,"* 73 Minn. L. Rev. 1023 (1989).

Third, extraterritorial application may refer to the reach of an American statute, such as RICO, to conduct occurring abroad. The RICO statute may be applied to conduct occurring in part outside the United States if there is a sufficient nexus between the RICO pattern and the United States. *Alfadda v. Fenn,* 935 F.2d 475 (2d Cir.), *cert. denied,* 502 U.S. 1005 (1991) (since "'the heart of any RICO complaint is the allegation of a *pattern* of racketeering activity' . . . predicate acts which occurred primarily in the United States . . . serve as a basis of subject matter jurisdiction for the RICO claims"); *North South Fin. Corp. v. Al-Turki,* 100 F.3d 1046 (2d Cir. 1996) (declining to specify precise test for determining jurisdiction; "we have no doubt that the district court was without

8. The constitutional imperative is satisfied if the defendant's contacts with the United States as a whole satisfy the traditional "minimum contacts" test. *See* § 4(A)(3), *supra.*

9. *See generally* the discussion in §§ 4(A)(1)–(2), *supra.* It should be observed that a domestic subsidiary of a foreign company may be the parent's "agent" (a § 1965(a) criterion) if the relationship between the two is sufficiently close to justify the exercise of jurisdiction over the parent. See Huang v. Sentinel Gov't Sec., 657 F. Supp. 485 (S.D.N.Y 1987) (insufficient domination and control by parent to permit assertion of jurisdiction over parent).

jurisdiction over a controversy involving foreign victims who sold a foreign entity to foreign defrauders in a foreign transaction lacking significant and material contact with the United States"); *Butte Mining P.L.C. v. Smith*, 76 F.3d 287 (9th Cir. 1996) (where underlying "securities fraud . . . occurred completely outside the jurisdiction of the United States" and plaintiff only generically alleges "that the mail and wire were used 'to further' the securities fraud" within the United States, "[t]here is no reason to extend the jurisdictional scope of RICO to make criminal the use of the mail and wire in the United States as part of an alleged fraud outside the United States. We do not suppose that Congress in enacting RICO had the purpose of punishing frauds by aliens abroad even if peripheral preparations were undertaken by them here"); *see also Republic of Philippines v. Marcos*, 818 F.2d 1473 (9th Cir. 1987), *vacated on other grounds*, 862 F.2d 1355 (9th Cir. 1988) (en banc), *cert. denied*, 490 U.S. 1035 (1989). This category of conduct—occurring primarily within the United States—may suffice to permit the court to assert personal jurisdiction over any foreign defendant who participated in it.[10]

5. Fiduciary Shield Doctrine Under the fiduciary shield doctrine, if an individual has contacts with the forum state only by virtue of his or her acts as a fiduciary (for example, an officer or director of a corporation), that individual may be personally shielded from the exercise of personal jurisdiction or venue in the forum state on the basis of that conduct. A creature of state law, this doctrine has been held inapplicable in RICO cases (1) because the RICO statute provides for nationwide service of process, (2) because it extends personal jurisdiction to the limits of due process, and (3) where the vehicle utilized to commit the RICO violation is the entity (for example, the corporation) of which the defendant is a fiduciary. *See generally Merchants Nat'l Bank v. Safrabank*, No. 90-4194-R, 1991 U.S. Dist. LEXIS 12380 (D. Kan. Aug. 28, 1991); *American Trade Partners, L.P. v. A-1 Int'l Importing Enters., Ltd.*, 755 F. Supp. 1292 (E.D. Pa. 1990); *Obee v. Teleshare, Inc.*, 725 F. Supp. 913 (E.D. Mich. 1989); *Abeloff v. Barth*, 119 F.R.D. 315 (D.

10. Among the unique, nonjurisdictional defenses that may defeat extraterritorial RICO claims are (1) the doctrine of sovereign compulsion, which is a complete defense if the defendant can demonstrate that a foreign government compelled the challenged misconduct (*see, e.g.*, Interamerican Ref. Corp. v. Texaco Maracaibo, Inc., 307 F. Supp. 1291 (D. Del. 1970)); (2) sovereign immunity, to the extent that the doctrine survives the Foreign Sovereign Immunities Act, 28 U.S.C. § 1602-11; and (3) the act of state doctrine, under which United States courts will decline to become embroiled in the affairs of a foreign nation whose acts are challenged. *See, e.g.*, Republic of Philippines v. Marcos, 862 F.2d 1355 (9th Cir. 1988) (en banc), *cert. denied*, 490 U.S. 1035 (1989) (finding defense factually inapposite).

Mass. 1988); *Rolls-Royce Motors, Inc v. Charles Schmitt & Co.*, 657 F. Supp. 1040 (S.D.N.Y. 1987); *Nordic Bank PLC v. Trend Group*, 619 F. Supp. 542 (S.D.N.Y 1985).

B. State Court Jurisdiction

State courts have concurrent jurisdiction over civil RICO claims under the Supreme Court's decision in *Tafflin v. Levitt*, 493 U.S. 455 (1990). The *Tafflin* Court perceived no "clear incompatibility" between state court jurisdiction over civil RICO actions and federal interests. On the contrary, it concluded that permitting state courts to entertain RICO claims would facilitate the enforcement of the rights afforded by the RICO statute and promote the broad remedial purposes envisioned by Congress. The Court did not perceive any significant danger of inconsistent application of federal criminal law. It observed that federal courts would not be bound by state court interpretations of the federal offenses constituting RICO predicate acts, and it remarked that state court judgments misconstruing federal criminal law would be subject to its review.

The existence of concurrent state and federal jurisdiction over RICO claims raises several issues relating to, among other things, removal, remand, abstention, arbitration (discussed in this chapter), and collateral estoppel (*see* § 30(B), *infra*).

C. Removal and Remand

If a plaintiff elects to commence RICO litigation in state court, as *Tafflin*[11] permits, the defendant may remove the action to federal court, in compliance with 28 U.S.C. §§ 1441–52. *See generally Lichtenberger v. Prudential-Bache Sec., Inc.*, 737 F. Supp. 43 (S.D. Tex. 1990) (declining to infer congressional intent to prohibit removal); *accord Weisman v. Fribush*, 911 F.2d 726, No. 89-154 (4th Cir. 1990) (unpublished opinion). Section 1441(a) permits removal of any civil action brought in a state court of which federal district courts have original jurisdiction.[12] Under section 1441(b), removal is permitted without regard to citizenship of the parties in federal question cases, such as RICO actions.[13]

---

11. 493 U.S. at 455.

12. § 1441(a) provides that

> [e]xcept as otherwise expressly provided by Act of Congress, any civil action brought in a State court of which the district courts of the United States have original jurisdiction, may be removed by the defendant . . . to the district court of the United States for the district and division embracing the place where such action is pending.

13. § 1441(b) provides that "[a]ny civil action of which the district courts have original

Section 1441(c) permits removal where, as in the typical RICO case, a removable claim is coupled with one or more otherwise nonremovable claims.[14] Under the 1990 amendment to section 1441(c), however, the federal district judge has the discretion to remand to state court "all matters in which state law predominates." *See, e.g., Holland v. World Omni Leasing, Inc.*, 764 F. Supp. 1442 (N.D. Ala. 1991) (remanding RICO claim "so intertwined with, and so indistinguishable from, the state law claims as to be very difficult, if not impossible, to treat separately"). Whether to remand is a matter vested in the trial judge's discretion. *Chamberlain v. State Farm Mut. Auto. Ins. Co.*, No. 90-7070, 1990 U.S. Dist. LEXIS 16646 (E.D. Pa. Dec. 7, 1990) (articulating presumption against remand).

D. Deferral Doctrines

The federal courts have developed a series of deferral doctrines under which they may decline to adjudicate cases brought before them even though they have jurisdiction. In appropriate circumstances, various abstention doctrines may apply in civil RICO actions. In addition, a federal court may find it appropriate to dismiss due to a plaintiff's failure to exhaust state or administrative remedies, for lack of primary jurisdiction, or under other established federal court doctrines.

1. Abstention If there are pending parallel state and federal actions in which substantially the same parties are contemporaneously litigating substantially the same issues, a federal district court may in "exceptional circumstances" abstain from exercising jurisdiction and defer to the state court. *See Colorado River Water Conservation Dist. v. United States*, 424 U.S. 800 (1976).

The court is to consider at least 10 factors in determining whether the exceptional-circumstances criterion is met: (1) whether the state court has assumed jurisdiction over pertinent property; (2) the convenience or inconvenience of the federal forum; (3) the desirability of avoiding piecemeal litigation; (4) the order in which jurisdiction was obtained by the concurrent forums; (5) the source

---

jurisdiction founded on a claim or right arising under the Constitution, treaties or laws of the United States shall be removable without regard to the citizenship or residence of the parties."

14. § 1441(c) provides that

> [w]henever a separate and independent claim or cause of action within the jurisdiction conferred by section 1331 of this title, is joined with one or more otherwise non-removable claims or causes of action, the entire case may be removed and the district court may determine all issues therein, or, in its discretion, may remand all matters in which state law predominates.

of governing law, state or federal; (6) the adequacy of state court action to protect the federal plaintiff's rights; (7) the relative progress of the state and federal proceedings; (8) the presence or absence of concurrent jurisdiction; (9) the availability of removal; and (10) any vexatious or contrived nature of the federal claim. *See, e.g., LaDuke v. Burlington N. RR,* 879 F.2d 1556 (7th Cir. 1989); *Romine v. CompuServe Corp.,* 160 F.3d 337 (6th Cir. 1998).

No single factor is determinative. The weight to be accorded to each depends on the circumstances before the court. The factors are "to be applied in a pragmatic, flexible manner with a view to the realities of the case at hand." *Moses H. Cone Memorial Hosp. v. Mercury Constr. Corp.,* 460 U.S. 1 (1983).

In *Quackenbush v. Allstate Ins. Co.,* 517 U.S. 706 (1996), the Supreme Court ruled that, in a damages action, the district court may order only a stay pending resolution of state proceedings and may not invoke abstention to dismiss the suit altogether. This limitation applies in civil RICO actions seeking damages. *DeMauro v. DeMauro,* 115 F.3d 94 (1st Cir. 1997). (As to the courts' power to award nonmonetary relief to private RICO litigants, *see* § 20, *infra.*)

Colorado River abstention may be appropriate regardless of whether the state court action explicitly includes a RICO claim. *See, e.g., Coopers & Lybrand v. Sun-Diamond Growers of Cal.,* 912 F.2d 1135 (9th Cir. 1990), *on remand,* No. C-88-4480-RFP, 1991 U.S. Dist. LEXIS 3995 (N.D. Cal. Mar. 28, 1991) (abstaining pursuant to *Colorado River* doctrine; no RICO claim stated in state court action); *see also P & P Mktg., Inc. v. Dinton,* 746 F. Supp. 1354 (N.D. Ill. 1990) (same; abstention appropriate upon the court's finding of "a substantial likelihood that the state-court action will dispose of all the claims presented in the federal case. This is especially true where [plaintiff's] civil RICO claim could have been brought as part of its state-court counterclaim and *res judicata* or collateral estoppel would likely operate to bar such a claim after resolution of these state-court proceedings").[15]

There is, however, a heavy presumption favoring the exercise of jurisdiction by the federal courts. Abstention is the exception, not the rule. *Colorado River,* 424 U.S. at 813. Even if the parties in both the state and federal actions are virtually identical, if different issues are raised and different remedies are sought, abstention may be unwarranted. *New Beckley Mining Corp. v. United Mine Workers of Am.,* 946 F.2d 1072 (4th Cir. 1991), *cert. denied,* 503 U.S. 971 (1992) (reversing abstention where (1) federal relief sought

---

15. For a discussion of res judicata and collateral estoppel in the RICO context as applied to state court litigation, *see* § 30(B), *infra.*

was monetary and state relief equitable and (2) the federal action was more encompassing than the state action in terms of factual misconduct alleged and legal violations asserted); *Rycoline Products, Inc. v. C & W Unlimited,* 109 F.3d 883 (3d Cir. 1997) ("Even assuming the two actions are sufficiently parallel for purposes of invoking the *Colorado River* doctrine, it would be an abuse of discretion for the court to abstain from hearing this matter").

A district court's decision to invoke *Colorado River* abstention necessarily contemplates that the federal court will have nothing further to do in resolving any substantive part of the case. As a result, the district court cannot simultaneously order *Colorado River* abstention and yet envisage further, concurrent federal proceedings on the RICO claim. *See Crotty v. Chicago Heights,* 857 F.2d 1170 (7th Cir. 1988).

Under the doctrine enunciated in *Burford v. Sun Oil Co.,* 319 U.S. 315 (1943), a federal court may abstain to avoid interfering in determinations of inherently local matters made by state courts or administrative agencies pursuant to complex state regulatory schemes. *Burford* abstention is appropriate (1) when there are difficult questions of state law bearing on policy problems of substantial public import or (2) where the exercise of federal review would be disruptive of state efforts to establish a coherent policy with respect to a matter of substantial public concern. *New Orleans Pub. Serv., Inc. v. Council of New Orleans,* 491 U.S. 350 (1989) (also noting the requirement that timely and adequate state court review be available where administrative agency action is at issue).

Burford abstention is the exception, not the rule, in RICO as in other actions. Where a regulated industry is involved, abstention is not ordinarily ordered in RICO cases unless the party before the federal court is itself the pertinent administrative agency, regulated entity, or an officer or agent of either. *See, e.g., University of Md. v. Peat, Marwick, Main & Co.,* 923 F.2d 265 (3d Cir. 1991) (reversing *Burford* abstention despite the pendency of state administrative proceedings involving the insolvent insurance company that the defendant had audited (allegedly in a fraudulent fashion); held, *Burford* abstention may be ordered "only when one of the parties to the action . . . is the insolvent insurer or its receiver, trustee, officers and the like"; also observing that *New Orleans Pub. Serv.* indicates that *Burford* abstention applies only to "a federal court sitting in equity," while civil RICO claims are legal, not equitable, in nature [*see* § 20, *infra*]); *Brandenburg v. Seidel,* 859 F.2d 1179 (4th Cir. 1988) (affirming *Burford* abstention to avoid disruption of comprehensive state regulatory apparatus for insolvent thrift institutions; former officers and directors of thrift institutions and regulatory agency named as defendants).

Even the presence of the regulated entity in the federal RICO action may be insufficient to warrant *Burford* abstention. A number of circuits have, for example, addressed the applicability of *Burford* abstention to public utilities faced with claims of fraud in rate-making proceedings. The Second and Eleventh Circuits have held *Burford* abstention is inappropriate in these circumstances. *County of Suffolk v. Long Island Lighting Co.*, 907 F.2d 1295 (2d Cir. 1990), and *Taffet v. Southern Co.*, 930 F.2d 847 (11th Cir. 1991), *vacated*, 958 F.2d 1514 (11th Cir. 1992), articulate the following as principal factors militating against *Burford* abstention: (1) the fact that RICO provides a federal basis for jurisdiction "raise[s] the level of justification needed for abstention" (*see Colorado River*, 424 U.S. at 815 n.21); (2) RICO actions primarily involve questions of federal, not state, law; (3) in examining the potential conflict between state and federal interests, RICO's treble-damage and lawyer's fee remedy, which cannot be awarded in any rate-making proceeding, demonstrate the gravity of the federal interest involved; and (4) the federal damages remedy will not disrupt the state's attempt to establish a coherent policy because, among other things, the federal court will not pass judgment upon a state regulatory decision nor act within the area of administrative expertise (in this context, prospective rate making). *County of Suffolk v. Long Island Lighting Co.*, 907 F.2d at 1308–9; *Taffet v. Southern Co.*, 930 F.2d at 853–54; *but see H.J. Inc. v. Northwestern Bell Tel. Co.*, No. 90-5245, 954 F.2d 485 (8th Cir.), *cert. denied*, 504 U.S. 957 (1992) (expressing contrary view in dicta; on remand from Supreme Court). Note that each of these factors is likely to apply in most regulated industry cases in which *Burford* abstention is urged.

The *Burford* doctrine also applies outside the sphere of regulated industries in certain areas traditionally regulated exclusively by the state courts. The First Circuit has thus concluded that *Burford* "abstention by use of a stay may be permissible where a RICO action is directed against concealment or transfer of property that is the very subject of a pending divorce proceeding." *DeMauro v. DeMauro*, 115 F.3d at 99. *See also Dubroff v. Dubroff*, 833 F.2d 557 (5th Cir. 1987) (ordering abstention because "there is perhaps no state administrative scheme in which federal court intrusions are less appropriate than domestic relations law"). *Compare Fregeau v. Instrument Assocs., Inc.*, No. 87 C 8924, 1988 U.S. Dist. LEXIS 14066 (N.D. Ill. Dec. 14, 1988) (*Burford* abstention inappropriate in domestic relations-related case where state court is incompetent to adjudicate the exclusively federal (ERISA) issues raised in the federal action).

2. Exhaustion and Other Doctrines The federal courts are equally strict in scrutinizing other proffered grounds for deferring to state courts or administrative agencies. In RICO actions brought against persons allegedly pillaging decedents' estates, for example, courts have rejected contentions that the plaintiffs are required to exhaust state probate remedies before filing their federal RICO actions. *Glickstein v. Sun Bank/Miami, N.A.*, 922 F.2d 666 (11th Cir. 1991) (rejecting exhaustion arguments under both federal and state law: "While Florida courts do have concurrent jurisdiction over RICO claims . . . the state does not have the power to impose a substantive exhaustion requirement on a federal claim"); *Gunther v. Dinger*, 547 F. Supp. 25 (S.D.N.Y. 1982) (labeling the exhaustion argument "frivolous on its face"). Primary jurisdiction, clear statement, and the remaining federal deferral doctrines apply in RICO cases but have not generally been urged successfully. *See, e.g., County of Suffolk v. Long Island Lighting Co.*, 907 F.2d at 1305–9; *Taffet v. Southern Co.*, 930 F.2d at 851–52, 854. *But see H.J. Inc. v. Northwestern Bell Tel. Co.*, 734 F. Supp. 879 (D. Minn. 1990), *aff'd*, No. 90-5245, 1992 U.S. App. LEXIS 452 (8th Cir. Jan. 15, 1992) (on remand from Supreme Court; applying filed-rate doctrine in dismissing action).

E. Arbitration

1. Arbitrability Civil RICO actions, including treble-damage claims, are arbitrable under the Supreme Court's decision in *Shearson/American Express, Inc. v. McMahon*, 482 U.S. 220 (1987) ("There is no hint in th[e] legislative debates that Congress intended for RICO treble damages claims to be excluded from the ambit of the [Federal] Arbitration Act," 9 U.S.C. §§ 1–16). The Supreme Court in *McMahon* adhered closely to the analysis it had applied in concluding that treble-damage antitrust claims were arbitrable in *Mitsubishi Motors Corp. v. Soler Chrysler-Plymouth, Inc.*, 473 U.S. 614 (1985). It emphasized the priority of the compensatory (as opposed to punitive) function of the RICO treble-damage remedy and concluded that the presence of the criminal provisions in the statute "do[es] not preclude arbitration of bona fide civil actions brought under § 1964(c)." *McMahon*, 482 U.S. at 240.

2. Agreement to Arbitrate Arbitration is a contractual matter. Whether a RICO claim is arbitrable turns solely on the question of whether the claim is within the scope of the parties' agreement to arbitrate. All doubts concerning the arbitrability issues, including problems concerning the construction of the language of the arbitration clause, are to be resolved in favor of arbitration. *Moses H. Cone Memorial Hosp. v. Mercury Constr. Corp.*, 460 U.S. 1 (1983).

Contractual arbitration clauses are commonly quite broad. The standard arbitration clause recommended by the American Arbitration Association, for example, calls for arbitration of "[a]ny controversy or claim arising out of or relating to this contract, or the breach thereof."[16]

Language of this breadth has consistently been construed as requiring arbitration of RICO claims that arise out of conduct relating to the parties' contractual relationship. *See, e.g., Genesco, Inc. v. T. Kakiuchi & Co.*, 815 F.2d 840 (2d Cir. 1987) (finding arbitrability where the "wire, mail and transportation fraud allegations which form the predicate acts of [the] RICO claim all derive from the parties' transactions under the sales agreements"; stressing that, "[i]f the allegations underlying the claims 'touch matters' covered by the parties' sales agreements, then those claims must be arbitrated, whatever the legal labels attached to them"); *Kerr-McGee Ref. Corp. v. M/T Triumph*, 924 F.2d 467 (2d Cir.), *cert. denied*, 502 U.S. 821 (1991) (holding that a broad arbitration clause mandates arbitration of RICO claims even where not all predicate acts forming part of the RICO pattern relate to the contract containing the arbitration clause).[17]

If a plaintiff sues not only another party to the contract containing the arbitration clause but third persons as well, the third persons cannot generally be compelled to arbitrate the dispute absent their agreement. That raises the prospect of multiple proceedings unless the arbitration is stayed. At the same time, the plaintiff ordinarily may not avoid its obligation to arbitrate by suing—in addition to the other party to the contract—third persons who have not agreed to arbitration. Yet, the scope of an arbitration clause between two parties may never have been intended to preclude litigation of multiparty RICO conspiracies in a single judicial forum. (*Cf.* § 5(C), *infra.*)

As these illustrations reflect, knotty arbitration issues have yet to be resolved in the RICO case law. The general arbitration case law is not fully developed in these areas either for that matter, and judicial resolution depends, in the last analysis, on the court's interpretation of the intended scope of the arbitration clause.

---

16. *See* AMERICAN ARBITRATION ASS'N, COMMERCIAL ARBITRATION RULES (Jan 1, 1999) (available on the Internet at http://www.adr.org/rules/commercial_rules.html).

17. In light of the potential breadth and ramifications of arbitration clauses, it has persuasively been argued that prudence dictates that special attention be paid when drafting them—with the possibility of a RICO claim in mind. *See generally* Offenkrantz, *Arbitrating RICO: Ten Years after* McMahon, 1997 COLUM. BUS. L. REV. 45. *See also* the discussion of judicial or arbitral appellate review at the end of this section.

The right to arbitrate may also be waived, as where a party does not seek to compel arbitration promptly but instead chooses to litigate in court before doing so (for example, to obtain the benefit of discovery). *See, e.g., Com-Tech Assocs., L.P. v. Computer Assocs. Int'l, Inc.*, 938 F.2d 1574 (2d Cir. 1991) ("To permit litigants to exercise their contractual rights to arbitrate . . . after they have deliberately chosen to participate in costly and extended litigation would defeat the purpose of arbitration").

3. Power to Award Treble or Punitive Damages Under the arbitration law of some states, arbitrators are not empowered to issue awards of punitive damages. *See, e.g., Garrity v. Lyle Stuart, Inc.*, 40 N.Y.2d 354, 353 N.E.2d 793, 386 N.Y.S.2d 831 (1976); *Anderson v. Nichols*, 359 S.E.2d 117 (W. Va. 1987); *Shaw v. Kuhnel & Assocs., Inc.*, 102 N.M. 607, 698 P.2d 880 (1985). At the same time, certain decisions hold that punitive damages may be awarded in addition to treble damages under RICO. (*See* § 19(A), *infra*.) Moreover, even treble damages may be construed as being punitive, or at least partially punitive, in nature. *See, e.g., Faircloth v. Finesod*, 938 F.2d 513 (4th Cir. 1991) ("In short, civil RICO is a square peg, and squeeze it as we may, it will never comfortably fit in the round holes of the remedy/penalty dichotomy"). The question, therefore, may arise as to whether an arbitrator is empowered to award either treble or punitive damages on a RICO claim.

The clear answer is that arbitrators are not inhibited, as a matter of arbitration law, from awarding either treble or punitive damages (to the extent that the latter may be legally permissible) in RICO actions. *See Kerr-McGee Ref. Corp. v. M/T Triumph*, 924 F.2d 467 (2d Cir. 1991); *Matter of NYSE Arbitration Between Fahnestock & Co. v. Waltman*, 935 F.2d 512 (2d Cir.), *cert. denied*, 502 U.S. 821 (1991). RICO provides federal question jurisdiction (which the Federal Arbitration Act does not) and preempts state arbitration law on this subject. *Fahnestock*, 935 F.2d at 519.

4. Judicial Review Judicial review of arbitration awards is ordinarily quite limited. *See generally* ABA Litigation section, *Commercial Arbitration for the 1990s* 95 (R. Medalie ed., 1991) ("In light of the strong federal policy in favor of voluntary commercial arbitration, judicial review of an arbitration award resulting from a motion to vacate or modify is 'severely limited'" (citations omitted)). Under section 10 of the Federal Arbitration Act, an award may be vacated only on grounds of fraud or corruption, evident partiality on the part of the arbitrators, arbitrator misconduct in refusing to hear relevant evidence or in otherwise prejudicing any party's rights, or the arbitrators' exceeding their powers.[18] State arbitration statutes—which may apply, as where the contract specifies a state court to enter judgment[19]—are generally to the same effect.[20]

The Supreme Court has indicated that the grounds for vacating an arbitration award are strictly confined to the statutorily specified categories.[21] That approach generally constricts judicial review of any arbitration award, but permits reversal on a showing of the arbitrators' "manifest disregard" of the law[22] or issuance of an award that is "arbitrary and capricious."[23] The "manifest disregard" standard has in recent years been applied more aggressively. *See generally* Posner, *Arbitration: Judicial Review of Arbitration Awards: Manifest Disregard of the Law*, 64 BROOKLYN L. REV. 471

---

18. § 10 of the Federal Arbitration Act, 9 U.S.C. § 10, provides that the federal district court in which the award was made may vacate it upon the application of any party only in the following circumstances:

(a) Where the award was procured by corruption, fraud, or undue means.
(b) Where there was evident partiality or corruption in the arbitrators, or either of them.
(c) Where the arbitrators were guilty of misconduct in refusing to postpone the hearing, upon sufficient cause shown, or in refusing to hear evidence pertinent and material to the controversy; or of any other misbehavior by which the rights of any party have been prejudiced.
(d) Where the arbitrators exceeded their powers, or so imperfectly executed them, that a mutual, final, and definite award upon the subject matter submitted was not made.

19. *See, e.g.*, 9 U.S.C. § 9.

20. *See, e.g.*, § 12(a) of the Uniform Arbitration Act, which authorizes a court to vacate an arbitration award only under the following circumstances:

(1) The award was procured by corruption, fraud, or other undue means;
(2) There was evident partiality by an arbitrator appointed as a neutral or corruption in any of the arbitrators or misconduct prejudicing the rights of any parties;
(3) The arbitrators exceeded their power;
(4) The arbitrators refused to postpone the hearing upon sufficient cause being shown therefor or refused to hear evidence material to the controversy or otherwise so conducted to hearing . . . as to prejudice substantially the rights of a party; or
(5) There was no arbitration agreement and the issue was not adversely determined in [judicial] proceedings . . . and the party did not participate in the arbitration hearing without raising the objection.

The Uniform Arbitration Act has been adopted in 34 states and the District of Columbia. *See* 7 U.L.A. 1 (1997; Supp. 1999). All but two of the remaining states, plus the Commonwealth of Puerto Rico, have modern arbitration laws similar in content to the Uniform Arbitration Act. *See* ABA LITIGATION SECTION, *COMMERCIAL ARBITRATION FOR THE 1990s* 178 (R. Medalie ed., 1991).

21. Wilko v. Swan, 346 U.S. 427, 436 & n.22 (1953).

22. *See, e.g.*, Shearson/American Express, Inc. v. McMahon, 482 U.S. 220, 231(1987); First Options of Chicago, Inc. v. Kaplan, 514 U.S. 938 (1995); Merrill Lynch, Pierce, Fenner & Smith, Inc. v. Bobker, 808 F.2d 930 (2d Cir. 1986); Jenkins v. Prudential-Bache Secs., Inc., 847 F.2d 631 (10th Cir. 1988).

23. *See, e.g.*, United States Postal Serv. v. National Ass'n of Letter Carriers, 847 F.2d 775 (11th Cir. 1988).

(1998) ("The courts are beginning to reject manifest disregard as the proper standard of review in favor of a broader standard of review of arbitration awards . . . although . . . purporting to be applying the standard").

To the extent that these additional grounds are applied, they necessarily involve the court in a more or less elaborate review of the arbitral record. That prospect is inconsistent with at least one principal reason why arbitration is encouraged: to relieve the federal courts of the burden of litigations that the parties have elected to resolve elsewhere. It should be noted, however, that a number of courts now recognize the enforceability of contractual provisions providing for broader judicial review than that otherwise afforded under the Federal Arbitration Act. *See, e.g., LaPine Tech. Corp. v. Kyocera Corp.*, 130 F.3d 884 (9th Cir. 1997); *Gateway Tech., Inc. v. MCI Tel. Corp.*, 64 F.3d 993 (5th Cir. 1995). Alternatively, an arbitration clause may provide for review of the award by an appellate arbitration panel. *See Chicago Typographical Union v. Chicago Sun-Times*, 935 F.2d 1501 (7th Cir. 1991). These options should be considered by the parties in the drafting process.

§ 5. Venue

A. Generally

Section 1965(a) authorizes the commencement of a RICO action in any district court in which a defendant "resides, is found, has an agent, or transacts his affairs." Residence and physical presence are relatively straightforward concepts,[24] but "agen[cy]" and "transact[ing] . . . affairs" are less so. It has been suggested that the phrase "has an agent" contemplates that the alleged agent "have engaged in purposeful activities in [the district] . . . for the benefit of and with the knowledge and consent of the non-domiciliary, and [that] the non-domiciliary [have] exercise[d] some element of control over the agent." *Rashid v. Reidel*, No. 88 Civ. 4876 (PKL) 1990 U.S. Dist. LEXIS 6965 (S.D.N.Y. June 8, 1990).[25] Further, the

---

24. *See generally* Burnham v. Superior Ct., 495 U.S. 604 (1990), for a discussion of these concepts in the context of due process constraints on the exercise of personal jurisdiction over nonresidents based on physical presence (held, assertion of personal jurisdiction over nonresidents served with process while physically present in the territory of the forum satisfies due process).

25. This "agen[cy]" phrase has also been construed as applying only to individuals and not to corporate defendants. *See, e.g.*, King v. Vesco, 342 F. Supp. 120 (N.D. Cal. 1972) (obiter); Rashid v. Reidel, *supra* (alternative holding). This interpretation appears to be more semantic than substantive in nature, however, since a corporation with an agent in a district will be "found" there and will be "transact[ing its] affairs" in that district as well.

"transacts his affairs" language, which was drawn from section 12 of the Clayton Act, 15 U.S.C. § 22, has been interpreted as requiring that the defendant regularly transact business of a substantial and continuous character within the district. *See, e.g., Abeloff v. Barth,* 119 F.R.D. 315 (D. Mass. 1988); *Dody v. Brown,* 659 F. Supp. 541 (W.D. Mo. 1987); *Miller Brewing Co. v. Landau,* 616 F. Supp. 1285 (E.D. Wis. 1985); *King v. Vesco,* 342 F. Supp. 120 (N.D. Cal. 1972).

Section 1965(b) "effectively operates as a waiver of the applicable venue requirements if the 'ends of justice' so require." *Anchor Glass Container Corp. v. Stand Energy Corp.,* 711 F. Supp. 325 (S.D. Miss. 1989). This section is applicable only if venue in the district is appropriate as to at least one defendant pursuant either to section 1965(a) or the general venue statute, 28 U.S.C. § 1391.[26] Where venue is appropriate as to at least one defendant and where no district represents a proper venue as to all defendants, the interests of justice weigh in favor of the original court's summoning all defendants before it under section 1965(b). *Southmark Prime Plus, L.P. v. Falzone,* 768 F. Supp. 487 (D. Del. 1991).[27] The interests of justice weigh all the more heavily in favor of the exercise of section 1965(b) power if more or most of the defendants are subject to venue in the original district. *See, e.g., United States v. Bonanno Organized Crime Family,* 695 F. Supp. 1426 (E.D.N.Y. 1988) (section 1965(b) power exercised where venue appropriate as to all but two defendants in original district).

As suggested in the preceding paragraph, aside from section 1965(a)–(b), the plaintiff may look to the general venue statute, 28 U.S.C. § 1391.[28] *Obee v. Teleshare, Inc.,* 725 F. Supp. 913 (E.D. Mich. 1989); *Wichita Fed. Sav. & Loan Ass'n v. Landmark Land Group, Inc.,* 674 F. Supp. 321 (D. Kan. 1987). Consequently, even if none of the prongs of section 1965(a) is satisfied, a RICO action may be maintained under section 1391(b)(2) if "a substantial part of the events

---

26. Where venue is not appropriate under either § 1965(a) or § 1391 as to any defendant, venue is improper. *See, e.g.,* Shuman v. Computer Assocs. Int'l, Inc., 762 F. Supp. 114 (E.D. Pa. 1991).

27. This is consonant with the underlying purpose of § 1965(b), which is to permit a plaintiff to bring all members of a nationwide RICO conspiracy before one court for a single trial. Butcher's Union Local No. 498 v. SDC Inv., Inc., 788 F.2d 535 (9th Cir. 1986).

28. The principal federal question venue provision, 28 U.S.C. § 1391(b), provides the following:

> A civil action wherein jurisdiction is not founded solely on diversity of citizenship may, except as otherwise provided by law, be brought only i[n] (1) a judicial district where any defendant resides, if all defendants reside in the same State, (2) a judicial district in which a substantial part of the events or omissions giving rise to the claim occurred, or a substantial part of property that is the subject of the action is situated, or (3) a judicial district in which any defendant may be found, if there is no district in which the action may otherwise be brought.

or omissions giving rise to the claim occurred, or a substantial part of the property that is the subject of the action is situated" in the district. *See, e.g.*, *American Trade Partners, L.P. v. A-1 Int'l Importing Enters., Ltd.*, 757 F. Supp. 545 (E.D. Pa. 1991); *cf. Obee*, 725 F. Supp. at 913 (construing to the same effect the predecessor provision to the present section 1391(b)).

B. Section 1404(a) and Forum Non Conveniens

Although venue may be appropriate, the judge may nonetheless (1) transfer venue within the United States pursuant to 28 U.S.C. § 1404(a) or (2) if another country (or, conceivably, a state court) is a more convenient forum, dismiss the action pursuant to the doctrine of forum non conveniens.

1. Section 1404(a) Section 1404(a)[29] reflects a "desire to have federal civil suits tried in the federal system at the place called for in a particular case by considerations of convenience and justice." *Van Dusen v. Barrack*, 376 U.S. 612, 616 (1964). In deciding transfer motions, the court weighs in the balance a number of case-specific factors. *Stewart Org., Inc. v. Ricoh Corp.*, 487 U.S. 22, 29 (1988). These include the residence and convenience of parties, the availability of compulsory process for the attendance of unwilling witnesses, the cost of obtaining witnesses' testimony, the location in which the operative facts occurred, and any other factor the court deems pertinent to the interests-of-justice inquiry. Transfer under section 1404(a) is available upon a lesser showing of inconvenience than that required for a forum non conveniens dismissal. *Norwood v. Kirkpatrick*, 349 U.S. 29 (1955); *Commodities Futures Trading Comm'n v. Savage*, 611 F.2d 270 (9th Cir. 1979). RICO actions are fully transferable under section 1404(a), in the district judge's discretion. *See, e.g.*, *Project 74 Allentown, Inc v. Frost*, 770 F. Supp. 207 (S.D.N.Y. 1991); *Walters v. Beavers*, No. 89-696-JJF, 1991 U.S. Dist. LEXIS 1432 (D. Del. Feb. 6, 1991); *Rolls-Royce Motors, Inc. v. Charles Schmitt & Co.*, 657 F. Supp. 1040 (S.D.N.Y. 1987); *Follett College Stores Corp. v. Fernandez*, 587 F. Supp. 1051 (N.D. Ill. 1984).

2. Forum Non Conveniens With the enactment of section 1404(a), the common law doctrine of forum non conveniens is applicable primarily in instances where another country (as distinct from another federal district court) is alleged to provide the more convenient forum. Unlike antitrust cases, RICO cases are

29. 28 U.S.C. § 1404(a) provides that "[f]or the convenience of parties and witnesses, in the interest of justice, a district court may transfer any civil action to any other district or division where it might have been brought."

subject to the doctrine of forum non conveniens. *Transunion Corp. v. PepsiCo, Inc.*, 811 F.2d 127 (2d Cir. 1987); *Kempe v. Ocean Drilling & Exploration Co.*, 876 F.2d 1138 (5th Cir.), *cert. denied*, 110 S. Ct. 279 (1989); *Lockman Found. v. Evangelical Alliance Mission*, 930 F.2d 764 (9th Cir. 1991).

Because the alternative forum is usually a foreign country, the impact of a dismissal on forum non conveniens grounds is often to preclude any RICO recovery.[30] However, the fact that the substantive law to be applied in an alternative forum is less favorable to the plaintiff than that applicable in the original forum is not a basis on which to deny a forum non conveniens motion. *Piper Aircraft Co. v. Reyno*, 454 U.S. 235 (1981) ("The possibility of a change in substantive law should ordinarily not be given conclusive or even substantial weight in the forum non conveniens inquiry"). The movant must establish only that (1) an alternative forum exists[31] and (2) this forum affords some not "clearly inadequate" remedy for the dispute set forth in the complaint. *Id.* at 254 n.22 ("dismissal would not be appropriate where the alternative forum does not permit litigation of the subject matter of the dispute"); *see also Lockman Found.*, 930 F.2d at 768; *Kempe*, 876 F.2d at 1144–45 (5th Cir. 1989). The absence of a RICO remedy abroad does not, without more, render a foreign court's remedies so clearly inadequate as to preclude dismissal on forum non conveniens grounds. As long as the foreign court is competent to adjudge claims arising out of the dispute articulated in the complaint, the fact that the potential damage award may be smaller does not foreclose application of forum non conveniens. *PT United Can Co. v. Crown Cork & Seal Co.*, 138 F.3d 65 (2d Cir. 1998) ("the nonexistence of a RICO statute there does not, by itself, preclude the use of another forum"; rather, the issue is "whether the laws enforceable in [the foreign country's] courts [a]re an adequate, not identical, alternative"); *Richards v. Lloyd's of London*, 135 F.3d 1289 (9th Cir.) (en banc), *cert. denied*, 119 S.Ct. 365 (1998) ("the loss of RICO claims does not suffice to bar dismissal for forum non conveniens"); *accord Kempe*, 876 F.2d at 1145; *Lockman Found.*, 930 F.2d at 768–69.

C. Forum Selection Clauses

Frequently in commercial and consumer transactions, a choice of forum is contractually specified. Under controlling Supreme

---

30. At least in theory, some foreign courts' choice of law rules may permit or require application of RICO. That prospect does not appear to have materialized.

31. The existence of an available alternative forum can be established, inter alia, by the defendant's consent to jurisdiction in that forum coupled with a waiver of any statute of limitations defense that may have accrued there. Jayaraman v. Salomon, Inc., No. 87 Civ. 2781 (MJL), 1991 U.S. Dist. LEXIS 4205 (S.D.N.Y. 1991).

Court authority, forum selection clauses are prima facie valid, whether they are negotiated or nonnegotiated in nature. *Carnival Cruise Lines, Inc. v. Shute,* 499 U.S. 585 (1991) (nonnegotiated; printed on back of passenger ticket); *Bremen v. Zapata Off-Shore Co.,* 407 U.S. 1 (1972) (contractually negotiated). A forum selection clause is not to be set aside unless the party challenging the clause can "clearly show that enforcement would be unreasonable and unjust." *Bremen,* 407 U.S. at 10. The fact that the selected forum (for example, one outside the United States) will not allow the plaintiff to proceed on a RICO theory of recovery and does not permit the same measure of damages that would be available under American law does not render the clause invalid as contrary to public policy. *Richards v. Lloyd's of London,* 135 F.3d 1289 (9th Cir.) (en banc), *cert. denied,* 119 S.Ct. 365 (1998); *Medoil Corp. v. Citicorp,* 729 F. Supp. 1456 (S.D.N.Y. 1990); *Winex, Ltd. v. Paine,* No. 89-2083, 1990 U.S. Dist. LEXIS 10834 (E.D. Pa. Aug. 15, 1990).

The construction of any forum selection clause begins and ends with its terms. As drafted, the clause may or may not apply to an alleged RICO violation. If the RICO claim involves allegations arising out of the contract containing the clause, or if the RICO claim can be fairly stated to derive from the relationship structured by that contract, the RICO claim is subject to the forum selection clause. *Crescent Int'l, Inc. v. Avatar Communities, Inc.,* 857 F.2d 943 (3d Cir. 1988); *Cinema Laser Technology, Inc. v. Hampson,* No. 91-101A, 1991 U.S. Dist. LEXIS 7215 (D.N.J. May 30, 1991).[32]

In multiparty cases, where not all parties are subject to the forum selection clause, questions may arise as to the scope and impact of the clause. *See, e.g., Snider v. Lone Star Art Trading Co.,* 672 F. Supp. 977 (E.D. Mich. 1987), *aff'd mem.,* 838 F.2d 1215 (6th Cir. 1988) (scope of forum selection clause between plaintiff and one defendant does not encompass a RICO action against multiple defendants). *Compare Friedman v. World Trans., Inc.,* 636 F. Supp. 685 (N.D. Ill. 1986) (enforcing a forum selection clause between the plaintiff and one of several RICO defendants). Enforcement of forum selection clauses is ultimately discretionary with the judge and rests on his or her assessment of the totality of circumstances. *See, e.g., First Interstate Credit Alliance, Inc. v. Alliance Leasing, Inc.,* No. 89 Civ. 4038 (JFK), 1990 U.S. Dist. LEXIS 5744 (S.D.N.Y. May 15, 1990).

D. Forum Shopping

Few, if any, other statutes have been in force as long as RICO and remain subject to as many conflicting interpretations. *See H.J.*

---

32. *Cf.* the discussion relating to construction of arbitration clauses in § 4(E), *supra.*

Inc. v. Northwestern Bell Tel. Co., 492 U.S. 229, 251 (1984) (Scalia, J., concurring). In several substantive respects, the circuits are, in Judge Mikva's words, "all over the lot" in construing the act.[33] *Yellow Bus Lines, Inc. v. Drivers, Chauffeurs & Helpers Local Union* 639, 913 F.2d 948, 957 (D.C. Cir. 1990), *cert. denied,* 501 U.S. 1222 (1991) (Mikva, J., concurring).

In light of the breadth of the jurisdiction and venue provisions discussed above and the plaintiff's freedom to seek to transfer venue under section 1404(a) while retaining the law of the transferor court,[34] substantial conflicts among the circuits are an invitation to forum shopping. Effectively, they require responsible plaintiffs' counsel to evaluate scrupulously the alternatives available in selecting the appropriate site for commencing suit. Simultaneously, they oblige defense counsel to monitor strict adherence to the jurisdictional and venue constraints that exist. Jurisdiction and venue determinations in RICO cases can have serious substantive repercussions and should not be treated casually by court or counsel.

33. *See, e.g.*, §§ 7, 9(C), 10, 11(B)(1)–(2), 11(D), 19(A), and 27, *infra*.

34. *Ferens v. John Deere Co.*, 496 U.S. 516 (1990).

Chapter 3
Standing

§ 6. Overview

A. Four-Factor Test

Generally, federal court standing requires injury in fact caused by the challenged conduct.[1] Under the Supreme Court's decision in *Sedima, S.P.R.L. v. Imrex Co., Inc.*, 473 U.S. 479, 496 (1985), a RICO "plaintiff only has standing if, and can only recover to the extent that, he has been injured in his business or property by the conduct constituting the violation."

The *Sedima* Court rejected a number of standing limitations that had been erected by lower courts in an attempt to stem the rising tide of civil RICO litigation. Specifically, it overruled earlier lower court decisions dictating, as a prerequisite to instituting a civil RICO action, that (1) the defendant have been convicted of the criminal offenses constituting the predicate acts and (2) the plaintiff have suffered a "racketeering injury" distinct from the harm inflicted by the predicate acts. Both the prior-conviction and racketeering-injury requirements were discarded as unwarranted interpolations into the statutory scheme, unsupported by the plain language of the RICO Act or its legislative history. *See* 473 U.S. at 488–90 ("a prior-conviction requirement cannot be found in the definition of 'racketeering activity.' Nor can it be found in § 1962") and *id.* at 496–97 ("the compensable injury necessarily is the harm caused by predicate acts sufficiently related to constitute a pattern").

Section 1964(c), which creates the civil RICO remedy, articulates the precise criteria for determining RICO standing: "Any person injured in his business or property by reason of a violation of section 1962 of this chapter may sue therefor in any appropriate

1. Association of Data Processing Serv. Orgs., Inc. v. Camp, 397 U.S. 150 (1970); Duke Power Co. v. Carolina Envtl. Study Group, Inc., 438 U.S. 59 (1978). *See generally* 15 Moore's Federal Practice §§ 101.20–22 (3d ed. 1997).

United States district court and shall recover threefold the damages he sustains and the cost of the suit, including a reasonable attorney's fee. . . ." 18 U.S.C. § 1964(c).

Therefore, section 1964(c) requires that four criteria be satisfied to establish standing to sue: (1) the plaintiff must be a "person" who has (2) suffered "injur[y]" to (3) his or her "business or property" (4) "by reason of" the defendant's violation of section 1962.

1. "Person" (Plaintiff) The term "person" is broadly defined in section 1961(3) to include "any individual or entity capable of holding a legal or beneficial interest in a property."

Governmental Entities. For standing purposes—that is, to determine who may bring suit under RICO[2]—the term "person" has been liberally construed to include not only people, partnerships, corporations, and joint ventures but also foreign governments and domestic state governmental units. *See, e.g., Republic of Philippines v. Marcos,* 862 F.2d 1355 (9th Cir. 1988) (en banc), *cert. denied,* 490 U.S. 1035 (1989) (foreign government); *Illinois Dep't of Revenue v. Phillips,* 771 F.2d 312 (7th Cir. 1985) (state tax agency); *cf. County of Oakland v. City of Detroit,* 866 F.2d 839 (6th Cir. 1989) (county).

There is one major omission from the plethora of potential governmental plaintiffs. The United States government has been held not to be a "person" within section 1961(3) capable of filing a section 1964(c) claim. In *United States v. Bonanno Organized Crime Family,* 879 F.2d 20 (2d Cir. 1989), the Second Circuit held that the federal government was not intended to be encompassed within section 1964(c), analogizing that provision to section 7 of the Sherman Act, under which the Supreme Court has held that the United States cannot maintain an action (*see United States v. Cooper Corp.,* 312 U.S. 600 (1941)). The Second Circuit painstakingly analyzed the language of section 1964 and emphasized that the United States is separately empowered to sue under section 1964(b), which does not afford a treble-damage remedy. It concluded that this omission was intentional, not inadvertent. *Bonnano,* 879 F.2d at 22–23.

Governmental parties must sue for injuries that they have themselves suffered, not as parens patriae on behalf of their citizens. *Dillon v. Combs,* 895 F.2d 1175 (7th Cir. 1990), *cert. denied,* 111 S. Ct. 670 (1991) ("RICO allows suits by the federal government, § 1964(b), but otherwise only by persons injured in their 'business

2. See § 11(A), *infra,* for a discussion of persons defendant.

or property,' § 1964(c), a phrase that does not include sovereign nor derivative interests"). Moreover, while governmental parties may be "persons" capable of suing, they may not be "persons" capable of being sued as RICO defendants.[3]

Unincorporated Associations. Unlike partnerships and corporations, unincorporated associations are not artificial entities with an existence independent of their membership, absent statutory recognition or authorization. Consequently, unincorporated associations ordinarily are unable to satisfy the requirements of section 1961(3). *See, e.g., Fleischhauer v. Feltner,* 879 F.2d 1290 (6th Cir.), *cert. denied,* 493 U.S. 1074 (1989) (entity for which corporate charter never filed). Where state or federal law permits an unincorporated association to hold an interest in property, that association satisfies the definition of "person" within section 1961(3). *See, e.g., Jund v. Town of Hempstead,* 941 F.2d 1271 (2d Cir. 1991) (holding local political party committees to be RICO "persons" because state law rendered them capable of holding property).

Ironically, at least one type of unincorporated entity that does not qualify as a "person" under section 1961(3) is the organized crime family. In the Second Circuit's view, an organized crime family may appropriately be pegged as the RICO enterprise but not as a RICO person because it is incapable of holding an interest in property. *United States v. Bonanno Organized Crime Family,* 879 F.2d 20 (2d Cir. 1989) ("even if the complaint could be amended to ascribe to the Bonnano Family the requisite features of a partnership or a joint venture, the organization described in the complaint lacks the capacity to hold a legal or beneficial interest in property for a more fundamental and obvious reason: in its purpose, structure and operations it is wholly and innately unlawful").

2. "Injur[y]" Absent damages, a RICO claim cannot be maintained. *Berg v. First Interstate Ins. Co.,* 915 F.2d 460 (9th Cir. 1990). The "injur[y]" requirement of section 1964(c) is given its plain meaning. In *Sedima, S.P.R.L. v. Imrex Co., Inc.,* 473 U.S. 479 (1985), the Supreme Court overruled prior lower court authority imposing, as a prerequisite for a private civil RICO action, the existence of "racketeering injury" independent of the harm caused by the predicate acts. The *Sedima* Court declared that "the compensable injury necessarily is the harm caused by predicate acts sufficiently related to constitute a pattern, for the essence of the violation is the commission of those acts in connection with the conduct as an enterprise." *Id.* at 497. In a footnote, the *Sedima*

---

3. See § 11(A), *infra.*

Court observed that injury would include, but is not limited to, "competitive injury." *Id.* at 497 n.15.

The RICO injury must be ripe and not contingent on future events that may or may not occur. *See, e.g., Lincoln House, Inc. v. Dupre,* 903 F.2d 845 (1st Cir. 1990) (claim dismissed where "the only injury alleged by [plaintiff] is the inability to satisfy a prospective state court judgment against [defendant], *if* [plaintiff] succeeds in securing such a judgment in its pending state action. The . . . claim of damages, at this point, [is] purely speculative, and not ripe for resolution"). Unless the plaintiff can demonstrate actual harm, it may not maintain an action.

3. "Business or Property" "The requirement that the injury be to the plaintiff's business or property means that the plaintiff must show a proprietary type of damage." *Grogan v. Platt,* 835 F.2d 844, 847 (11th Cir.), *cert. denied,* 488 U.S. 981 (1988) (quoting *Banker's Trust Co. v. Rhoades,* 741 F.2d 511 (2d Cir. 1984), *vacated on other grounds,* 473 U.S. 922 (1985)). While the Supreme Court has held that the "business or property" phrase in the Clayton Act refers only to commercial interests and competitive injuries,[4] the same language in RICO is not so limited. *Schact v. Brown,* 711 F.2d 1343 (7th Cir.), *cert. denied,* 464 U.S. 1002 (1983). Competitive injury represents one type of injury to business or property, but anticompetitive effect is not required for suits under this statute. *Sedima, S.P.R.L. v. Imrex Co., Inc.,* 473 U.S. 479, 497 n.15 (1985); *Illinois Dep't of Revenue v. Phillips,* 771 F.2d 312 (7th Cir. 1985); *County of Oakland v. City of Detroit,* 866 F.2d 839 (6th Cir. 1989).

Personal Injury. Physical injury and mental or emotional suffering do not constitute RICO "injury to business or property." *Rylewicz v. Beaton Servs., Ltd.,* 888 F.2d 1175 (7th Cir. 1989) ("the requirement that RICO injury be shown 'to his business or property' . . . would not permit the [plaintiffs] to recover for personal injuries"); *Berg v. First Interstate Ins. Co.,* 915 F.2d 460 (9th Cir. 1990) ("personal injury, including emotional distress, is not compensable under § 1964(c) of RICO"). *Accord Fleischhauer v. Feltner,* 879 F.2d 1290 (6th Cir. 1989), *cert. denied,* 493 U.S. 1074 (1990); *Drake v. B.F. Goodrich Co.,* 82 F.2d 638 (6th Cir. 1986).

Nor are the economic aspects of personal injuries—such as loss of earnings due to physical injury or pecuniary loss due to emotional distress—compensable under RICO. *Grogan v. Platt,* 835 F.2d at 847 ("pecuniary losses are so fundamentally a part of personal injuries that they should be considered something other than

4. Hawaii v. Standard Oil Co. of Cal., 405 U.S. 251 (1972).

injury to 'business or property'"); *Berg v. First Interstate Ins. Co.*, 915 F.2d at 464 ("pecuniary losses from emotional distress [are] not compensable under RICO").

Direct Versus Derivative Injury. A principal constraint on standing is the direct/derivative dichotomy. A plaintiff may sue for injury that it directly suffers by reason of a RICO violation. If, however, the injury is mediated through another entity (for example, a corporation, trust, union) in which the plaintiff holds an interest, that derivative injury does not suffice to confer standing to bring an individual suit absent a particularized injury unique to the plaintiff. This is a critical component of the proximate cause analysis under *Holmes v. Securities Investor Protection Corp.*, 503 U.S. 258 (1992). *See* § 6(A)(4), *infra*.

Shareholders. A RICO claim for damage to a corporation is a corporate asset. Consequently, shareholders do not have standing to prosecute individually RICO claims for diminution in the value of their stock caused by racketeering activities that harm the corporation. Only the corporation may sue for those damages. *See, e.g., Sears v. Likens*, 912 F.2d 889 (7th Cir. 1990); *Warner v. Alexander Grant & Co.*, 828 F.2d 1528 (11th Cir. 1987); *Roeder v. Alpha Indus., Inc.*, 814 F.2d 22 (1st Cir. 1987); *Rand v. Anaconda-Ericsson, Inc.*, 794 F.2d 843 (2d Cir.), *cert. denied*, 479 U.S. 987 (1986); *Warren v. Manufacturers Nat'l Bank of Detroit*, 759 F.2d 542 (6th Cir. 1985).[5] It has been suggested that a different rule—permitting individual actions by shareholders—might apply in the context of close corporations.[6]

The rationale underlying these decisions is that it is the corporation that is "injured in [its] business or property" within the meaning of section 1964(c). *Rylewicz v. Beaton Servs., Ltd.*, 888 F.2d 1175 (7th Cir. 1989); *Sears*, 912 F.2d at 892. The shareholders have not suffered any injury to their property distinct from the injury suffered by the corporation. *Leach v. Federal Deposit Ins. Corp.*, 860 F.2d 1266 (5th Cir. 1988). The claim therefore belongs to the corporation, and the shareholders' remedy is to commence a derivative suit if the corporation inappropriately declines to take action directly. Fed. R. Civ. P. 23.1; *Grand Cent. Sanitation, Inc. v. First Nat'l*

---

5. For the same reason, a promoter of a corporation may not file a RICO action where the injury was suffered by the corporation and its shareholders. Bennett v. Centerpoint Bank, 761 F. Supp. 908 (D.N.H.), *aff'd*, 953 F.2d 634 (1st Cir. 1991) (rejecting argument that the "responsibilities of a promoter to a corporation, its stock subscribers, and its creditors, give him standing as an organizer of [the corporation] to sue the defendants under RICO").

6. *See* Rylewicz, 888 F.2d 1179 (declining to consider the close corporation argument because it was not made below and because "[n]o serious attempt has been made to show that [the corporation] was truly a close corporation"). *Compare* Swerdloff v. Miami Nat'l Bank, 584 F.2d 54, 58–59 (5th Cir. 1978).

Bank, No. 90-0533, 1990 U.S. Dist. LEXIS 10590 (M.D. Pa. July 31, 1990) (former shareholders squeezed out in merger permitted to prosecute derivative RICO claim to remedy misconduct occurring in the merger transaction); *Grafman v. Century Broadcasting Corp.,* 743 F. Supp. 544 (N.D. Ill. 1990) (derivative RICO action by current shareholders).

There are primarily three exceptions to the rule precluding shareholder actions. First, a shareholder who suffers a particularized injury may sue individually. *Grafman,* 743 F. Supp. at 549 (shareholder's suit alleging (1) fraudulent nonpayment of loan owed him by corporation and (2) breach of corporate agreement relating to his compensation); *Powers v. British Vita, P.L.C.,* 57 F.3d 176 (2d Cir. 1995) (former CEO of acquired corporation had RICO standing to sue defendants who fraudulently induced him to rescind an existing agreement and resign his corporate office in return for stock options which defendants secretly intended to dilute massively by recapitalizing the corporation). Second, there has been some recognition of a limited "fiduciary duty" exception. Under this exception, a parent corporation (a shareholder) has been permitted to maintain an action against an officer or director who has breached fiduciary duties owed to one of the corporation's subsidiaries, thus causing the parent's stock in the subsidiary to decline in value. *Qantel Corp. v. Niemuller,* No. 91 Civ. 0371 (PKL), 1991 U.S. Dist. LEXIS (S.D.N.Y. Aug. 22, 1991). This exception—assuming its viability—must be limited to its facts if it is not to swallow the general preclusion of shareholder lawsuits against corporate officers and directors. Factually, the parent and subsidiary corporations are subject to common control. There seems, therefore, little need to recognize this exception since the subsidiary is generally in a position to commence the action directly (or the parent through a derivative action). Third, as mentioned above, assuming compliance with state corporation law, a shareholder (like the parent corporation in the preceding scenario) may file a derivative action, which would render the corporation—the directly injured party—the plaintiff and beneficiary of any award. See, e.g., *Bivens Gardens Office Bldg., Inc. v. Barnett Banks of Fla.,* 140 F.3d 898 (11th Cir. 1998).

Thrift Depositors. Persons standing in a position analogous to that of a shareholder have similarly been denied standing to sue under section 1964(c). For example, savings and loan depositors may not sue for RICO damage to their thrift because the recoverable damages constitute an asset of the institution. *See, e.g., In re Sunrise Secs. Litig.,* 916 F.2d 874 (3d Cir. 1990) ("claims by depositors based on injuries sustained primarily by the financial institution or by depositors generally belong to the financial institutions initially through their receiver"); *Brandenburg v. Seidel,* 859

F.2d 1179 (4th Cir. 1988) (depositors' RICO action against officers of failed savings and loan for misfeasance properly belongs to state receiver rather than to depositors).

Trust/Estate Beneficiaries. Similarly, beneficiaries of trusts and estates have been held to lack standing to sue for diminution of value in the particular corpus in question as a result of RICO violations. Since the injuries are directly suffered by the trust or estate, they can be remedied in a RICO action brought by the appropriate fiduciary on behalf of the injured entity. *Firestone v. Galbreath,* 747 F. Supp. 1556 (S.D. Ohio 1990) ("[a]ny injuries allegedly sustained by plaintiffs and the Family Trust were not directly caused by the alleged wrongful acts and were at most 'merely incidental' to the injuries of [the decedent] and her estate"), *aff'd,* 976 F.2d 279 (6th Cir. 1992).

Union Members. In *Bass v. Campagnone,* 838 F.2d 10 (1st Cir. 1988), the First Circuit ruled that union members had no standing to assert that an officer's RICO violation financially damaged the local, even though the court recognized that—unlike shareholders—the plaintiffs could not have initiated a derivative suit on behalf of the union. 838 F.2d at 12–13 ("the plaintiffs' claim cannot be sustained because it alleges no injury *'peculiar'* to [the plaintiffs] alone [which] does not fall alike upon all other [members of the local]"). The Fifth Circuit reached a similar conclusion in *Adams-Lundy v. Association of Professional Flight Attendants,* 844 F.2d 245 (5th Cir. 1988) (denying union members' standing to sue union; assuming without deciding that the district court was correct in analogizing the plaintiffs' claim to a shareholder derivative action).

Taxpayers. Taxpayers have been precluded from filing RICO actions seeking recovery of excess taxes paid as a result of alleged RICO violations. The Seventh Circuit, in *Carter v. Berger,* 777 F.2d 1173 (7th Cir. 1985), held that the taxpayers lacked standing to sue a defendant whose bribery resulted in lower tax assessments for his clients and a consequent tax increase for the plaintiffs. The *Carter* court concluded that the taxpayers' injury was purely derivative of damage to the public entity, whose remedy it was to sue.

Creditors and Guarantors. Creditors, including guarantors, are generally held to have no more standing to sue than shareholders for RICO violations perpetrated on a debtor corporation. The prevailing rationale is that since the debtor corporation is entitled to litigate in its own name to collect the entirety of any damage it suffered, actions by other participants in the venture—be they equity or debt holders (or, for that matter, employees)—would amount to "a form of double counting." *Mid-State Fertilizer Co. v. Exchange Nat'l Bank of Chicago,* 877 F.2d 1333 (7th Cir. 1989) (the alternative, to permit multiple lawsuits by the various corporate constituencies to recover the same sum in proportion to their various interests, "would be a nightmare"). In the context of a close corporation, however, more leeway may be extended to guarantors and creditors, just as it may be extended to shareholders. *Id.* at 1340–41 & n.1 (concurring opinion). The most expansive standard recognizing creditor standing appears to be that of the Second Circuit, which accords a creditor standing to pursue a RICO claim if harm to that creditor was "reasonably foreseeable or anticipated as a natural consequence." *See GICC Capital Corp. v. Technology Fin. Grp.*, 30 F.3d 289, 292–93 (2d Cir. 1994), *cert. denied*, 518 U.S. 1017 (1996). Other circuits take a more restrictive view. *See, e.g., Bivens Gardens Office Bldg., Inc. v. Barnett Banks of Fla.*, 140 F.3d 898 (11th Cir. 1998) (opining that "the Second Circuit's broad interpretation of RICO standing is inconsistent with the Supreme Court's proximate cause analysis in *Holmes* [*v. Securities Investor Protection Corp.*, 503 U.S. 258 (1992)]").

A creditor victimized by a fraudulent conveyance has been accorded standing to file a RICO claim asserting as predicate acts the fraud giving rise to the conveyance, even though the same fraudulent acts also injured the corporation-borrower, provided that any corporate recovery leading to a partial payment to the creditor is taken into account in computing damages. *Bankers Trust Co. v. Rhoades*, 859 F.2d 1097 (2d Cir. 1988) (the recoverable damages are in part a function of the extent to which the borrower succeeds in recovering the amounts of which it was defrauded; the extent of the creditor's potential recovery is ascertainable only after the borrower has succeeded or failed in its attempt at recovering and the creditor has thereafter been paid in whole or in part out of any proceeds).

Standing under *Bankers Trust* has been limited, however, to situations in which the fraudulent misconduct (1) was specifically aimed at the creditor filing suit and (2) formed only one of the wrongful means by which the defendant sought to thwart the creditor-plaintiff. *Wooten v. Loshbough*, 951 F.2d 768 (7th Cir. 1991) ("corporate creditors, like shareholders, cannot sue under RICO when their only injury comes about through the depletion of corporate assets").

As with shareholders, creditors may also pursue individual RICO claims for any particularized injury they have suffered. *Ashland Oil, Inc. v. Arnett*, 875 F.2d 1271 (7th Cir. 1989) (permitting action where "the facts show[ed] an injury to the plaintiffs significantly different from the injuries to creditors in general resulting from the diversion of corporate assets"). Creditors in bankruptcy proceedings, for example, have been held to have standing to sue for losses caused by sales of the debtor's assets at submarket prices. *See, e.g., Bivens Gardens Office Bldg., Inc. v. Barnett Banks of Fla.*, 140 F.3d at 908 ("The sale of the hotel for a higher price would have directly benefitted major creditors such as [plaintiff], because they would have been able to recover a greater percentage of the debts owed to them. In contrast, the sale of the hotel for a higher price would have little impact on the shareholders and the corporation, since the additional funds from the sale would have been used to satisfy creditors instead of going to shareholders. Therefore, the sale of the hotel at a lower price affected creditors in a manner distinct from shareholders, and in a manner sufficiently direct to confer RICO standing on [plaintiff] in his capacity as a creditor").

Policyholders. An insured may pursue a RICO claim against the agent who defrauded him or her into taking out a policy from an insolvent insurer. *Ocean Energy II, Inc. v. Alexander & Alexander, Inc.*, 868 F.2d 740 (5th Cir. 1989) (plaintiff was injured individually and not derivatively, as from fraud perpetrated on corporation; damages cannot be characterized as property of the bankruptcy estate). Similarly, policyholders may sue a failed insurance company's auditors whose alleged RICO violations resulted in losses to each of them when the carrier collapsed. *University of Md. v. Peat, Marwick, Main & Co.*, 923 F.2d 265 (3d Cir. 1991) (class action).

Utility Customers. Money lost by customers of utilities in paying fraud-induced rates as a result of RICO violations does not constitute compensable injury to "business or property." Recovery is barred by the filed rate doctrine. *Taffet v. Southern Co.*, 967 F.2d 1483 (11th Cir.) (en banc), *cert. denied*, 506 U.S. 1021 (1992); *Wegoland Ltd. v. NYNEX Corp.*, 27 F.3d 17 (2d Cir. 1994).

4. "By Reason Of" The "by reason of" language of section 1964(c) imposes a proximate cause requirement on the plaintiff. That is, the section 1962 violation must proximately cause the plaintiff's injury to business or property. *See Holmes v. Securities Investor Protection Corp.*, 503 U.S. 258 (1992) ("Proximate cause is . . . required"); *Steamfitters Local Union No. 420 Welfare Fund v. Philip Morris, Inc.*, 171 F.3d 912 (3d Cir. 1999) ("proximate cause [is] a necessary element for bringing . . . RICO claims"); *Haroco, Inc. v. American Nat'l Bank & Trust Co.*, 747 F.2d 384 (7th Cir. 1984), *aff'd per curiam*, 473 U.S. 606 (1985) ("As we read this 'by reason of' language, it simply imposes a proximate cause requirement on plaintiffs. The criminal conduct in violation of § 1962 must, directly or indirectly, have injured the plaintiff's business or property"); *Old Time Enters., Inc. v. International Coffee Corp.*, 862 F.2d 1213 (5th Cir. 1989) ("proximate causal relationship"); *Pelletier v. Zweifel*, 921 F.2d 1465 (11th Cir.), *cert. denied*, 502 U.S. 855 (1991) ("a proximate cause requirement"); Kaiser, *Extortion in the Workplace,* 61 BROOKLYN L. REV. 965, 978 (1995) (citing **Treatise**).

Proximate cause is satisfied if the RICO pattern is a substantial factor in causing the plaintiff's injury, provided that the injury is reasonably foreseeable as a natural consequence of those acts. *Cox v. Administrator,* 17 F.3d 1386 (11th Cir. 1994), *cert. denied,* 513 U.S. 1110 (1995) ("A proximate cause is not . . . the same thing as a sole cause. Instead, a factor is a proximate cause if it is 'a substantial factor in the sequence of responsible causation'"); *Hecht v. Commerce Clearing House, Inc.,* 879 F.2d 21 (2d Cir. 1990) ("the RICO pattern or acts proximately cause a plaintiff's injury if they are a substantial factor in the sequence of responsible causation, and if the injury is reasonably foreseeable or anticipated as a natural consequence").

The proximate cause requirement means that legal liability does not extend as far as factual causation—that, at some point, the causal link is too attenuated to warrant the imposition of RICO liability. *See, e.g., Chisolm v. TranSouth Fin. Corp.,* 95 F.3d 331 (4th Cir. 1996) ("it is not enough that a civil RICO plaintiff prove that, but for the defendant's violation, he would not have been injured; he must also show that the violation proximately caused the harm"); *In re American Express Co. Shareholder Litig.,* 39 F.3d 395 (2d Cir. 1994) ("By itself, factual causation (*e.g.,* 'cause-in-fact' or 'but for' causation) is not sufficient") (quotation omitted). The critical question is at what point to draw the line. The cases provide guidance by articulating factors for the court's consideration and by applying them to certain recurring factual scenarios, but the inquiry remains inherently factual and case-specific. The Supreme Court's opinion in *Holmes* is instructive.

The plaintiffs in *Holmes* were customers of defunct brokerage houses (suit was brought on their behalf by a governmental agency). The brokerage firms had been driven to insolvency by a massive stock manipulation scheme. None of the customer-plaintiffs had purchased any of the manipulated stock—they were injured solely by virtue of the brokerage firms' consequent insolvency. In denying recovery under RICO, the Supreme Court looked to the antitrust laws for guidance and emphasized the indirect nature of the plaintiffs' injury, articulating three rationales for denying recovery: (1) "the less direct an injury is, the more difficult it becomes to ascertain the amount of a plaintiff's damages attributable to the [RICO] violation, as distinct from other, independent factors"; (2) allowing recovery by indirectly injured plaintiffs "would force courts to adopt complicated rules apportioning damages among plaintiffs removed at different levels of injury . . . to obviate the risk of multiple recoveries"; and (3) "directly injured victims can generally be counted on to vindicate the law," rendering unnecessary recognition of a cause of action on the part of those only indirectly injured. *Holmes,* 503 U.S. at 269–270.

Since *Holmes,* the directness of injury to the RICO plaintiff has been the paramount consideration guiding proximate-cause determinations.

Examining the nuances of this issue, courts consider whether, among other things:

1. The plaintiff's injury was a direct result of the alleged RICO violation, as opposed to being derivative of injury to another.
2. The plaintiff was the intended target of the RICO offense.
3. Injury to the plaintiff was a reasonably foreseeable consequence of the RICO violation.
4. Independent causes have, or may have, intervened between the RICO violation and the injury to the plaintiff.
5. There is risk of multiple recoveries.
6. The plaintiff's injury was caused by the RICO offense itself or merely by public disclosure of the offense.

See, e.g., Khurana v. Innovative Health Care Sys., Inc., 130 F.3d 143, 149 (5th Cir. 1997), *vacated as moot,* 119 S. Ct. 442 (1998) ("The proximate cause determination for RICO standing is guided by indications of preconceived purpose, specifically intended consequence, necessary or natural result, reasonable foreseeability of result, the intervention of independent causes, whether the defendant's acts are a substantial factor in the sequence of responsible causation and the factual directness of the causal connection") (citations omitted); *In re American Express Co. Shareholder Litig.,* 39 F.3d at 399–400 (no RICO recovery where plaintiffs "were 'neither the target of the racketeering enterprise nor the competitors nor the customers of the racketeer'"; where the harm was not a direct result of the offense but resulted "only because it was publicly exposed"; and where, as a result, "[t]he injuries . . . were neither the 'preconceived purpose' nor the 'specifically-intended consequence' of the RICO defendants' acts") (citations omitted); *accord Laborers Local 17 Health & Benefit Fund v. Philip Morris, Inc.,* 172 F.3d 223 (2d Cir. 1999).

Chief Judge Winter of the Second Circuit has persuasively emphasized that the phrase "proximate cause" is not helpful, and can be pernicious, when invoked in the context of a statute like RICO, because it may misleadingly connote the common law doctrine of the same name. The real issue, he observes, is twofold: "[W]as the plaintiff in the category of people meant by the statute to be safeguarded, and was the harm that which the act meant to avoid?" *Abrahams v. Young & Rubicam, Inc.,* 79 F.3d 234, 237 n.3 (2d

Cir.), *cert. denied,* 519 U.S. 816 (1996). The answers to these questions may lead to different results than those dictated by the common law doctrine of proximate cause, which will govern any attendant common law claims, as *Abrahams* observes.

In that vein, Chief Judge Becker of the Third Circuit has stressed the significance of the Supreme Court's reliance in *Holmes* on the antitrust precedent in assessing proximate cause questions. *Steamfitters Local Union No. 420 Welfare Fund v. Philip Morris, Inc.,* 171 F.3d 912 (3d Cir. 1999) ("In *Holmes* . . . the Supreme Court held that its discussion of proximate cause and remoteness in cases such as *McCready* [*Blue Shield v. McCready,* 457 U.S. 465 (1982)] and *AGC* [*Associated Gen. Contractors, Inc. v. California State Council of Carpenters,* 459 U.S. 519 (1983)] applied to the analysis of proximate cause RICO cases as well"). This observation serves as a reminder not only of the existence of a co-existing body of precedent that must be considered but also of why directness of injury is so important in deciding proximate cause questions.

While directness of injury has assumed paramount importance in proximate cause determinations, injuries characterized as "indirect" may be deemed proximately caused in unusual circumstances. *See, e.g., Israel Travel Advisory Serv. v. Israel Identity Tours, Inc.,* 61 F.3d 1250 (7th Cir. 1995), *cert. denied,* 517 U.S. 1220 (1996) (*Holmes* "did not mean to preclude all possibility of recovery for injury that was transmitted indirectly"; held, business rivals' campaign of misinformation directed at plaintiffs' customers proximately harmed plaintiffs by influencing choices of customers who themselves suffered no harm (but see below)); *accord Mid Atlantic Telecom, Inc. v. Long Distance Services, Inc.,* 18 F.3d 260 (4th Cir.), *cert. denied,* 513 U.S. 931 (1994).

The salience of directness of injury—and of the plaintiff being the intended target of the RICO violation—are illustrated in two recurring factual scenarios.

Whistleblowing. The courts have consistently declined to accord standing under section 1962(c) to employees who have been discharged either for "whistleblowing" activities or for personally refusing to participate in the RICO violation. *See, e.g., Shearin v. E.F. Hutton Group, Inc.,* 885 F.2d 1162 (3d Cir. 1989) (neither the plaintiff's being hired away from her previous job nor her firing "when she refused to play the good soldier . . . can fairly be said to have resulted from the violations of any of RICO's first three subsections or from the predicate acts necessary to establish these"); *Hecht,* 897 F.2d at 24 (neither loss of employment nor loss of commissions due to retaliatory firing was proximately caused by the RICO violation); *Cullom v. Hibernia Nat'l Bank,* 859 F.2d 1211 (5th Cir. 1988) (allegation of constructive discharge for refusal to participate in RICO violation fails to state an adequate "causal nexus between [the] injury and the predicate acts"); *Kramer v. Bachan Aerospace Corp.*, 912 F.2d 151 (6th Cir. 1990) (whistleblower's discharge is an incidental consequence of the RICO violations, which were not directed at the whistleblower); *Reddy v. Litton Indus., Inc.*, 912 F.2d 291 (9th Cir. 1990), *cert. denied*, 502 U.S. 921 (1991) ("All of the circuits that have considered this issue have held that an employee who was wrongfully discharged for refusing to participate in an alleged pattern of racketeering activity lacks standing to sue under § 1962(c)"); *accord Camelio v. AFSCME*, 137 F.3d 666 (1st Cir. 1998); *Beck v. Prupis*, 162 F.3d 1090 (11th Cir. 1998), *cert. granted*, 119 S. Ct. 2046 (1999); *Tarr v. Credit Suisse Asset Mgmt., Inc*, 1997 U.S. Dist. LEXIS 5000 at 35 n.13 (E.D.N.Y. Mar. 21, 1997) (citing **Treatise**).

Mail Fraud. Two circuits have held that a business competitor may not predicate a RICO claim against a rival on alleged mail frauds perpetrated on customers, on the ground that only the customers are the beneficiaries of the statutory protection. *See Israel Travel Advisory Serv. v. Israel Identity Tours, Inc.*, 61 F.3d 1250 (7th Cir. 1995), *cert. denied*, 517 U.S. 1220 (1996); *Lancaster Community Hosp. v. Antelope Valley Hosp. Dist.*, 940 F.2d 397 (9th Cir. 1991), *cert. denied*, 502 U.S. 1094 (1992). This is consistent with the general rule that a civil RICO claim may not be predicated on a mail or wire fraud not directed at the RICO plaintiff but rather at third parties. (*See* the general discussion of mail and fraud as RICO predicates in § 11(C)(2)(a), *infra*.) Generalizations in this area are difficult, however, because the analysis in each case is driven by the facts alleged or proved.

The courts' focus on the "target and victims" of the RICO violations, *Zervas v. Faulkner*, 861 F.2d 823, 832 (5th Cir. 1988), echoes Chief Judge Cardozo's analysis in *Palsgraf v. Long Island R.R.*, 248 N.Y. 339, 162 N.E. 99 (1928) ("The risk reasonably to be perceived defines the duty to be obeyed, and risk imports relations; it is risk to another or to others within the range of apprehension"). Proximate cause inquiries routinely involve a thicket of factual issues that must be addressed on a case-by-case basis.

Causation is inescapably a fact-driven inquiry. While commentators have criticized a perceived lack of judicial or legislative guidance in this area,[7] it may be that general statements (admittedly on the order of platitudes), coupled with an identification of

7. *See, e.g.*, Ginger, *Causation and Civil RICO Standing: When Is a Plaintiff Injured "By Reason of" a RICO Violation?* 64 ST. JOHN'S L. REV 849 (1990); Comment, *Civil RICO Standing: Direct/Indirect Distinction Should Not Be Taken Sitting Down*, 64 TUL. L. REV. 1239 (1990).

relevant factors and reliance on sound judgment, are inescapable. That is effectively the situation presented by tort law generally, and RICO is in substance a "federal business tort statute." *Finne v. Dain Bosworth, Inc.*, 648 F. Supp. 337 (D. Minn. 1986).

B. Predicate Act Standing

If the four RICO standing criteria are satisfied, must the plaintiff independently meet the technical standing requirements of each underlying predicate act? That question was left unanswered by the Supreme Court in *Holmes v. Securities Investor Protection Corp.*, 503 U.S. 258 (1992). The Ninth Circuit ruled in *Holmes* that the Securities Investor Protection Corporation and the trustees of defunct stock brokerage firms were entitled to pursue RICO claims predicated on violations of the federal securities laws (section 10(b) of the Securities Exchange Act of 1934, 15 U.S.C. § 78j(b), and SEC rule 10b-5) even though none of the plaintiffs satisfied the technical standing requirements of those underlying provisions (none was a purchaser or seller of the securities involved).[8] *See Securities Investor Protection Corp. v. Vigman*, 908 F.2d 1461 (9th Cir. 1990), *rev'd on other grounds*, 503 U.S. 258 (1992). The Ninth Circuit concluded that the RICO text does not require that a plaintiff have standing to sue for the predicate acts forming the pattern "so long as the plaintiff suffered injury 'by reason of' the alleged" RICO violation. 908 F.2d at 1466. The Supreme Court granted certiorari on this issue, but the majority declined to address it. Four members of the Court (Justices O'Connor, White, Stevens, and Scalia), however, joined in concurrences agreeing with the Ninth Circuit's resolution of the issue.[9]

The Ninth Circuit reached the correct result for two reasons. First, RICO standing requires only harm resulting proximately from the predicate offenses—it does not also require that this harm necessarily give rise to a civil claim based on those predicate offenses. Second, the RICO plaintiff need not have suffered harm from each predicate offense comprising the pattern.

---

8. The *Holmes* case was litigated prior to the adoption of the Private Securities Litigation Reform Act of 1995 (PSLRA), Pub.L. 104-67, on Dec. 22, 1995. The PSLRA amended 18 U.S.C. § 1964(c) to bar civil RICO plaintiffs from relying on any alleged violation of the federal securities laws as a RICO predicate act in the absence of a criminal conviction for the alleged violation. In the wake of the PSLRA, the issue of predicate act standing has taken on diminished practical significance.

9. The Eleventh Circuit came to the same conclusion as the Ninth in Warner v. Alexander Grant & Co., 828 F.2d 1528 (11th Cir. 1987). The Fourth and Eighth Circuits reached the opposite conclusion in International Data Bank, Ltd. v. Zepkin, 812 F.2d 149 (4th Cir. 1987), and Brannan v. Eisenstein, 804 F.2d 1041 (8th Cir. 1986).

Harm from Predicate Offenses. Under *Sedima,* the plaintiff need only demonstrate—or at least plead—"compensable injury [consisting of] harm caused by predicate acts sufficiently related to constitute a pattern." *Sedima, S.P.R.L. v. Imrex Co.,* 473 US. 479, 497 (1985). If that injury has properly been pleaded and the other elements of RICO standing are satisfied, the plaintiff should be permitted to proceed with its RICO claim. *See, e.g., Ford Motor Co. v. Summit Motor Prods., Inc.,* 930 F.2d 277 (3d Cir.), *cert. denied,* 502 U.S. 939 (1991) (permitting a RICO claim based on violation of a court order to which the claimant was not a party: the "standing inquiry in any civil RICO case depends solely on demonstrating injury to business or property, and not on satisfying any standing requirement attached to the predicate act").

In many cases, standing to sue on the RICO violation will go hand in glove with standing to sue on the predicate acts. Because the RICO violation consists of the predicate offenses (in "pattern" form) and because the "compensable injury" under *Sedima* must be "caused by [the] predicate acts," the RICO injury and underlying injury will often be identical. Where standing limitations would bar a civil claim based on the predicate offenses, those limitations—and the reasons animating them—should be scrutinized carefully to see whether they square with the generous remedy that RICO is designed to supply. To the extent that predicate-act standing requirements do little more than measure the actuality of harm suffered by the plaintiff, they may be a valuable gauge of whether RICO injury has been sustained. To the extent that they have been imposed for other reasons (for example, to contain an implied right of action, as under SEC rule 10b-5), they may have no place in circumscribing RICO standing. In the final analysis, it is important to bear in mind that RICO incorporates predicate offenses—criminal violations (*see* section 1961)—not their civil counterparts and whatever baggage they import.[10]

Harm from All Predicate Offenses. That a plaintiff need not have standing to sue on each predicate offense is further illustrated by the fact that the plaintiff need not suffer injury from each predicate act comprising the pattern. This may seem counterintuitive. Under section 1964(c), a plaintiff may proceed only if it has been "injured in [its] business or property by reason of a violation of section 1962." *Sedima* teaches that "the compensable injury necessarily is the harm caused by predicate acts sufficiently related to constitute a pattern." *Sedima, S.P.R.L. v. Imrex Co., Inc.,* 473 U.S. 479,

10. Thus, it is irrelevant if the statute of limitations on the predicate act has expired, as long as the four-year RICO statute has not lapsed. See § 29, *infra.*

497 (1985). This might appear to lead to the conclusion that the plaintiff must be injured by each predicate act forming the pattern.

That conclusion would be incorrect. The classic illustration: a hoodlum extorts "protection" money from each of several shopkeepers. To state a pattern, it may be necessary for any one plaintiff shopkeeper to allege the defendant's extortion of others as well. But the plaintiff will not have been injured by the defendant's extortion of others. (That this hypothetical states a viable RICO claim is certain because it is drawn from the Supreme Court's opinion in *H.J. Inc. v. Northwestern Bell Tel. Co.*, 492 U.S. 229, 242 (1989).) Additionally, any individual predicate act may fizzle and, to no credit of the defendant, not cause the harm intended. The unsuccessful predicate acts are viable components of the plaintiff's pattern as well.

As long as the pattern of racketeering activity has caused harm to the plaintiff's business or property, the plaintiff has RICO standing. The plaintiff is not obliged to plead or prove that it has been injured by multiple predicate acts: "[N]o requirement exists that the plaintiff must suffer an injury from two or more predicate acts, or from all of the predicate acts. Thus, a RICO verdict can be sustained when a pattern of racketeering acts existed, but when only one act caused injury." *Deppe v. Tripp*, 863 F.2d 1356, 1366 (7th Cir. 1988) (citation omitted) ("Stated differently, merely because one of the racketeering acts was not successful does not mean that it is unavailable to establish a pattern"); *see also Banks v. Wolt* 918 F.2d 418 (3d Cir. 1990) ("the fact that [plaintiff] was not a victim of the additional frauds [he alleges were part of the pattern] should not carry much weight. The reference to 'similar victims' in *H.J. Inc.* cannot be read to require that a plaintiff be injured by more than one predicate act"); *Town of Kearny v. Hudson Meadows Urban Renewal Corp.*, 829 F.2d 1263 (3d Cir. 1987) ("Reading into the statute a requirement that a civil plaintiff prove injury from the entire pattern rather than from any predicate act would . . . be inconsistent with the core congressional purposes behind its enactment"). *Accord Terminate Control Corp. v. Horowitz*, 28 F.3d 1335 (2d Cir. 1994) (dicta).[11]

The key is that some predicate act must injure the plaintiff.[12] If so, the plaintiff will have standing to sue under RICO. If not, section 1964(c)'s injury requirement is not satisfied and the plaintiff

---

11. It should be noted, however, that if a plaintiff has not been injured by all predicate acts, a question may arise as to whether those acts not causing injury are sufficiently connected to those acts causing injury so as to satisfy the relatedness prong of the pattern requirement. *See generally* § 11(D), *infra*.

12. This language may need qualification depending on the outcome of the Supreme Court's pending decision in Beck v. Prupris, 119 S. Ct. 2046 (1999) (granting certiorari),

lacks standing. *Landry v. Air Line Pilots Ass'n,* 892 F.2d 1238 (5th Cir.), *cert. denied,* 498 U.S. 895 (1990) (acknowledging that "[a]ny injury to business or property caused by a violation . . . is sufficient" but nonetheless dismissing RICO claim because all alleged predicate acts operated to benefit, and not harm, the plaintiffs).

C. Abatement and Survival

RICO claims are generally held not to abate upon the death of an individual plaintiff but, rather, to survive. The Fourth Circuit definitively so ruled in *Faircloth v. Finesod,* 938 F.2d 513 (4th Cir. 1991), on the rationale that RICO—including its treble-damage remedy—is predominantly remedial (rather than punitive) in nature.[13] *See* 938 F.2d at 518 ("Construing [RICO] liberally, as Congress directed, we think that civil RICO claims should survive"). The Fourth Circuit's conclusion is compelling, at least in the case of individuals. It would be anomalous to permit RICO defendants—who by definition include real racketeers—to create their own safe harbor if they have "the foresight to kill their victims." *Id.* at 518. Survival is the rule, abatement the exception.[14]

---

in which the issue is whether the injuy-producing act, in a RICO conspiracy case, need be a predicate act or may be any overt act.

13. The federal rule is that an action for a penalty does not survive, Schreiber v. Sharpless, 110 U.S. 76, 80 (1884), but remedial actions do survive. United States v. Grannis, 172 F.2d 504, 514 (4th Cir.), *cert. denied,* 337 U.S. 918 (1949). In assessing whether an action is penal or remedial, the court considers whether (1) the purpose of the action is to redress individual wrongs or wrongs to the public; (2) recovery runs to the individual or to the public; and (3) the authorized recovery is proportionate or disproportionate to the harm suffered. Smith v. No. 2 Galesburg Crown Fin. Corp, 615 F.2d 407, 414 (7th Cir. 1980); *accord* James v. Home Constr. Co. of Mobile, Inc., 621 F.2d 727 (5th Cir. 1980). Note that the conclusion that RICO's treble-damage remedy is predominantly punitive, not remedial, has been reached by some courts in the context of deciding whether governmental entities are immune from suit under RICO. *See* § 11(A), *infra.*

14. *Compare* State Farm Fire & Casualty Co. v. Estate of Caton, 540 F. Supp. 673 (N.D. Ind. 1982); Costello v. Cooper, No. 86 Civ. 3264 (JFK), 1990 U.S. Dist. LEXIS 946, 1990 WL 9856 (S.D.N.Y. Jan. 31, 1990); Republic Pension Servs., Inc. v. Finger, No. CV 87-0255 (LDW), 1988 U.S. Dist. LEXIS 1848, 1988 WL 22579 (E.D.N.Y. Feb. 11, 1988) (magistrate judge's opinion) (all holding RICO claims survive) *with* Washburn v. Brown, No. 81-C-1475, 1988 U.S. Dist. LEXIS 13474, 1988 WL 130021 (N.D. Ill. Nov. 23, 1988) (citing other unreported Northern District of Illinois decisions holding that RICO claims abate). (Since the Seventh Circuit, like the Supreme Court and other courts of appeals, has expressly acknowledged the generally remedial nature of the civil RICO remedy, it is not unlikely that the Northern District of Illinois—whose precedents largely antedate the Seventh Circuit authority on this issue—might come to a different conclusion if the issue were revisited.) *See, e.g.,* Shearson/American Express, Inc. v. McMahon, 482 U.S. 220, 240 (1987) ("The legislative history of § 1964(c) reveals [an] emphasis on the remedial role of the treble-damages provision"), and Liquid Air Corp. v. Rogers, 834 F.2d 1297 (7th Cir.), *cert. denied,* 492 U.S. 917 (1989) ("Although there is some sense in which RICO treble damages are punitive, they are largely compensatory in the special sense that they ensure that wrongs will be redressed in light of the recognized difficulties in itemizing damages").

On the same analysis—that a civil RICO claim is predominantly remedial, not punitive—RICO claims are generally held not to abate upon the death of the defendant. *See, e.g., Epstein v. Epstein*, 966 F. Supp. 260 (S.D.N.Y. 1997) (Rakoff, J.) ("Congress viewed the private civil RICO claim as a victim's remedy, first and foremost, and so it has proven to be. By operation of settled principles of federal common law, it follows a fortiori that such claims survive a party's demise, whether the party be a plaintiff, or, as here, a defendant"); *Holford USA Ltd., Inc. v. Harvey*, 169 F.R.D. 41 (S.D.N.Y. 1996) (same); *First American Corp. v. Al-Nahyan*, 948 F. Supp. 1107 (D.D.C. 1996) (same); *but see Confederation Life Ins. Co. v. Goodman*, 842 F. Supp. 836 (E.D.Pa. 1994), and *Ball v. Marshall Field V*, 1993 U.S. Dist. LEXIS 4273 (N.D.Ill. Apr. 2, 1993) (both contra).

D. Assignability and Subrogation

Most courts hold that RICO claims are assignable, on an analogy to antitrust damages claims. *See, e.g., Federal Ins. Co. v. Parello*, 767 F. Supp. 157 (N.D. Ill. 1990) ("There is very little room to argue that Congress would intend to allow the assignment of antitrust claims and would prohibit the assignment of RICO claims"); *In re National Mortgage Equity Corp. Mortgage Pool Certificate Secs. Litig.*, 636 F. Supp. 1138 (C.D. Cal. 1986) (because antitrust damages claims are assignable and the goals of the RICO and antitrust statutes are similar—deterring interference with free competition—RICO claims are similarly assignable); *Flinn Found. v. Petro-Lewis Corp.*, [1985] CCH Fed. Sec. L. Rep. & 92,449 (D. Colo. 1985) (same); *Nicolls Pointing Coulson Ltd. v. Transportation Underwriters of La., Inc.*, No. 90-2951 (E.D. La. Oct. 31, 1991) (RICO claims assignable; assignment ineffective under state law).[15]

This conclusion comports with those cases recognizing that a subrogated insurance company's loss constitutes RICO injury conferring standing to sue. *See, e.g., Federal Ins. Co. v. Ayers*, 760 F. Supp. 1118 (E.D. Pa. 1990) (subrogated surety's monetary loss, which flows directly from the predicate acts, "constitutes an injury to plaintiff's business sufficient to satisfy the requirements for standing under the Federal RICO statute"); *accord General Accident Ins. Co. v. Fidelity & Deposit Co.*, 598 F. Supp. 1223 (E.D. Pa. 1984) (fidelity bond surety properly pleaded RICO violation by asserting

---

15. There is, however, contrary authority in the Northern District of Illinois, premised on the analysis that "the survival of a claim does determine its assignability" and relying on the case law in that district (discussed in § 6(C), above) holding that RICO claims do not survive a plaintiff's death. *With Parello*, 767 F. Supp. at 157, *compare* Lincoln Nat'l Life Ins. Co. v. Silver, No. 86 C 7175, 1990 U.S. Dist. LEXIS 13669 (N.D. Ill. Oct. 4, 1990).

racketeering injury to its bondholder); *Levey v. E. Stewart Mitchell, Inc.*, 585 F. Supp. 1030 (D. Md. 1984), *aff'd mem.*, 762 F. Supp. 998 (4th Cir. 1985) (recognizing that payment bond surety could be a proper RICO plaintiff for injuries sustained as a result of making payments under the bond). There can be little doubt about the standing of a subrogee to bring a RICO action since the plaintiff before the Supreme Court in *Holmes v. Securities Investor Protection Corp.*, 503 U.S. 258 (1992), was a governmental entity subrogated to the claims of customers of defunct brokerage firms.

§ 7. Section 1962(a) Standing

Section 1962(a) prohibits any person who has received income from a pattern of racketeering activity or through collection of an unlawful debt from "us[ing] or invest[ing], directly or indirectly, any part of such income, or the proceeds of such income, in acquisition of any interest in, or the establishment or operation of, any enterprise."[16] There is a split in the circuits as to the type of injury necessary to confer standing under section 1962(a). The majority rule holds that the plaintiff must allege injury from the "use or invest[ment]" of racketeering income or unlawful debt proceeds. Under this analysis, simple injury caused by the predicate racketeering acts is inadequate. The majority approach requires that the investment-use itself proximately cause the plaintiff's injury. *See, e.g., Ouaknine v. MacFarlane*, 897 F.2d 75 (2d Cir. 1990) ("Under the plain language of this section, a violation of § 1962(a) consists of investing income derived from a pattern of racketeering activity to acquire an interest in, establish, or operate an enterprise; the violation is not established by mere participation in predicate acts of racketeering"); *Grider v. Texas Oil & Gas Corp.*, 868 F.2d 1147 (10th

16. In full, § 1962(a) provides the following:

> It shall be unlawful for any person who has received any income derived, directly or indirectly, from a pattern of racketeering activity or through collection of an unlawful debt in which such person has participated as a principal within the meaning of section 2, title 18, United States Code, to use or invest, directly or indirectly, any part of such income, or the proceeds of such income, in acquisition of any interest in, or the establishment or operation of, any enterprise which is engaged in, or the activities of which affect, interstate or foreign commerce. A purchase of securities on the open market for purposes of investment, and without the intention of controlling or participating in the control of the issuer, or of assisting another to do so, shall not be unlawful under this subsection if the securities of the issuer held by the purchaser, the members of his immediate family, and his or their accomplices in any pattern of racketeering activity or the collection of an unlawful debt after such purchase do not amount in the aggregate to one percent of the outstanding securities of any one class, and do not confer, either in law or in fact, the power to elect one or more directors of the issuer.

Cir.), *cert. denied*, 493 U.S. 820 (1989) ("we find no justification for disregarding the clear language of § 1962(a), which prohibits the use or investment of income from racketeering activity); *accord Rose v. Bartle*, 871 F.2d 331 (3d Cir. 1989); *Craighead v. E.F. Hutton & Co.*, 899 F.2d 485 (6th Cir. 1990); *Old Time Enters., Inc. v. International Coffee Corp.*, 862 F.2d 1213 (5th Cir. 1989); *Danielson v. Burnside-Ott Aviation*, 941 F.2d 1220 (D.C. Cir. 1991); *Nugget Hydroelectric, L.P. v. Pacific Gas & Elec. Co.*, 981 F.2d 429 (9th Cir. 1992), *cert. denied*, 508 U.S. 908 (1993); *Compagnie de Reassurance d'Ile de France v. New England Reinsurance Corp.*, 57 F.3d 56 (1st Cir.), *cert. denied*, 516 U.S. 1009 (1995); *Lewicky v. Chou*, 1993 U.S. Dist. LEXIS 4127 at *14 (N.D. Ill. Mar. 30, 1993) (citing **Treatise**).

It is insufficient, under the majority approach, to allege or prove that the defendant merely reinvested the racketeering proceeds in its ongoing business activities, thus permitting the alleged violations to continue. The link between the investment and the injury cannot be that remote. *Brittingham v. Mobil Corp.*, 943 F.2d 297 (3d Cir. 1991) ("If this remote [reinvestment] connection were to suffice, the use-or-investment injury requirement would be almost completely eviscerated when the alleged pattern of racketeering is committed on behalf of a corporation. . . . Over the long term, corporations generally reinvest their profits, regardless of source").

The Fourth Circuit has rejected the majority view and holds that no investment-use injury is required. Under the Fourth Circuit's analysis, to allege a violation of section 1962(a), a plaintiff must show both (1) the defendant's receipt of income from a pattern of racketeering activity (or through collection of an unlawful debt) and (2) the defendant's use or investment of this income in an enterprise. However, the plaintiff's injury may result from either item (1) or item (2). "Nothing in the 'by reason of' language of § 1964(c) . . . limits the compensable racketeering activities to those sustained . . . after the investment and/or use of the income." *Busby v. Crown Supply, Inc.*, 896 F.2d 833, 837 (4th Cir. 1990) (also opining that the investment-use rule "conflicts with the explicit policy that RICO be liberally interpreted").

Both the majority and minority rules derive a two-prong approach from the structure of section 1962(a). Under the majority's approach, both prongs must be satisfied before the plaintiff may sue: not only must the offender have received income from a pattern of racketeering activity (or through collection of an unlawful debt), but he or she must also have used or invested that income in a fashion that harms the plaintiff. The Fourth Circuit approach severs the two steps and contemplates that a plaintiff may pursue a section 1962(a) claim if it has been injured by either prong.

In practice, the second prong effectively becomes surplusage under the Fourth Circuit approach. All income not stuffed under a mattress is ultimately invested, and it is difficult for the investment not to affect interstate commerce under the liberal test that is applied.[17] The majority rule is more consonant with the structure of section 1962(a) and more consistent with the legislative intent of the provision—to halt the investment of racketeering proceeds into legitimate businesses.[18]

§ 8. Section 1962(b) Standing

Section 1962(b) renders it unlawful for any person "to acquire or maintain, directly or indirectly, any interest in or control of any enterprise" through a pattern of racketeering activity or collection of an unlawful debt.[19] Standing for section 1962(b) purposes requires an injury to the plaintiff resulting from the defendant's acquisition or maintenance of an interest in, or control over, the pertinent enterprise. *See, e.g., Danielsen v. Burnside-Ott Aviation Training Center, Inc.*, 941 F.2d 1220 (D.C. Cir. 1991) ("plaintiffs must allege an 'acquisition' injury, analogous to the 'use or investment injury' required under § 1962(a) to show injury by reason of a § 1962(b) violation"); *Kehr Packages, Inc. v. Fidelcor, Inc.*, 926 F.2d 1406 (3d Cir. 1991) ("under § 1962(b), a plaintiff must allege a specific nexus between control of a named enterprise and the alleged racketeering activity"); *Compagnie de Reassurance d'Ile de France v. New England Reinsurance Corp.*, 57 F.3d 56 (1st Cir. 1995) ("Under § 1962(b), the plaintiffs had to show that they were harmed by reason of [defendant's] acquisition or maintenance of control of an enterprise through a pattern of racketeering activity"); *Discon, Inc. v. NYNEX Corp.*, 93 F.3d 1055 (2d Cir. 1996), *vacated on antitrust grounds*, 119 S.Ct. 493 (1998) ("'acquisition injury' [is] necessary to state a claim under subsection 1962(b)"); *Advocacy Org. for Patients v. Auto Club Ins. Ass'n*, 176 F.3d 315 (6th Cir. 1999) ("a complaint for violation of § 1962(b) must allege an 'acquisition or maintenance' injury separate and apart from the injury suffered as a result of the predicate acts of racketeering").

---

17. *See* § 11(E), *infra*.

18. *See, e.g.*, 116 CONG. REC. 35,199 (1970) (remarks of Rep. St. Germain); 116 CONG. REC. 607 (1970) (remarks of Sen. Byrd); 115 CONG. REC. 6993 (1969) (remarks of Sen. Hruska).

19. § 1962(b) provides in full that "[i]t shall be unlawful for any person through a pattern of racketeering activity or through collection of an unlawful debt to acquire or maintain, directly or indirectly, any interest in or control of any enterprise which is engaged in, or the activities of which affect, interstate or foreign commerce."

Injury in fact is insufficient to confer section 1962(b) standing unless that injury has been caused by the acquisition or maintenance of the interest in, or control of, an enterprise through a pattern of racketeering activity (or collection of an unlawful debt). *See, e.g., Shearin v. E.F. Hutton Group, Inc.*, 885 F.2d 1162 (3d Cir. 1989) (plaintiff who was fired for "refus[ing] to play the good soldier" in her employer's section 1962(b) fraudulent scheme did not have standing to sue under that section because her injury was not caused by the employer's acquisition or maintenance of control over the enterprise through the alleged pattern of racketeering activity); *Protter v. Nathan's Famous Sys., Inc.*, 925 F. Supp. 947, 955 (E.D.N.Y. 1996) (citing **Treatise**); *Lewicky v. Chou*, 1993 U.S. Dist. LEXIS 4127 at *14 (N.D. Ill. Mar. 30, 1993) (citing **Treatise**).[20]

Whether a person has "acquire[d] or maintain[ed], directly or indirectly, any *interest* in . . . any enterprise" is a fairly straightforward, objective determination. In contrast, whether someone has "acquire[d] or maintain[ed], directly or indirectly, any . . . *control* of any enterprise" is not subject to a bright line test. One court has drawn a persuasive distinction between a defendant's merely "influenc[ing] and affect[ing]" an enterprise and its exercising "control" over the enterprise. Under this analysis, control for section 1962(b) purposes is essentially "managerial" in nature and requires proof that the defendant "participat[ed] in the operation or management of the enterprise itself." *Rosemount Cogeneration Joint Venture v. Northern States Power Co.*, 1991-1 Trade Cas. (CCH) & 69,351, 1991 U.S. Dist. LEXIS 1504 (D. Minn. Jan. 18, 1991) (quoting and relying in part on section 1962(c) precedent (from the Eighth Circuit) on the theory that both subsections (b) and (c) "prohibit 'persons' from engaging in racketeering activity via RICO 'enterprises'").

"Control" has many meanings in the law and is largely context sensitive. Hands-on managerial control is an appropriate touchstone, but others may be equally valid. If a person "ha[s] the power to control or influence" an enterprise or actually exerted "influence over the policy and decision-making process" of that enterprise—tests applied under section 20(a) of the Securities Exchange Act of 1934, 15 U.S.C. § 78t(a), to determine "controlling

20. There are a few district court decisions to the contrary, *see, e.g.*, Avirgan v. Hull, 691 F. Supp. 1357 (S.D. Fla. 1988), *aff'd on other grounds*, 932 F.2d 1572 (11th Cir. 1991), *cert. denied*, 502 U.S. 1048 (1992) (requiring only that the plaintiff "be injured by the defendant's pattern of racketeering activity, that was used to either acquire or maintain any interest in . . . any enterprise" and rejecting the contention that the injury must be "caused by . . . the acquisition or maintenance of [the] interest"); *In re* Sahlen & Assocs., Inc. Secs. Litig., 773 F. Supp. 342 (S.D. Fla. 1991) (same). No court of appeals has adopted this analysis; all have held to the contrary.

persons"[21]—a court could conclude that section 1962(b) has been satisfied. In other situations, the perpetrators of a broad, fraudulent scheme might be said to "control" an enterprise even though they are committing the fraud as outsiders rather than as insiders. *See, e.g., Sutliff, Inc. v. Donovan Cos.*, 727 F.2d 648 (7th Cir. 1984) (two individuals who took advantage of the distraught mental state of the owner of a small business operated out of the home and effectively ran the operation and "control[led]" it for section 1962(b) purposes). *Compare Cooperativa de Ahorro y Credito Aguada v. Kidder, Peabody & Co.*, 758 F. Supp. 64 (D.P.R. 1991) (defendant brokerage firms did not "control" an enterprise "by fraudulently causing [it] to make bad investment decisions").

In the discussion of section 1962(a), it was noted that reinvestment of the proceeds of alleged racketeering activity in the ongoing business enterprise—permitting it to continue to do business and, thus, to continue the alleged RICO scheme—does not satisfy the investment-injury requirement of section 1962(a). Reinvestment of the proceeds of alleged racketeering activity may satisfy section 1962(b)'s requirement that the defendant acquire or maintain an interest in, or control over, the enterprise through a pattern of racketeering activity or collection of an unlawful debt. However, unless the plaintiff's injury results directly from the defendant's maintenance of that financial interest or exertion of that control, the plaintiff will lack section 1962(b) standing as well. *See, e.g., American Millworks v. Mellon Bank Corp.*, No. 88-5163, 1991 U.S. Dist. LEXIS 8393, 1991 WL 112015 (E.D. La. June 13, 1991) (dismissing section 1962(b) claim because "[p]laintiffs allege[d] that they were injured by the [RICO] scheme, not by [defendant's] ability to maintain control over" the enterprise).

§ 9. Section 1962(c) Standing

Under section 1962(c), it is unlawful for any person who is "employed by or associated with any enterprise . . . to conduct or participate . . . in the conduct of such enterprise's affairs through a pattern of racketeering activity or collection of unlawful debt."[22] The Supreme Court declared in *Sedima, S.P.R.L. v. Imrex Co.*, 473

21. *See, e.g.*, Wool v. Tandem Computers, Inc., 818 F.2d 1433, 1441 (9th Cir. 1987).

22. In full, § 1962(c) provides that "[i]t shall be unlawful for any person employed by or associated with any enterprise engaged in, or the activities of which affect, interstate or foreign commerce, to conduct or participate, directly or indirectly, in the conduct of such enterprise's affairs through a pattern of racketeering activity or collection of unlawful debt."

U.S. 479 (1985), that a "plaintiff only has standing [under section 1962(c)] if, and can only recover to the extent that, he has been injured in his business or property by the conduct constituting the violation." In the Supreme Court's words, the violation "requires (1) conduct (2) of an enterprise (3) through a pattern (4) of racketeering activity." *Id.* at 496–97.

Section 1962(c) standing is both the simplest and most complex to evaluate. On the one hand, under *Sedima,* it requires only proof of injury caused proximately by the violation, without additional hurdles such as the investment-injury requirement of section 1962(a) or the interest-or-control requirement of section 1962(b). On the other hand, the section 1962(c) violation entails a series of difficult analytical distinctions and relationships, and it is by far the most heavily litigated subsection of section 1962. The most diffuse aspects of the pertinent law—the "pattern" and "enterprise" requirements—apply to all substantive subsections of section 1962 and are discussed elsewhere.[23] Three criteria for standing discussed in this section are (1) that the "person" and the "enterprise" be distinct under section 1962(c), (2) what constitutes being "associated with" an enterprise for section 1962(c) purposes, and (3) what it means "to conduct or participate . . . in the conduct of [an] enterprise's affairs."

A. "Person" Versus "Enterprise"

The "person" who allegedly violates section 1962(c) must be distinct from the "enterprise" whose affairs that person is allegedly "conduct[ing] or participat[ing]" in conducting.[24] The reason for this distinction is that section 1962(c) applies only to a person *associated with or employed by* an enterprise who has wrongfully conducted or participated in the enterprise's affairs. Because, in Chief Judge Posner's words, "you cannot associate with yourself" (*McCullough v. Suter,* 757 F.2d 142, 144 (7th Cir. 1985)) and because only the person and not the enterprise is liable under section 1962(c), the "person" and "enterprise" must be separate entities. *Haroco* v. *American Nat'l Bank & Trust Co.,* 747 F.2d 384 (7th Cir. 1984), *aff'd,* 473 U.S. 606 (1985) ("The use of the terms 'employed by' and 'associated with' appears to contemplate a person distinct from the enterprise. If Congress had meant to permit the same entity to be the liable person and the enterprise under section 1962(c), it would have required only a simple change in language

---

23. *See* § 11(B) and (D), *infra.*

24. "Person" is defined in § 1961(3) and is discussed in §§ 6(A)(1), *supra,* and 11(A), *infra.* "Enterprise," which is defined in § 1961(4), is discussed in § 11(B) *infra.*

to make that intention crystal clear"); *Arzuaga-Collazo v. Oriental Fed. Sav. Bank,* 913 F.2d 5 (1st Cir. 1990) ("the word 'person,' as used in the statute to describe one who 'conducts' an 'enterprise,' does not apply to the enterprise itself. . . . Hence the unlawful enterprise itself cannot also be the person the plaintiff charges with conducting it"); *Old Time Enters., Inc. v. International Coffee Corp.,* 862 F.2d 1213 (5th Cir. 1989) ("The violator of § 1962(c) who commits the pattern of predicate racketeering acts must be distinct from the enterprise whose affairs are thereby conducted"); *accord Banks v. Wolk,* 918 F.2d 418 (3d Cir. 1990); *Yellow Bus Lines, Inc. v. Drivers, Chauffeurs & Helpers Local Union 639,* 913 F.2d 948 (D.C. Cir. 1990) (en banc), *cert. denied,* 501 U.S. 1222 (1991); *Bennett v. United States Trust Co.,* 770 F.2d 308 (2d Cir. 1985), *cert. denied,* 474 U.S. 1058 (1986); *but see Cox v. Administrator,* 17 F.3d 1386 (11th Cir. 1994), *cert. denied,* 513 U.S. 1110 (1995) (noting that the Eleventh Circuit does not enforce the person/enterprise distinction under section 1962(c)).[25]

This distinction between the "person" defendant and the "enterprise" under section 1962(c) is particularly significant because it is not required under either section 1962(a) or (b). Neither of those subsections is drafted to require that the person and the enterprise be separate. *See, e.g., Busby v. Crown Supply, Inc.,* 896 F.2d 833 (4th Cir. 1990) ("Unlike subsection (c), which requires the relationship between the 'person' and the 'enterprise' (i.e., employer-employee), subsection (a) requires only the use of an 'enterprise' by a 'person.' . . . [T]he offender and the enterprise need not be separate."); *Official Publications, Inc. v. Kable News Co.,* 884 F.2d 664 (2d Cir. 1989) ("under § 1962(a), it may be possible for a defendant to be the enterprise"); *D & S Auto Parts, Inc. v. Schwartz,* 838 F.2d 964 (7th Cir. 1988) ("If it perpetrates illegal conduct, a corporation-enterprise can be sanctioned under § 1962(a), which, unlike subsection (c), contains no language indicating that the enterprise cannot itself be a liable 'person' "); *Landry v. Air Line Pilots Ass'n,* 901 F.2d 404 (5th Cir.), *cert. denied,* 498 U.S. 895 (1990) ("In contrast to the language of subsection (c) which 'requires a relationship between the "person"' and the "enterprise," subsection . . . (b) require[s] only the *use* of an "enterprise" by a "person."' Thus the RICO person and the enterprise need not be distinct for a person to be held liable under subsection (b)" (court's emphasis)); *Schreiber Distrib. Co. v. Serv-Well Furniture Co.,* 806 F.2d 1393 (9th Cir. 1986) (holding that the "person" may also be the "enterprise"

25. At the same time, nothing would necessarily preclude an entity from functioning both as the enterprise on certain claims and as a person perpetrating RICO violations through another enterprise on other claims. Rose v. Bartle, 871 F.2d 331 (3d Cir. 1989).

under either section 1962(a) or (b) if it is also "the direct or indirect beneficiary of the pattern of racketeering activity").

Since the "person" defendant and the "enterprise" must be distinct under section 1962(c), the question arises whether there is a sufficient distinction if the complaint alleges that the defendant is one member of an "associated-in-fact" enterprise. The circuits conflict at least nominally on this question, but the conflict may be more apparent than real. Some courts have ruled it insufficient under section 1962 for a plaintiff simply to allege that the defendant is—rather than the enterprise itself—a member of an associated-in-fact enterprise. *See, e.g., Yellow Bus Lines, Inc. v. Drivers, Chauffeurs & Helpers Local Union 639*, 913 F.2d at 951 ("leav[ing] . . . undisturbed" the prior panel opinion (883 F.2d at 141) that "an organization cannot join with its own members to do that which it normally does and thereby form an enterprise separate and apart from itself"); *Entre Computer Centers, Inc. v. FMG of Kansas City, Inc.*, 819 F.2d 1279 (4th Cir. 1987) (rejecting contention that a corporation that was the "person" could also be a member of the "enterprise" consisting of itself and its officers and directors).

Other courts have expressed the opposite view, declaring that a defendant may be a member of an associated-in-fact enterprise without transgressing the distinction required by section 1962(c). *See, e.g., Atlas Pile Driving Co. v. DiCon Fin. Co.*, 886 F.2d 986 (8th Cir. 1989) ("A collective entity is something more than the members of which it is comprised. If five persons form an association in fact and engage in a pattern of racketeering activity such as drug smuggling and murder, an individual member could never be prosecuted for violating RICO under the [opposite] reasoning because he or she would not be considered distinct from the enterprise"); *Cullen* v. *Margiotta*, 811 F.2d 698 (2d Cir.), *cert. denied*, 483 U.S. 1021 (1987) ("we see no reason why a single entity could not be both the RICO 'person' and one of a number of members of the RICO 'enterprise'").

These authorities may be less divergent than they appear. At one extreme, a transparent subterfuge—such as the plaintiff's allegation in *Yellow Bus Lines* that a union together with its business agent constituted an "enterprise" distinct from the union itself—provides a compelling argument against the finding of any distinction in fact. *Entre's* purported enterprise, composed of the defendant corporation together with its officers and directors, is another case in point. To the same effect, *see, e.g., Atkinson v. Anadarko Bank & Trust Co.*, 808 F.2d 438 (5th Cir.), *cert. denied*, 483 U.S. 1032 (1987) (the required distinction between "person" and "enterprise" is not established where the alleged violator is a corporation and the "enterprise" consists of the corporation, its holding company parent, and three corporate employees).

In contrast, *Atlas* presented an enterprise composed of two defendants—a corporation and a partnership in which the corporation served as general partner—and three other companies. Based on a jury verdict, the Eighth Circuit in *Atlas* found that the two defendants "were distinct from the enterprise." 886 F.2d at 995. *Cullen*, like *Atlas*, involved the review of a jury's verdict finding the existence of an enterprise composed of three entities—a town, that town's Republican committee, and the local county Republican committee. That the two committees were also defendants was not, in the Second Circuit's opinion, inconsistent with its prior section 1962(c) holding "that a solitary entity cannot . . . simultaneously constitute both the RICO 'person' whose conduct is prohibited and the entire RICO 'enterprise' whose affairs are impacted by the RICO person." 811 F.2d at 729.

While there is plainly linguistic tension among certain of these opinions, it is not altogether certain that the analytic approaches are incompatible, much less irreconcilable. The appropriate test should be whether, in fact, the defendant and the enterprise are distinct, regardless of the artistry with which the pleading may be drafted. If they are distinct in fact, the claim should be sustained. If not, it should be dismissed.

This issue becomes most pointed when the named defendant is a collective entity—one that can act only through its agents or constituent parts—and the alleged enterprise is composed of the entity and its agents or other constituents. With perhaps a rare exception, this is held to blur impermissibly the person/enterprise distinction. *Fitzgerald v. Chrysler Corp.*, 116 F.3d 225 (7th Cir. 1997) ("Read literally, RICO would encompass every fraud case against a corporation, provided only that a pattern of fraud and some use of the mails or of telecommunications to further the fraud were shown; the corporation would be the RICO person and the corporation plus its employees the 'enterprise.' The courts have excluded this far-fetched possibility by holding that an employer and its employees cannot constitute a RICO enterprise"). *See also* § 11(B)(4), *infra*.

There are visible differences among the circuits. The Third Circuit, for example, reexamined its precedent in this area in 1995 and concluded that *Reves v. Ernst & Young*, 507 U.S. 170, 183 (1993), foreclosed any absolute prohibition against finding that corporate managers were appropriate defendants when the enterprise was a corporation because *Reves* requires that the defendants operate or manage the corporation. *See Jaguar Cars Inc. v. Royal Oaks Motor Car Co.*, 46 F.3d 258 (3d Cir. 1995) (criminal fraud perpetrated by president and general manager through corporate enterprise stated viable section 1962(c) claim, preserving the essential distinction between the defendant "person[s]" and the "enterprise"). The

Seventh Circuit tends to hew to a stricter line, reasoning that "it is one thing to allege that criminals are using a corporation to commit crimes, a natural meaning to impress on the statutory language of conducting an enterprise's affairs through a pattern of racketeering activity, and another to assert merely that since the corporation's unlawful scheme must have been hatched by someone connected to the corporation, the scheme (provided it satisfies the statute's pattern requirement) violates RICO." *Emery v. American Gen. Fin. Inc.*, 134 F.3d 1321, 1324–25 (7th Cir.), *cert. denied*, 119 S.Ct. 57 (1998). The practical import of the distinction between these approaches—to the extent there is a difference—may be felt most immediately at the pleading stage, where particularity is mandated. (*See* § 23, *infra*.) *See also Fitzgerald*, 116 F.3d at 227 (in evaluating RICO allegations, the court should "determine how close to the prototyp[ical civil RICO case] the case before the court is—how close, in other words, the family resemblance is between the prototypical case and the case at hand. . . . The prototypical RICO case is one in which a person bent on criminal activity seizes control of a previously legitimate firm and uses the firm's resources, contacts, facilities, and appearance of legitimacy to perpetrate more, and less easily discovered, criminal acts than he could do in his own person, that is, without channeling his criminal activities through the enterprise that he has taken over"); *accord Brannon v. Boatmen's First Nat'l Bank*, 153 F.3d 1144 (10th Cir. 1998).

Sole Proprietorships. A related question is whether an individual defendant is sufficiently distinct from his or her sole proprietorship to satisfy the person/enterprise distinction under section 1962(c). This, too, is a factual question, and it will turn largely on the nature and substance of the sole proprietorship. *See, e.g., McCullough v. Suter*, 757 F.2d 142 (7th Cir. 1985) ("a sole proprietorship is a recognized legal entity, and, provided it has any employees, is in any event a 'group of individuals associated in fact.' . . . There would be a problem if the sole proprietorship were strictly a one-man show. . . . But if the man has employees or associates, the enterprise is distinct from him, and it then makes no difference, so far as we can see, what legal form the enterprise takes"); *United States v. London*, 66 F.3d 1227 (1st Cir. 1995), *cert. denied*, 517 U.S. 1155 (1996) (entity, "though a sole proprietorship, had at least one employee other than [the defendant/owner]. No more is required to establish the separateness required by RICO").

Plaintiff "Person" and Enterprise. The requirement under section 1962(c) that the "person" be distinct from the "enterprise" applies only to "persons" named as defendants, not to persons as plaintiffs. There is no section 1962(c) bar to a suit by the victimized enterprise against the responsible defendants in which the plaintiff and the enterprise are identical. *See, e.g., United Energy Owners Comm., Inc. v. United States Energy Management Sys., Inc.*, 837 F.2d 356 (9th Cir. 1988) ("plaintiffs are free to allege that they or one of their members is a RICO enterprise or part of a RICO enterprise"); *Com-Tech Assocs., L.P. v. Computer Assocs. Int'l, Inc.*, 753 F. Supp. 1078 (E.D.N.Y. 1990), *aff'd*, 938 F.2d 1574 (2d Cir. 1991) ("Even though the plaintiffs themselves are also the 'enterprise,' it is permissible for the victimized enterprise to sue for damages under RICO, so long as it is alleged that the *defendants* conducted the enterprise through a pattern of racketeering activity" (emphasis in original)). This is consistent with the language of section 1962(c), which requires only that the "person" defendant be employed by or associated with the victimized enterprise such that the two must be distinct.

B. "Associated With"

Section 1962(c) dictates that the culpable person be "employed by or associated with" the enterprise whose affairs are conducted through a pattern of racketeering activity. While the "employed by" side of the equation is relatively straightforward, the phrase "associated with" is a bit more nebulous. It is plainly intended to expand the horizon of culpable persons beyond insiders, such as employees, to include others having some relationship with the enterprise. *See, e.g., Shulton, Inc. v. Optel Corp.*, 1987-1 Trade Cas. (CCH) ¶ 67,436 (D.N.J. 1986) ("It is well established that the compass of persons 'associated with' an enterprise includes 'outsiders' as well as 'insiders' of the enterprise"). The question is how wide a net it casts. In the absence of a statutory definition, the cases have adopted a common sense reading of the term "associat[ion]," focusing on the business of the enterprise and the relationship of the defendant to that business. *United States v. Yonan*, 800 F.2d 164 (7th Cir. 1986), *cert. denied*, 479 U.S. 1055 (1987) ("The cases make clear that the defendant need not have a stake in the enterprise's 'goals,' but can associate with the enterprise by conducting business with it, even if in doing so the defendant is subverting the enterprise's goals").

The courts approach the "associat[ing] with" question as one of fact. The plaintiff is required to prove the existence of the defendant's "associat[ion] with" the enterprise or its section 1962(c) claim is lost. *See, e.g., Avirgan v. Hull*, 932 F.2d 1572 (11th Cir. 1991), *cert. denied*, 502 U.S. 1048 (1992) (defendants properly awarded summary judgment where, among other things, plaintiffs failed to offer evidence proving that individual wrongdoer was associated with the alleged enterprise); *Verges v. Babovich*, No. 86-2382 (E.D. La. Nov. 26, 1986) ("Even assuming [the existence of] an enterprise within the meaning of RICO, no evidence has been presented by which a jury could possibly conclude that [defendant] was associated in any meaningful manner with [that enterprise]").

Association with an enterprise may be established by evidence that the defendant participated in, or managed aspects of, the enterprise's affairs or was simply held out, with his or her acquiescence, as a member of the enterprise. *See, e.g., Casperone v. Landmark Oil & Gas Corp.,* No. 86-1367, 1987 U.S. App. LEXIS 12253 (5th Cir. 1987) (per curiam) (first defendant's "association with the enterprise is shown by [another defendant's] introduction of [the first defendant] as his partner. . . . an introduction that [the first defendant] did not deny, correct or modify"; first defendant also acted as counsel for the enterprise and made material misrepresentations relating to it); *Pappas v. Arfaras,* No. B-90-326 (WWE), 1991 U.S. Dist. LEXIS 14840 (D. Conn. Aug. 28, 1991) ("The complaint alleges that [the individual defendants] were associated with the . . . enterprise through their participation and management of each corporate entity. The corporate entities are alleged to have been associated with the enterprise through participation in various fraudulent schemes").

Engaging in the RICO violation with agents, employees, or members of an enterprise also constitutes "associat[ing] with" that enterprise within the meaning of section 1962(c). *City of New York v. Joseph L. Balkan, Inc.,* 656 F. Supp. 536 (E.D.N.Y. 1987) ("by scheming with and bribing [enterprise] employees . . . the [defendants] associated with the [enterprise]").

The defendant's "associat[ion] with" the enterprise must involve the unlawful activities at issue. Mere association with a legitimate entity, not involving any of the alleged wrongdoing or participation in any predicate acts, does not constitute "associat[ion] with" the enterprise for section 1962(c) purposes. *Gussin v. Shockey,* 725 F. Supp. 271 (D. Md. 1989), *aff'd mem.,* 933 F.2d 1001 (4th Cir. 1991) ("The mere fact [a defendant] could be described as an agent for the . . . partnership [i.e., the enterprise] does not give rise to that relationship with an enterprise which is encompassed by RICO. . . . [The defendant] must associate with an enterprise to carry on a pattern of racketeering activity. That association must include an aspect of purpose to violate the act").

Similarly, wrongdoing unassociated with the enterprise, even though independently actionable or punishable, does not give rise to section 1962(c) liability. *Banks v. Wolk,* 918 F.2d 418 (3d Cir. 1990) ("the amended complaint alleges no connection between either enterprise and" two of seven purported schemes. In light of the absence of any alleged "relationship between th[ese] scheme[s] and the named enterprises . . . neither of these schemes can form part of a pattern of acts underlying the § 1962(c) violation").

C. "Conduct or Participate . . . in the Conduct"

In *Reves v. Ernst & Young,* 507 U.S. 170, 183 (1993), the Supreme Court interpreted the requirement that a defendant "conduct or participate, directly or indirectly, in the conduct of [the] enterprise's affairs," an interpretive issue on which the circuits had been, in Judge Mikva's accurate appraisal, "all over the lot."[26] *Yellow Bus Lines, Inc. v. Drivers, Chauffeurs & Helpers Local Union 639,* 913 F.2d 948, 957 (D.C. Cir. 1990) (Mikva, J., concurring), *cert. denied,* 501 U.S. 1222 (1991).

The *Reves* Court affirmed the Eighth Circuit's view that the phrase "conduct or participate" contemplates that the defendant must be involved in the operation or management of the enterprise. "Once we understand the word 'conduct' to require some degree of direction and the word 'participate' to require some part in that direction, the meaning of § 1962(c) comes into focus." *Reves,* 507 U.S. at 179. Analyzing the statutory imperative in a case in which the civil RICO plaintiff was a bankruptcy trustee suing the outside auditor of the debtor, the *Reves* Court elaborated:

> In order to "participate, directly or indirectly, in the conduct of such enterprise's affairs," one must have some part in directing those affairs. Of course, the word "participate" makes clear that RICO liability is not limited to those with primary responsibility for the enterprise's affairs, just as the phrase "directly or indirectly" makes clear that RICO liability is not limited to those with a formal position in the enterprise, *but some part in directing the enterprise's affairs is required.*

Id. (emphasis added; footnote omitted).

---

26. The interpretation ultimately adopted by the Supreme Court in *Reves* was originally articulated in Bennett v. Berg, 710 F.2d 1364 (8th Cir.) (en banc), *cert. denied,* 464 U.S. 1008 (1983) ("A defendant's participation must be in the conduct of the affairs of a RICO enterprise, which ordinarily will require some participation in the operation or management of the enterprise itself"). The District of Columbia and Fourth Circuits had adopted the Eighth Circuit's operation-and-management test prior to *Reves.* Yellow Bus Lines, Inc. v. Drivers, Chauffeurs & Helpers Local Union 639, 913 F.2d at 953–54; United States v. Mandel, 591 F.2d 1347 (4th Cir. 1979), *cert. denied,* 445 U.S. 961 (1980), although *Reves* did disavow the D.C. Circuit's "significant control" application of that test (507 U.S. at 1170 n.4). The Second and Ninth Circuits, in contrast, had merely required *either* that (1) the defendant be "enabled to commit the predicate offenses solely by virtue of [his or her] position in the enterprise or involvement in or control over the affairs of the enterprise, *or* (2) the predicate offenses [be] related to the activities of that enterprise." *United States v. Scotto,* 641 F.2d 47, 54 (2d Cir. 1980), *cert. denied,* 452 U.S. 961 (1981) (emphasis added); *accord* United States v. Yarbrough, 852 F.2d 1522 (9th Cir.), *cert. denied,* 488 U.S. 866 (1988). The Fifth and Seventh Circuits took an intermediate position, essentially adapting the Second Circuit's *Scotto* standard by substituting the conjunctive "and" for the disjunctive "or" in *Scotto's* two-pronged test. See, e.g., Overnite Transp. Co. v. Truck Drivers, Oil Drivers, Filling Station & Platform Workers Union Local No. 705, 904 F.2d 391 (7th Cir. 1990); United States v. Cauble, 706 F.2d 1322 (5th Cir. 1983), *cert. denied,* 465 U.S. 1005 (1984). The Eleventh Circuit applied a unique interpretation, concluding that the word "conduct" "simply mean[t] the performance of activities necessary or helpful to the operation of the enterprise." Bank of Am. v. Touche Ross & Co., 782 F.2d 966 (11th Cir. 1986). *Reves* supersedes all of these interpretations, rendering pre-*Reves* precedent suspect.

Reves observed that section 1962(c) does not "requir[e] '*significant* control' over or within an enterprise." *Id.* at 179 n.4 (emphasis added). The opinion reasoned that "liability under § 1962(c) is not limited to upper management" of an enterprise because "[a]n enterprise is 'operated' not just by upper management but also by lower rung participants in the enterprise who are under the direction of upper management." The *Reves* Court concluded, however, that it "need not decide . . . how far § 1962(c) extends down the ladder of operation" of an enterprise (*id.* at 184 n.9). As to defendants outside the enterprise, *Reves* observed that "[a]n enterprise also might be 'operated' or 'managed' by others 'associated with' the enterprise who exert control over it as, for example, by bribery." *Id.* at 184 (footnote omitted).

Neither passive acquiescence nor persuasive power constitute "operation or management" within *Reeves. Schmidt v. Fleet Bank,* 16 F. Supp.2d at 347 ("allowing [an employee] to loot the escrow accounts of his investors" does not state operation or maintenance on the part of the corporate employer, within *Reves,* even though plaintiff "alleged wrongful acts that were allegedly of real importance to [the employee's] scheme," including "allowing [him] access to the escrow accounts, approving [his] overdrafts on 500 separate occasions, failing to notify the relevant authorities of the irregularities in [his] accounts, misrepresenting to investors the status of the accounts and helping [him] to conceal the scheme generally"—all of which, "when reduced to their essentials, . . . are really allegations of assistance to the alleged RICO enterprise, not direction of it"); *Vickers Stock Research Corp. v. Quotron Sys.,* 1997 U.S. Dist. LEXIS 10837 at *9–*10 (S.D.N.Y. 1997), *aff'd mem.,* 1998 U.S. App. LEXIS 22046 (2d Cir. Aug. 24, 1998) ("a defendant will not be found to participate in the management or operation of the enterprise simply because he enjoys 'substantial persuasive power to induce the alleged enterprise to take certain actions'").

The post-*Reves* case law has drawn a dichotomy between outsiders, like the auditor-defendants in *Reves,* and insiders, such as employees of a corporate enterprise. The First Circuit, which draws this distinction most starkly, has opined that "*Reves* is a case about the liability of *outsiders* who may assist the enterprise's affairs. Special care is required in translating *Reves'* concern with 'horizontal' connections—focusing on the liability of an outside adviser—into the 'vertical' question of how far RICO liability may extend within the enterprise but down the organizational ladder. In our view, the reason the accounts were not liable in *Reves* is that . . . [they] were outside the chain of command. . . ." *United States v. Oreto,* 37 F.3d 739, 750 (1st Cir. 1994) (emphasis in original), *cert. denied,* 513 U.S. 1177 (1995), *quoted with approval in MCM Partners v. Andrews-Bartlett & Assocs.,* 62 F.3d 967, 978 (7th Cir. 1995).

This distinction between insiders and outsiders should not be overstated. *Reves* was interpreting a statutory requirement—that "one *must* participate in the operation or management of the enterprise itself." 507 U.S. at 185 (emphasis added). The "operation or management" requirement applies to all putative RICO defendants, whether they are insiders or outsiders. The distinction between insiders and outsiders is made in recognition of the fact that operation or management does not necessarily mean the same thing for those, in *Oreto's* words, inside and those "outside the chain of command." 37 F.3d at 750.

Lower-level persons within the chain of command of an enterprise have been held to operate or manage, within *Reves,* if they exercise broad discretion or knowingly implement criminal decisions. Since illegal drug rings and gangs are paradigmatic association-in-fact enterprises, courts have expansively interpreted *Reves'* mandate in criminal cases. *See, e.g., United States v. Diaz,* 176 F.3d 52, (2d Cir. 1999) ("even if a defendant is not acting in a managerial role . . . he can still be liable for directing the enterprise's affairs if he 'exercised broad discretion' in carrying out the instructions of his principal. . . . [But] 'the simple taking of directions and performance of tasks that are "necessary or helpful" to the enterprise, without more, is insufficient to bring a defendant within the scope of § 1962(c)'"); *United States v. Posada-Rios,* 158 F.3d 832 (5th Cir. 1998), *cert. denied,* 119 S.Ct. 1792 (1999) ("Although [a mid-level distributor] did not operate the enterprise as a whole, he participated in its operation at his level by deciding how much cocaine to buy and what prices and terms to charge to the lower-level distributors to whom he redistributed"). In light of the contextual nature of this issue, the Second Circuit has aptly concluded that "the only principle to be drawn from th[e] array of holdings and [judicial] statements is that the commission of crimes by lower level employees of a RICO enterprise may be found to indicate participation in the operation or management of the enterprise but does not compel such a finding." *United States v. Allen,* 155 F.3d 35 (2d Cir. 1998).

The analysis has extended to civil cases—for example, to employees of a corporate enterprise—to encompass active "lower-rung participants who are under the direction of upper management."[27] *See, e.g., MCM Partners,* 62 F.3d at 978 (two businesses that committed crimes at the behest of three controlling

27. If the legal entity is alleged to be the enterprise and its officers or other agents are the named defendants—or if the entity together with its officers or agents are alleged to constitute an association-in-fact enterprise—the court will have to satisfy itself that the person/enterprise distinction has been preserved and that the enterprise is in fact discrete and separable from the collective entity (*see generally* §§ 9(A), 11(B)(4), infra).

members of the enterprise held to have "participate[d] in the conduct of an enterprise 'by knowingly implementing decisions'") (citation omitted).

Where the defendants are not lower-rung corporate employees or others acting "under the direction of [the enterprise's] upper management" (*Reves,* 507 U.S. at 184) but, rather, unaffiliated persons outside the chain of command, the requirement that they actively direct the affairs of the enterprise is rigorously enforced, particularly in civil cases. This is true even if the outsiders are nominally (conclusorily) alleged to be participants in the enterprise, unless they are factually alleged to have either exercised decision-making authority for the enterprise or committed crimes on behalf of the enterprise. Any other result would permit *Reves* to be circumvented by the simple expedient of alleging summarily that the enterprise embraces unaffiliated defendants. *See, e.g., Redtail Leasing, Inc. v. Bellezza,* 1999 U.S. Dist. LEXIS 486 at *11 (S.D.N.Y. Jan. 21, 1999) ("the 'operation and management' test . . . is a very difficult test to satisfy. . . . There is a 'difference between actual control over an enterprise and association with an enterprise in ways that do not involve control; only the former is sufficient under *Reves* because 'the test is not involvement but control'") (quotations and citations omitted); *Schmidt v. Fleet Bank,* 16 F.Supp.2d 340, 347 (S.D.N.Y. 1998) ("There is a 'substantial difference between actual control over an enterprise and association with an enterprise in ways that do not involve control; only the former is sufficient under Reves because "the test is not involvement but control"'"); *Goren v. New Vision Int'l, Inc.,* 156 F.3d 721, 728 n.3 (7th Cir. 1998) (nonemployees hired by corporate enterprise to perform specific tasks "cannot be said to conduct the affairs of the enterprise" but are instead "best characterized as contractors hired by the enterprise"). *See generally MCM Partners,* 62 F.3d at 978 ("the accountants were not liable in *Reves* . . . [because], while they were undeniably involved in the enterprise's decisions, they neither made those decisions nor carried them out; in other words, the accountants were outside the chain of command through which the enterprise's affairs were conducted"), *quoting Oreto,* 37 F.3d 750.

A prime example of persons outside the chain of command are professionals, like the defendants in *Reves.* Professionals are routinely held not to operate or manage a enterprise simply by providing customary services to the enterprise, regardless of whether they are conclusorily alleged to be participants in the enterprise. *Handeen v. Lemaire,* 112 F.3d 1339 (8th Cir. 1997) ("Furnishing a client with ordinary professional assistance, even when the client happens to be a RICO enterprise, will not normally rise to the level of participation sufficient to satisfy the Supreme Court's pronouncements in *Reves*") (attorney); *Azrielli v. Cohen Law Offices*, 21 F.3d 512 (2d Cir. 1994) (lawyer who "merely acted as an attorney for the other individual defendants" not shown to have "participated in the management or direction of a RICO enterprise"); *Univ. of Md. v. Peat, Marwick, Main & Co.*, 996 F.2d 1534 (3d Cir. 1993) ("It cannot be said that by merely performing what are generic financial and related services to [a client], even if they are later found to be deficient, an accounting firm has opened itself to liability under the federal racketeering statute").

But this analysis is not limited to professionals. It applies to all who are not factually alleged to be within the chain of command of the enterprise. *See generally Goren*, 156 F.3d at 728 ("simply performing services for an enterprise, even with knowledge of the enterprise's illicit nature, is not enough to subject an individual to RICO liability under § 1962(c); instead, the individual must have participated in the operation and management of the enterprise itself").

In this area, artful pleading is common. Complaints frequently cast a broad net, naming unaffiliated defendants who are not factually alleged to have participated meaningfully in directing the enterprise's affairs. Conclusory, boilerplate allegations do not determine whether a defendant is properly named as a participant in an enterprise, much less whether the defendant operated or managed the enterprise. The complaint must contain factual allegations that would lead to the conclusion that each defendant was actually involved in directing the affairs of the enterprise; otherwise dismissal is appropriate. *See, e.g., Goren*, 156 F.3d at 727; *accord Reynolds v. Condon*, 908 F. Supp. 1494, 1527 (N.D. Iowa 1996) ("giving [plaintiff] all reasonable inferences due his allegations of fact, he failed to alleged 'conduct' of the alleged RICO enterprise by the RICO defendants"). *See generally* § 23, *infra*.

§ 10. Section 1962(d) Standing

Section 1962(d) outlaws any conspiracy to violate any of the other subsections of section 1962.[28] The principal standing question arising under section 1962(d) is whether a person has standing to sue for a RICO conspiracy if the injury-producing wrongful

28. § 1962(d) provides that "[i]t shall be unlawful for any person to conspire to violate any of the provisions of subsection (a), (b), or (c) of this section."

acts alleged do not constitute "predicate acts" as defined in section 1961(1). The majority rule is that standing does require a plaintiff to allege injury from overt acts that are themselves prohibited by the RICO statute. *See Hecht v. Commerce Clearing House, Inc.*, 897 F.2d 21 (2d Cir. 1990) ("Because a conspiracy . . . cannot by itself cause any injury, we think that Congress presupposed injury-causing overt acts as the basis of civil standing to recover for RICO conspiracy violations. [A]lthough an overt act by itself (whether or not injury ensues) is not a requisite element of a § 1962(d) criminal conspiracy violation, we hold that injury from an overt act is necessary and sufficient to establish civil standing for a RICO conspiracy violation") (citations omitted); *accord Miranda v. Ponce Fed. Bank*, 948 F.2d 41, 48 (1st Cir. 1991); *Bowman v. Western Auto Supply Co.*, 985 F.2d 383 (8th Cir.), *cert. denied*, 508 U.S. 957 (1993); *Reddy v. Litton Indus., Inc.*, 912 F.2d 291 (9th Cir. 1990), *cert. denied*, 502 U.S. 921 (1991); *Beck v. Prupis*, 162 F.3d 1090 (11th Cir. 1998), *cert. granted*, 67 U.S.L.W. 3747 (U.S. June 7, 1999).

The Third Circuit arrived at the opposite conclusion in *Shearin v. E.F. Hutton Group, Inc.*, 885 F.2d 1162 (3d Cir. 1989), a decision subsequently followed by the Fifth and Seventh Circuits. *Khurana v. Innovative Health Care Sys., Inc.*, 130 F.3d 143 (5th Cir. 1997), *vacated as moot*, 119 S. Ct. 442 (1998); *Schiffels v. Kemper Fin. Servs., Inc.*, 978 F.2d 344 (7th Cir. 1992). Stressing that *Sedima* requires only injury from the RICO violation and that "[p]redicate acts for conspiracy do not of necessity consist of § 1961(1) racketeering activity," the minority approach reasons that: "Acts that further a § 1962(d) conspiracy thus may cause harm [and afford standing] even when they do not themselves qualify as racketeering activity." *Shearin*, 885 F.2d at 1169.

Both the majority and minority views reflect principled approaches to the issue. The minority view is certainly consistent with the Supreme Court's decision in *Salinas v. United States*, 522 U.S. 52 (1997), which stresses that no overt act is necessary to state a criminal RICO conspiracy. There is, though, a key difference between a criminal RICO conspiracy (like that at issue in *Salinas*) and a civil RICO conspiracy—namely, the injury requirement imposed on civil plaintiffs by section 1964(c). That is a requirement without analog in the criminal sphere, in which the existence of the conspiracy, as such, is considered a public ill.

Under conventional conspiracy analysis, the act of conspiring means agreeing to "facilitat[e] . . . acts leading to the substantive offense." *Salinas*, 522 U.S. at 65. The majority rule—limiting section 1962(d) standing to persons injured by overt acts that are predicate acts—effectively takes the view that only predicate acts specified in section 1961(1) proximately lead to the substantive offenses in section 1962(a), (b), and (c). Stated another way, the majority considers that preliminary or underlying conduct which merely facilitates predicate acts is too remote to permit recovery under section 1964(c), within the proximate cause precepts of *Holmes v. Securities Investor Protection Corp.*, 503 U.S. 258 (1992) (*see* § 6(A)(4), *supra*).

Although the first edition of this book took the position that what is now the minority rule was the "more compelling," the majority rule is easier to reconcile with the Supreme Court's intervening analysis in *Holmes*—it does "not . . . go beyond the first step." *Id.*, 503 U.S. at 271 (quotations and citations omitted). Its bright line also has practical benefits. The majority view has the virtue of discouraging litigants from arguing that purely non-RICO conduct was, in fact, intended to further a predicate act; that it was thus intended, in some remote way, to facilitate a section 1962(a), (b), or (c) violation; and, therefore, that it presents a civil RICO conspiracy claim—even though there is no substantive RICO offense in sight.

Underlying Violation Requirement. Section 1962(d) is violated by "conspir[ing] to violate any of the provisions of subsection (a), (b), or (c) of this section." Accordingly, if the allegations of a substantive violation of subsection (a), (b), or (c) are infirm, the subsection (d) claim fails. *Edwards v. First Nat'l Bank*, 872 F.2d 347 (10th Cir. 1989) ("the conspiracy claim falls when the substantive claim . . . is deficient"); *Grider v. Texas Oil & Gas Corp.*, 868 F.2d 1147 (10th Cir.), *cert. denied*, 493 U.S. 820 (1989) ("Because [plaintiff] has not alleged injury from the substantive violations, he has failed to show how the alleged conspiracy to commit those violations caused him injury"); *R.C.M. Executive Gallery Corp. v. Rols Capital Co.*, 1997 U.S. Dist. LEXIS 565 at *36 (S.D.N.Y. Jan. 18, 1997) (Koeltl, J.) (citing **Treatise**).

Consummation of Underlying Violation. Under *Salinas*, it is not necessary that the substantive violation (of subsection (a), (b), or (c)) actually be consummated for the conspiracy violation to be complete. It is sufficient that the defendant has agreed to further an endeavor which, if consummated, would satisfy all of the elements of a RICO offense. This raises the question whether, if the substantive offense is not consummated, civil standing lies to sue for treble damages for injury to business or property resulting from an overt act taken in furtherance of the conspiracy.

Under the preceding analysis, that depends on whether the overt act is a predicate act within section 1961(1). If it is an overt act, then, under the majority rule, the injury would appear to have been proximately caused by the conspiracy to commit a substantive RICO offense, and standing would exist. If not, the proximate cause requirement of *Holmes v. Securities Investor Protection Corp.*, 503 U.S. 258 (1992), would not be satisfied and the plaintiff would lack standing to sue. Minority-rule courts likely would not adhere to this analysis because they do not generally require that the injury be caused by a predicate act. However, the introduction of a requirement of injury from an overt act that is also a predicate act where the underlying violation has not been consummated might be acceptable in minority-rule jurisdiction because the absence of a consummated violation of section 1962(a), (b), or (c) introduces further remoteness to the alleged RICO injury.

Operation or Management. The question whether the operation-and-management test of *Reves v. Ernst & Young*, 507 U.S. 170, 183 (1993), applies to alleged conspiracies to violate section 1962(c) is discussed in § 15, *infra*.

Chapter 4

Elements of Cause of Action

§ 11. Common Components

A. "Person" (Defendant)

The statutory definition of "person" contained in section 1961(3) applies whether the person is a plaintiff bringing an action under section 1964(c) or a defendant whose malediction is proscribed by section 1962(a), (b), (c), or (d). As a result, the discussion of persons as plaintiff (*see* § 6(A)(1), *supra*) generally applies to persons as defendant as well. There is, however, one significant distinction.

Governmental entities, which may bring suit as persons-plaintiff under section 1964(c), are not subject to RICO liability as defendants. There is some disparity in the case law as to whether governmental entities should be deemed not to be "persons" or should be recognized as "persons" but simply immune ones. For practical purposes, this is a distinction without a difference. The result is the same: they cannot successfully be sued.

Most courts reason that state and local governments are immune from RICO liability because they are incapable of forming the mens rea necessary to commit a predicate act.[1] *Lancaster Community Hosp. v. Antelope Valley Hosp. Dist.*, 940 F.2d 397 (9th Cir. 1991), *cert. denied*, 502 U.S. 1094 (U.S. Feb. 24, 1992) ("The RICO claims against [a government hospital and hospital district] fail because government entities are incapable of forming a malicious intent"); *Call v. Watts*, 1998 U.S. App. LEXIS 6875 (6th Cir. April 2, 1998) ("Counties are not persons under RICO because they lack 'the capability to form the mens rea requisite to the commission of the predicate acts'") (unpublished opinion), *quoting Smallwood v.*

1. For a discussion of mens rea generally, *see* § 11(G), *infra*.

Jefferson County Gov't, 743 F. Supp. 502 (W.D. Ky. 1990) (a county, like a municipal corporation, "cannot be considered a person under 18 U.S.C. § 1961(3) because [it] is an artificial person and lack[s] the capability to form the mens rea requisite to the commission of the predicate acts"); *Biondolillo v. City of Sunrise*, 736 F. Supp. 258 (S.D. Fla. 1990) ("although a municipality can be a person under RICO, it c[an]not be liable for the predicate acts necessary to establish [liability] under RICO. A municipality is incapable of the criminal intent necessary to support the alleged predicate offenses"); *accord North Star Contracting Corp. v. Long Island R.R*, 723 F. Supp. 902 (E.D.N.Y. 1989); *In re CitiSource, Inc. Secs. Litig.*, 694 F. Supp. 1069 (S.D.N.Y. 1988); *Massey v. Oklahoma City*, 643 F. Supp. 81 (W.D. Okla. 1986).

The Third Circuit has taken issue with this analysis, although reaching the same result—that state governmental entities enjoy immunity from RICO claims. In *Genty v. Resolution Trust Corp.*, 937 F.2d 899 (3d Cir. 1991), the Third Circuit determined that the foregoing reasoning "does not distinguish adequately those situations where municipal corporations are indeed held liable for the tortious or criminal acts of [their] officials, even where such acts require a malicious, willful or criminal intent." At the same time, however, the Third Circuit concluded that governmental entities' immunity from punitive damages extends to RICO's "mandatory award of treble damages, which are punitive in character." *Id.* at 914 ("we perceive no intention of Congress to abrogate the long-established and salutary principle of common law prohibiting punitive damages against municipalities").

The federal government is also immune from RICO liability, although this result has been reached on a slightly different rationale. Section 1961(1) defines "racketeering activity" in terms of a defendant being "chargeable," "indictable," or "punishable" for violations of specific state and federal offenses. The Sixth Circuit has declared that this is a requirement that the federal government cannot satisfy. *Berger v. Pierce*, 933 F.2d 393 (6th Cir. 1991) ("it is self-evident that a federal agency is not subject to state or federal criminal prosecution").

Regardless of the rationale, immunity is plainly the correct result. Particularly where the misconduct has already harmed the public, a RICO award would require taxpayers to pony up potentially the same sums a second time. *See, e.g., Lancaster Community Hosp. v. Antelope Valley Hosp. Dist.*, 940 F.2d at 404 ("The 'body politic,' that is, the taxpayers, will pay if [plaintiff's] RICO claim is successful. Yet the 'body politic' was the target of the deception perpetrated. Thus, the 'body politic' was not even aware of any dishonest activities, and plainly lacked the specific intent to deceive which is an element of mail fraud [which formed the predicate offenses]"). Where the misconduct has harmed others, there is no need or warrant to penalize citizens threefold. Compensatory damages, available under traditional theories of recovery, are sufficient. *Genty,* 937 F.2d at 913 (to permit RICO awards against governmental entities "would impose punitive damages upon the innocent taxpayers in favor of the plaintiffs who already may have recourse for their full compensation in a non-RICO cause of action against the [governmental entity] and a RICO action against [its] officers themselves").[2]

B. "Enterprise"

Section 1961(4) provides that the term "'enterprise' includes any individual, partnership, corporation, association, or other legal entity, and any union or group of individuals associated in fact although not a legal entity." This language is expansive; the word "includes" renders the statutory listing illustrative, not exhaustive. *See, e.g., United States v. Huber,* 603 F.2d 387 (2d Cir. 1979), *cert. denied,* 445 U.S. 927 (1980) ("The definition of 'enterprise' is a list beginning with the word 'includes.' This indicates that the list is not exhaustive but merely illustrative"). The term is liberally interpreted. *See, e.g., United States v. Masters,* 924 F.2d 1362 (7th Cir.), *cert. denied,* 508 U.S. 906 (1991) ("The statute says '"enterprise" includes'—not '"enterprise" means.' The point of the definition is to make it clear that it need not be a formal enterprise").

In *United States v. Turkette,* 452 U.S. 576 (1981), the Supreme Court ruled that the term "enterprise" encompasses both legitimate and illegitimate organizations without distinction. The *Turkette* Court also identified three characteristics of any RICO enterprise. An enterprise, it declared, "is proved *[first]* by evidence of an ongoing organization, formal or informal, and *[second]* by

---

2. There is an apparent conflict in the cases as to whether governmental entities may be held vicariously liable for RICO offenses committed by their agents or employees. *Compare* Lancaster Community Hosp. v. Antelope Valley Hosp. Dist., 940 F.2d at 404 (barring application of respondeat superior because "public policy is offended if all the citizens of a state are made liable for extraordinary damages as a result of the actions of a few dishonest officials"; relying on Newport v. Fact Concerts, Inc., 453 U.S. 247 (1981) (barring vicarious municipal liability under 42 U.S.C. § 1983)), *with* Genty v. Resolution Trust Corp.), 937 F.2d at 913 (remarking in dicta that, notwithstanding municipal immunity, "plaintiffs . . . may have . . . a RICO action against the municipal officers themselves"). *See generally* the discussion of vicarious liability in § 16, *infra.* In certain circumstances, ordinary principles of immunity will also attach to governmental officers and obviate the vicarious liability issue. *See, e.g.,* Connor v. City of Philadelphia, No. 90-6390, 1991 U.S. Dist. LEXIS 8058 (E.D. Pa. June 11, 1991) (state prosecutor). In those circumstances, the officer remains a RICO "person" but is not subject to liability under the act.

evidence that the various associates function as a continuing unit." *Third,* the *Turkette* opinion stressed the distinction between the "enterprise" and "pattern" requirements: "The 'enterprise' is not the 'pattern of racketeering activity', it is an entity separate and apart from the pattern of activity in which it engages." *Id.* at 583.

When an alleged enterprise is an "individual, partnership, corporation, association, or other legal entity," the *Turkette* criteria are easily satisfied. When, however, it is an "association in fact," as in *Turkette,* serious doubts may arise. Most enterprise-related questions arise in the context of alleged "associations in fact," and the *Turkette* analysis has bred conflicting lines of cases in the circuits and, indeed, within some circuits.

1. Structure Requirement A principal, if perhaps nominal, conflict among the circuits centers on whether, or to what extent, an associated-in-fact enterprise must bear an element of "structure." The leading case advancing the thesis that an enterprise must exhibit an independent "structure" is *United States v. Bledsoe,* 674 F.2d 647 (8th Cir. 1982), *cert. denied,* 459 U.S. 1040 (1983). In *Bledsoe,* the Eighth Circuit reasoned that unless the enterprise element is seen to require proof of "some structure separate from the racketeering activity and distinct from the organization which is a necessary incident to the racketeering," RICO would be punishing merely the commission of two specified (and related) crimes within a 10-year period—a result, in the Eighth Circuit's view, that Congress did not intend. The *Bledsoe* court held that a RICO enterprise is characterized by "concepts of continuity, unity, shared purpose and identifiable structure"—that it is earmarked by "commonality of purpose," "continuity of both structure and personality," and "an 'ascertainable structure' distinct from that inherent in the conduct of a pattern of racketeering activity." 674 F.2d at 664–65.

The Eighth Circuit continues to adhere to this analysis. *See, e.g., Atlas Pile Driving Co. v. DiCon Fin. Co.,* 886 F.2d 986 (8th Cir. 1989) ("a RICO enterprise must exhibit three basic characteristics: (1) a common or shared purpose; (2) some continuity of structure and personnel; and (3) an ascertainable structure distinct from that inherent in a pattern of racketeering").

The Third, Fourth, Fifth, Seventh, Ninth, and Tenth Circuits have reached substantially the same result, although the amount of structure required by any of these courts is not great. *See, e.g., United States v. Riccobene,* 709 F.2d 214 (3d Cir.), *cert. denied,* 464 U.S. 849 (1983) (requiring proof "that some sort of structure exists within the group for the making of decisions, whether it be hierarchical or consensual. There must be some mechanism for controlling and directing the affairs of the group on an ongoing, rather than an ad hoc, basis"); *Town of Kearny v. Hudson Meadows Urban Renewal Corp.*, 829 F.2d 1263 (3d Cir. 1987) (affirming trial court conclusion that "enterprise" requirement satisfied where "the enterprise had a structure for decisionmaking"); *United States v. Tillett*, 763 F.2d 628 (4th Cir. 1985) (focusing on "the operational structure . . . within the group, within which the various associates operated according to their specific function . . . financiers, organizers and associates"); *United States v. Padgett*, 1996 U.S. App. LEXIS 4209 (4th Cir. Mar. 1, 1996) (unpublished opinion) ("The enterprise can be formal or informal, and embody the concepts of continuity, unity, shared purpose and an identifiable structure"); *Calcasieu Marine Nat'l Bank v. Grant*, 943 F.2d 1453 (5th Cir. 1991) (requiring that a RICO associated-in-fact enterprise "be shown to have continuity" and "incorporat[ing] this notion of continuity into our definition of such enterprises. An association-in-fact enterprise (1) must have an existence separate and apart from the pattern of racketeering, (2) must be an ongoing organization, and (3) its members must function as a continuing unit as shown by a hierarchical or consensual decision-making structure"); *Shaffer v. Williams*, 794 F.2d 1030 (5th Cir. 1986) ("A RICO enterprise must have an ongoing organization, with associates functioning as a continuing unit. An 'ongoing organization' is shown by the existence of a decision-making structure, whether hierarchical or consensual. The RICO enterprise must have a common or shared purpose and continuity of structure and personnel" (citations omitted)); *Bonner v. Henderson*, 147 F.3d 457 (5th Cir. 1998) ("An association-in-fact consists of personnel who share a common purpose and collectively form a decision-making structure"); *United States v. Rogers*, 89 F.3d 1326 (7th Cir.), *cert. denied*, 519 U.S. 999 (1996) ("The hallmark of an enterprise is 'structure.' It includes informal organizations such as criminal gangs, and 'there must be some structure, to distinguish an enterprise from a mere conspiracy, but there need not be much'") (citations omitted); *Chang v. Chen*, 80 F.3d 1293 (9th Cir. 1996) ("a RICO enterprise must have an ascertainable structure separate and apart from the structure inherent in the conduct of the pattern of racketeering activity"); *United States v. Sanders*, 928 F.2d .940, 944 (10th Cir.), *cert. denied*, 502 U.S. 845 (1991) ("For purposes of this appeal, we will employ the Third Circuit Court of Appeal's elaboration of a framework for analyzing the existence of an enterprise as stated in *Riccobene*").

The Second, Eleventh, and District of Columbia Circuits have rejected any independent structure requirement, although that may be a bit misleading since they are still guided by the precepts of the Supreme Court's decision in *United States v. Turkette*, 452 U.S. 576 (1981), as discussed below. *See, e.g.*, *United States v. Bagaric*, 706 F.2d 42 (2d Cir.), *cert. denied*, 464 U.S. 840 (1983) ("a group of individuals may join together and therefore be 'associated in fact' . . . although not a legally cognizable entity in one of the traditional forms . . . solely for the purpose of conducting their activities. That is, it is logical to characterize any associative group in terms of what it *does,* rather than by abstract analysis of its structure"); *United States v. Coonan,* 938 F.2d 1553 (2d Cir. 1991), *cert. denied,* 503 U.S. 941 (1992) (same); *United States v. Indelicato,* 865 F.2d 1370 (2d Cir.), *cert. denied,* 491 U.S. 907 (1989) (stressing "that the concepts of relatedness and continuity are attributes of activity [i.e., of a RICO pattern], not of a RICO enterprise"); *United States v. Weinstein,* 762 F.2d 1522 (11th Cir. 1985), *cert. denied,* 475 U.S. 1110 (1986) (expressly rejecting any requirement that "a RICO enterprise must possess an 'ascertainable structure' distinct from the associations necessary to conduct the pattern of racketeering activity"); *United States v. Perholtz,* 842 F.2d 343 (D.C. Cir.), *cert. denied,* 488 U.S. 821 (1988) (rejecting structure requirement and requiring only "pro[of] that the associates are bound together by some form of organization so that they function as a unit"); *but see United States v. Richardson,* 167 F.3d 621 (D.C.Cir. 1999) ("a RICO enterprise may be 'any union or group of individuals associated in fact although not a legal entity,' so long as it involves 'some structure, to distinguish an enterprise from a mere conspiracy'") (citation omitted); *United States v. Hoyle,* 122 F.3d 48 (D.C.Cir. 1997) ("we do not believe that the government must show, under [21 U.S.C. § 848], the structure of a continuing organization equivalent to a RICO 'enterprise'").

Yet other courts have either not confronted or not yet consistently resolved the issue. *See, e.g., United States v. Owens,* 167 F.3d 739 (1st Cir. 1999). *See generally* Note, *The Enterprise Requirement: Getting to the Heart of Civil RICO,* 1988 WIS. L. REV. 663; Note, *Functions of the RICO Enterprise Concept,* 64 NOTRE DAME L. REV. 646 (1989); Annotation, 52 A.L.R. Fed. 818 (Supp. 1999).

This disparity of opinion is substantive in the sense that courts rejecting the "structure" requirement believe that they are verbalizing a looser standard than those that adhere to it, and ultimately this linguistic conflict may warrant Supreme Court clarification. However, the degree of divergence between these views should not be overstated. Whether or not a "structure" exists is a matter of characterization; it is the product of a court's application of a metaphysical construct to a given set of facts. Since "structure" means somewhat different things even among those circuits adhering to a "structure" analysis, it is conceivable that courts applying distinct variants of the "structure" analysis could come to diverse conclusions on substantially the same set of facts. At the same time, depending on the judges and the facts, a "structure" analysis may lead to the same conclusion as a "structure"-less analysis in any given case.

Under either approach, whether a specific set of facts reflects an associated-in-fact enterprise "depends on objective interconnections and requires a careful scrutiny of the facts." *United States v. Feldman*, 853 F.2d 648, 658 (9th Cir. 1988), *cert. denied*, 489 U.S. 1030 (1989). The value of the "structure" analysis—really, a characterization or conclusion more than an analytic tool—lies principally in its capturing, in a short locution, the basic criteria provided by the Supreme Court in *Turkette*: (1) "ongoing organization, formal or informal"; (2) various "associates function[ing] as a continuing unit"; and (3) "an entity separate and apart from the pattern of activity in which it engages." *United States v. Turkette*, 452 U.S. 576, 583 (1981).

2. Economic Motivation Prior to the Supreme Court's decision in *National Org. for Women, Inc. v. Scheidler*, 510 U.S. 249 (1994), the circuits were also split concerning whether RICO requires that the enterprise or underlying predicate acts be economically motivated.[3] In *Scheidler*, 501 U.S. at 252, the Supreme Court resolved the conflict, ruling that RICO did not require either that the racketeering enterprise or the predicate acts of racketeering be motivated by an economic purpose.

The *Scheidler* Court reasoned that (1) "[n]owhere in either § 1962(c) or the RICO definitions in § 1961 is there any indication that an economic motivation is required" (*id.* at 257); (2) an enterprise that is not economically motivated is as capable of "affect[ing]" interstate or foreign commerce as any other (*id.* at 258); (3) the use of the term "enterprise," in subsections (a) and (b), to connote a profitable (for-profit) victim of racketeering did not compel that

3. For example, the Second and Eighth Circuits previously considered that some financial dimension or economic motivation was a prerequisite to any RICO enterprise. *See, e.g.*, United States v. Ivic, 700 F.2d 51 (2d Cir. 1983) ("an 'enterprise' . . . is evidently an organized profit-seeking venture"); United States v. Bagaric, 706 F.2d 42 (2d Cir.), *cert. denied*, 464 U.S. 840 (1983) (requiring "an economic dimension sufficient to bring [the offenses] within the language and intention of § 1962," although simultaneously declining to hold "that economic gain must be the sole motive of every RICO enterprise"); United States v. Flynn, 852 F.2d 1045 (8th Cir.), *cert. denied*, 488 U.S. 974 (1988) ("For purposes of RICO, an enterprise must be directed toward an economic goal"); United States v. Anderson, 626 F.2d 1358 (8th Cir. 1980), *cert. denied*, 450 U.S. 912 (1981) (the enterprise must exist "for the purpose of maintaining operations directed toward an economic goal"). (So, too, did the Seventh Circuit in the opinion reversed by the Supreme Court in *Scheidler*). In contrast, the Third Circuit, in Northeast Women's Center, Inc. v. McMonagle, 868 F.2d 1342 (3d Cir.), *cert. denied*, 493 U.S. 901 (1989), held that the plaintiff was not required to prove economic motivation underlying a RICO predicate act.

connotation in subsection (c), where the enterprise is the vehicle of criminality. *Id.* at 259.

The *Scheidler* decision is plainly correct. No persuasive statutory basis exists for imposing the economic motivation requirement. Prior to *Scheidler,* the Second Circuit had reasoned that, as used in subsections (a) and (b), "the term 'enterprise' quite clearly refers to the sort of entity in which funds can be invested and a property interest of some sort acquired, and hence the sort of entity which one joins to make money." *United States v. Ivic,* 700 F.2d at 60. It concluded that the same connotation should attach to any subsection (c) "enterprise" because "[w]hen the same word is used in the same section of an act more than once, and the meaning is clear in one place, it will be assumed to have the same meaning in other places." *Id.*

This approach failed to distinguish between the quite different roles of the RICO enterprise under section 1962(a) or (b), on the one hand, and under section 1962(c), on the other. In subsections (a) and (b), the enterprise is an investment vehicle or target, sometimes denominated the "prize" or "victim" of the RICO defendant's misconduct. Quite distinctly, under subsection (c), the enterprise is itself the malefactor. Section 1962(c) is, therefore, directed at preventing or punishing a different ill than that targeted by section 1962(a) or (b)—namely, enterprise misbehavior (persons conducting an enterprise's affairs through a pattern of racketeering activity). There is no apparent need or warrant to require that the culprit enterprise of subsection (c) bear the earmarks of the financial plum or plundered booty envisaged in subsections (a) and (b). The Second Circuit's conclusion was, at best, the procrustean product of a perceived consistency at odds with the structure of the statute.[4]

But even this perceived consistency was illusory. The fact that the defendant (under subsection (a) or (b)) may eye an enterprise as a financial plum or booty to plunder reflects a motivation on the part of the defendant (the "person"), not a necessary characteristic of the enterprise. It is no more than a truism that most criminals are in it for the money. If a defendant has the requisite mens rea,[5] however, it is irrelevant whether his or her motivation is financial. In any case, it is the motivation of the defendant, not the enterprise, that is at issue.

This conclusion (that an enterprise need not be economically motivated) is reinforced by the fact that a legal entity identified as

---

4. *See, e.g.,* Beretsky, *Civil RICO and Anti-Abortion Protest: Must Protestors Profit?* 30 CAL. W. L. REV. 119, 135 n.123 (1993) (quoting **Treatise**).

5. *See* § 11(G), *infra,* for a discussion of mens rea.

an "enterprise" within section 1962(a), (b), or (c) need not be a profit-making or profit-generating entity. Perhaps the classic illustration is the governmental office or bureau, which has consistently been held to comprise a RICO "enterprise" under section 1962(c) when conducted through a pattern of racketeering activity. *See, e.g., Averbach v. Rival Mfg. Co.*, 809 F.2d 1016 (3d Cir.), *cert. denied*, 482 U.S. 915 (1987) ("a court may be an enterprise within the meaning of RICO"); *United States v. Goot*, 894 F.2d 231 (7th Cir.), *cert. denied*, 111 S. Ct. 45 (1990) (prosecutor's office held an enterprise for RICO purposes); *United States v. Hocking*, 860 F.2d 769 (7th Cir. 1988) ("'governmental or public entities fit within the definition of "enterprise" for purposes of RICO'" (Illinois Department of Transportation)).

Since nonprofit legal entities can clearly be "enterprises" within sections 1961(4) and 1962(c), it follows that the economic motivation test would necessarily have been limited to associated-in-fact enterprises. There is no statutory basis for distinguishing this type of enterprise from any other by imposing a unique motivational requirement—even assuming that the motivation of the enterprise, rather than that of the defendant, were somehow statutorily relevant.

The pre-*Scheidler* Eighth Circuit approach was infirm on an independent ground as well. That court construed the term "enterprise" in light of the type of offenses selected by Congress to comprise "racketeering activity" in section 1961(1). Under the Eighth Circuit's former approach, "[t]he offenses chosen reflect an economic orientation, reinforcing the view that Congress intended RICO to aim at the target of organized crime's infiltration of the American economy." *United States v. Anderson*, 626 F.2d 1358, 1368 (8th Cir. 1980). On that statutory ground, and in deference to legislative history to the same effect, the Eighth Circuit determined that a RICO enterprise must exist "for the purpose of maintaining operations directed toward an economic goal." *Id.* at 1372.

This approach was subject to challenge on two grounds. First, it is not true that all of the "racketeering activity" offenses set forth in section 1961(1) "reflect an economic orientation." Obvious contrary examples include murder; obstruction of justice; obstruction of criminal investigations; obstruction of state or local law enforcement; tampering with a witness, victim, or informant; retaliating against a witness, victim, or informant; and transporting a minor for illicit sexual activity. Second, to the extent that the Eighth Circuit's analysis was grounded in the legislative intention of eradicating organized crime's influence on American economic life, the statutory language is far more encompassing than that goal would require, and the Supreme Court precedent repeatedly directs that the statute's plain meaning be given its due. *See, e.g., H.J. Inc. v.*

Northwestern Bell Tel. Co., 492 U.S. 229 (1989) (rejecting, due to "evident textual problem[s,]" the "suggestion . . . that Congress intended [any] organized crime limitation").

As *Scheidler* concluded, there is no Robin Hood exception to RICO. There is no "safe harbor" for miscreant enterprises, whatever their motivation. If all the statutory criteria are satisfied (*see* chapter 4, *passim*), the statute has been violated. "Economic motivation" is beside the point.

3. Multiple Corporations or Entities Under section 1961(4), a question occasionally arises as to whether multiple corporations or other legal entities can, in the aggregate, form an association-in-fact enterprise. The question usually arises under section 1961(c) as a function of creative pleading attempting to satisfy the person/enterprise dichotomy (discussed in § 9(A), *supra*). The statutory reason that a question exists lies in section 1961(4), which—in describing associated-in-fact enterprises—refers only to "any union or group of *individuals* associated in fact although not a legal entity" (emphasis added). Occasional decisions have construed this reference to "individuals"—which, in RICO, refers to people only—as precluding a group of corporations or other legal entities from constituting an association-in-fact enterprise. *See, e.g., Benard v. Hoff,* 727 F. Supp. 211 (D. Md. 1989) ("Corporations cannot under RICO associate in fact to constitute an enterprise").

That analysis, however, has been rejected by all those circuits that have examined the issue. The appellate courts have so concluded on the theory that (1) the use of the word "includes" at the beginning of the definition set forth in section 1961(4) ("'enterprise' includes . . . ") renders the statutory list illustrative and (2) the language should in all events be construed liberally, as Congress specified. *See, e.g., United States v. London,* 66 F.3d 1227 (1st Cir. 1995) ("two or more legal entities can form or be part of an association-in-fact RICO enterprise"); *United States v. Blinder,* 10 F.3d 1468 (9th Cir. 1993) ("a group or union consisting *solely* of corporations or other legal entities can constitute an 'associated in fact' enterprise") (court's emphasis); *Dana Corp. v. Blue Cross & Blue Shield Mut. of N. Ohio,* 900 F.2d 882 (6th Cir. 1988) ("in view of the broad construction of RICO, a group of corporations can form an enterprise"); *United States v. Huber,* 603 F.2d 387 (2d Cir. 1979), *cert. denied,* 445 U.S. 927 (1980) (to exclude a group of corporations from the definition of "enterprise" would "perversely insulate the most sophisticated racketeering combinations from RICO's sanctions, the precise opposite of Congress' intentions"); *United States v. Navarro-Ordas,* 770 F.2d 959 (11th Cir. 1985), *cert. denied,* 475 U.S.

1016 (1986) ("a group of corporations can be a 'group of individuals associated in fact' within the meaning of the 'enterprise' definition of 18 U.S.C. § 1961(4)"); *Shearin v. E.F. Hutton Group, Inc.*, 885 F.2d 1162 (3d Cir. 1989) ("nothing precludes an association of [two or more] corporations for illicit purposes from constituting an enterprise").

4. Legal Entities Plus Their Agents or Constituents

Legal entities, such as corporations, can act only through agents, officers, employees, and constituent parts. In some sense, most corporate acts are accomplished through an "association" of individuals and, not infrequently, through entities (for example, subsidiaries, independent contractors). The question arises whether activity performed by agents, officers, and employees in the course and scope of their employment—or by a subsidiary, affiliate, or independent contractor (or by some combination of the foregoing)—can constitute an association-in-fact enterprise distinct from the entity itself.

As previously discussed (*see* § 9(A), *supra*), this issue often arises under section 1962(c) when the court is confronted with the question of whether the defendant and the enterprise are sufficiently distinct to satisfy the rigors of that subsection. Generally, the individual officers and employees of a corporation acting in the course and scope of their duties—when viewed together with the corporation or other affiliates or agents of the corporation acting within the scope of their agency—do not constitute an association-in-fact enterprise distinct from the corporation. *Khurana v. Innovative Health Care Sys.*, 130 F.3d 143 (5th Cir. 1997), *vacated as moot*, 119 S. Ct. 442 (1998) ("While it is theoretically possible for a corporation to play a separate active role in RICO violations committed by its employees and agents, when the alleged associate-in-fact entity is in reality no different from the association of individuals or entities that constitute a defendant 'person' and carry out its activities, the distinctiveness requirement is not met in regard to that defendant") (citations omitted); *Fitzgerald v. Chrysler Corp.*, 116 F.3d 225 (7th Cir. 1997) ("Where a [corporation] deals with its dealers and other agents in the ordinary way, so that their role in the manufacturer's illegal acts is entirely incidental, differing not at all from what it would be if these agents were . . . employees . . . , the [corporation] . . . (or any subset of the members of the corporate family) do not constitute an enterprise within the meaning of the statute."); *Riverwoods Chappaqua Corp. v. Marine Midland Bank, N.A.*, 30 F.3d 339 (2d Cir. 1994) ("by alleging a RICO enterprise that consists merely of a corporate defendant associated with its own employees or agents carrying on the regular affairs of the defendant, the distinctness requirement may not be circumvented"); *see also NRB Indus. v. R.A. Taylor & Assocs.*, 1998 U.S. Dist. LEXIS 25 (S.D.N.Y. Jan. 6, 1998) ("While 'a single entity simultaneously can be both the person and one of a number of members of the enterprise,' this is so only when the 'enterprise . . . is *distinct* from each of' the RICO 'persons.' An enterprise that 'consists merely of a corporate defendant associated with its own employees or agents' is not sufficiently distinct") (court's emphasis; citations omitted). On the same analysis, subsidiaries and affiliates of a corporation—alone or together with the corporation or other agents of the corporation acting within the scope of their agency—generally do not constitute an association-in-fact enterprise distinct from the parent corporation. *Discon, Inc. v. NYNEX Corp.*, 93 F.3d 1055 (2d Cir. 1996), *vacated on antitrust grounds,* 525 U.S. 128 (1997) (distinctiveness requirement not satisfied where the three corporate defendants constituted the alleged enterprise; although they were legally separate entities, the three affiliates "operated within a unified corporate structure" and were "guided by a single corporate consciousness"); *accord Katzman v. Victoria's Secret Catalogue,* 167 F.R.D. 649 (S.D.N.Y. 1996), *aff'd mem.*, 113 F.3d 1229 (2d Cir. 1997) (association-in-fact enterprise consisting of parent company, subsidiaries, and their employees "ignores the required distinction between the culpable 'person' and the 'enterprise'").

Chief Judge Edward R. Becker of the Third Circuit has properly observed that, when an organizational entity is involved, it is important to bear in mind the directive of *Reves v. Ernst & Young,* 507 U.S. 170, 183 (1993), that the defendant must be involved in the operation and management of the enterprise (discussed in § 9(c), *supra*). Certainly, a corporation or other entity can be run by its managers as an enterprise for palpably illicit ends. *Jaguar Cars Inc. v. Royal Oaks Motor Car Co.,* 46 F.3d 258 (3d Cir. 1995) (where alleged enterprise consisted of corporation alone, criminal fraud perpetrated by president and general manager through the corporate entity presented a viable section 1962(c) claim, preserving the essential distinction between the defendant "person[s]" and the "enterprise"). At the same time, as Chief Judge Richard A. Posner of the Seventh Circuit has noted, an organization can act only through its agents, so to permit routine allegations that insiders are responsible under RICO for every corporate dereliction "would eliminate any separate function for the 'conducts the affairs of through' language of the statute if the perpetrator is a firm." *Emery v. American Gen. Fin. Inc.,* 134 F.3d 1321, 1324–25 (7th Cir.), *cert. denied,* 119 S.Ct. 57 (1998) ("it is one thing to allege that criminals are using a corporation to commit crimes, a natural meaning to impress on the statutory language of conducting an enterprise's affairs through a pattern of racketeering activity, and another to assert merely that since the corporation's unlawful scheme must have been hatched by someone connected to the corporation, the scheme (provided it satisfies the statute's pattern requirement) violates RICO").

The ultimate issue is whether the alleged association-in-fact is merely a pleading subterfuge to reach the deep pockets of a target, collective defendant. This is always a fact-specific inquiry. (*See generally* § 9(A), *supra.*) If a corporation alone cannot serve both as defendant and enterprise, the corporation and its president are generally not an "association in fact" separate from the corporation permitting the two of them to be sued successfully under section 1962(c). As various individuals or entities are added to the mix, it may become a closer question whether an "enterprise" that is distinct from the defendant "person" has been stated.

It will always remain a judgment call whether the alleged association-in-fact is discrete and separable from the collective entity—or whether the pleader has engaged in a sophistic parsing exercise designed to create the illusion of many from the reality of one. Among the relevant factors for the court to consider are

1. the number and identity of persons comprising the alleged association-in-fact;
2. the relationship of the individuals to one another (for example, coworkers) and to the collective entities among them (for example, principals, agents, officers, employees);
3. the relationship between named collective entities (for example, parent-subsidiary, affiliates, general partner-partnership, principal-agent, customer-vendor); and
4. the relationship between (a) the acts alleged, (b) the ordinary course of business or affairs of any named collective entity, and (c) any duties owed by the individuals (or affiliated or subordinate collective entities) to any collective entity in the ordinary course of business or affairs, without regard to the existence of the purported association-in-fact (for example, were the acts performed in the ordinary course of business by a corporate officer? By the corporation's advertising agency?).

The closer the nexus between the individuals (and any affiliated or subordinate entities), the acts, and the ordinary course of business of the target (collective) defendant among them, the less likely that a substantial association-in-fact has been stated.

Bear in mind that distinguishing between collective entities and their officers, agents, and employees is important only when the person and enterprise must be kept distinct. This distinction must be drawn only under section 1962(c), not under section

1962(a) or (b).[6] Moreover, even under section 1962(c), a corporation may act together with its own officers and agents to conduct the affairs of another corporate enterprise in violation of section 1962(c) without transgressing the person/enterprise distinction. *Ashland Oil, Inc. v. Arnett*, 875 F.2d 1271 (7th Cir. 1989). *Compare Arzuaga-Collazo v. Oriental Fed. Sav. Bank*, 913 F.2d 5 (1st Cir. 1990) ("The complaint does not charge that they [the parent company and its wholly owned subsidiary] were conducting some other unlawful enterprise" (court's emphasis)).

5. Inanimate Objects Although section 1961(4) is construed as providing an illustrative, not an exhaustive, list of potential "enterprises," the statutory definition is not broad enough to include inanimate objects. Inanimate objects are of a character distinct from those identified on the statutory list—they are neither individuals nor legal entities staffed by individuals—and by definition are incapable of satisfying the *Turkette* criteria. *See generally Elliott v. Foufas*, 867 F.2d 877 (5th Cir. 1989) ("An inanimate object such as an apartment cannot constitute a RICO enterprise"); *Old Time Enters., Inc. v. International Coffee Corp.*, 862 F.2d 1213 (5th Cir. 1988) ("it is evident that inanimate objects, such as coffee, or intangible rights, such as contract rights, cannot possibly constitute a RICO 'enterprise' which be either an individual or a 'legal entity,' such as a corporation, or an association of 'individuals'"); *Guidry v. Bank of LaPlace*, 740 F. Supp. 1208 (E.D. La. 1990) ("A bank account fits most closely into the category of inanimate objects . . . called contract rights [and, t]hus, . . . is not a valid RICO enterprise"); *Creed Taylor, Inc. v. CBS Inc.*, 718 F. Supp. 1171 (S.D.N.Y. 1989) ("A RICO enterprise must be an association of natural persons or legal entities. It cannot be a collection of inanimate objects or a technology"—in this case, the "Masters Catalog" of the plaintiff record company).

6. "Enterprise" Versus "Person" *See* §§ 9(A) and 11(B)(4), *supra*.

7. "Enterprise" Versus "Pattern" *Turkette* teaches that an enterprise is not a "pattern of racketeering activity" and must be "an entity separate and apart from the pattern of activity in which it engages." *United States v. Turkette*, 452 U.S. 576, 583 (1981). This teaching is carefully attended to by the courts. *See, e.g., McDonough v. Nat'l Home Ins. Co.*, 108 F.3d 174 (8th Cir. 1997); *Montesano v. Seafirst Commercial Corp.*, 818 F.2d 423 (5th Cir. 1987).

---

6. *See* §§ 7–8, *supra*.

The distinction is relatively straightforward, although the evidence offered to establish one may also establish the other. *See Turkette,* 452 U.S. at 583 ("the proof used to establish these separate elements may in particular cases coalesce"). The pattern of racketeering activity is a series of criminal acts as defined in section 1961(1). The focus is on the relationship between the offenses alleged. *United States v. Indelicato,* 865 F.2d 1370 (2d Cir.) (en banc), *cert. denied,* 491 U.S. 907 (1989) ("the concept 'pattern' focuses on the relationship between acts of racketeering") (quoting Blakey & Gettings, *Racketeer Influenced and Corrupt Organizations (RICO): Basic Concepts—Criminal and Civil Remedies,* 53 Temp. L.Q. 1009 (1980)). The enterprise, in contrast, is a person, an entity, or a group of persons or entities associated together for a common purpose of engaging in a course of conduct. *See Procter & Gamble Co. v. Big Apple Indus. Bldgs., Inc.,* 879 F.2d 10 (2d Cir. 1989), *cert. denied,* 493 U.S. 1022 (1990) ("A pattern of racketeering activity is a series of *criminal acts* as defined in § 1961(1), and the enterprise is generally *a group of persons* associated together for a common purpose of engaging in a course of conduct" (emphasis in original)).

C. "Racketeering Activity"

1. Generally Under section 1961(1),[7] "'racketeering activity' consists of no more and no less than the commission of a predicate act." *Sedima, S.P.R.L. v. Imrex Co., Inc.,* 473 U.S. 479, 495 (1985).

---

7. As set forth in § 1961(1):

> "racketeering activity" means (A) any act or threat involving murder, kidnapping, gambling, arson, robbery, bribery, extortion, dealing in obscene matter, or dealing in a controlled substance or listed chemical (as defined in section 102 of the Controlled Substances Act), which is chargeable under State law and punishable by imprisonment for more than one year; (B) any act which is indictable under any of the following provisions of title 18, United States Code: Section 201 (relating to bribery), section 224 (relating to sports bribery), sections 471, 472, and 473 (relating to counterfeiting), section 659 (relating to theft from interstate shipment) if the act indictable under section 659 is felonious, section 664 (relating to embezzlement from pension and welfare funds), sections 891–894 (relating to extortionate credit transactions), section 1029 (relating to fraud and related activity in connection with access devices), section 1084 (relating to the transmission of gambling information), section 1341 (relating to mail fraud), section 1343 (relating to wire fraud), section 1344 (relating to financial institution fraud), section 1425 (relating to the procurement of citizenship or nationalization unlawfully), section 1426 (relating to the reproduction of naturalization or citizenship papers), section 1427 (relating to the sale of naturalization or citizenship papers), sections 1461–1465 (relating to obscene matter), section 1503 (relating to obstruction of justice), section 1510 (relating to obstruction of criminal investigations), section 1511 (relating to the obstruction of State or local law enforcement), section 1512 (relating to tampering with a witness, victim, or an informant), section 1513 (relating to retaliating against a witness, victim, or an informant), section 1542 (relating to false statement in application and use of passport), section 1543 (relating to forgery or false use of passport), section 1544 (relating to misuse of passport), section 1546 (relating to fraud and

Exhaustive List. Section 1961(1) sets forth an exhaustive list of predicate offenses. Unlike section 1961(4), which provides that the term "'enterprise' *includes*" the list that follows (and is thus deemed to be purely illustrative),[8] section 1961(1) delineates what the phrase "'racketeering activity' *means*" (emphasis added). Since all predicate acts are enumerated in section 1961(1), no unenumerated act can constitute a predicate offense, regardless of how similar it may be to any specified offense. *See, e.g., Miranda v. Ponce Fed. Bank,* 948 F.2d 41 (1st Cir. 1991) ("Congress painstakingly enumerated a complete list of predicate acts in 18 U.S.C. § 1961(1)").

No Prior-Conviction Requirement. There is no requirement that the defendant have been convicted of any of the underlying predicate acts before a civil RICO action may be commenced. *Sedima,* 473 U.S. at 493 (a prior-conviction requirement cannot be found in the definition of "racketeering activity" nor elsewhere in the statute, and the legislative history does not reflect any intention to impose such a requirement).

Single Action/Multiple Violations. Where a single action violates more than one of the statutes recited in section 1961(1), it constitutes only a single predicate act for RICO purposes, not mul-

---

misuse of visas, permits, and other documents), sections 1581–88 (relating to peonage and slavery), section 1951 (relating to interference with commerce, robbery, or extortion), section 1952 (relating to racketeering), section 1953 (relating to interstate transportation of wagering paraphernalia), section 1954 (relating to unlawful welfare fund payments), section 1955 (relating to the prohibition of illegal gambling businesses), section 1956 (relating to the laundering of monetary instruments), section 1957 (relating to engaging in monetary transactions in property derived from specified unlawful activity), section 1958 (relating to use of interstate commerce facilities in the commission of murder-for-hire), sections 2251, 2251A, 2252, and 2260 (relating to sexual exploitation of children), sections 2312 and 2313 (relating to interstate transportation of stolen motor vehicles), sections 2314 and 2315 (relating to interstate transportation of stolen property), section 2321 (relating to trafficking in certain motor vehicles or motor vehicle parts), section 2318 (relating to trafficking in counterfeit labels for phonorecords, computer programs or computer program documentation or packaging and copies of motion pictures or other audiovisual works), section 2319 (relating to criminal infringement of a copyright), section 2319A (relating to unauthorized fixation of and trafficking in sound recordings and music videos of live musical performances), section 2320 (relating to trafficking in goods or services bearing counterfeit marks), sections 2341–2346 (relating to trafficking in contraband cigarettes), sections 2421–24 (relating to white slave traffic), (C) any act which is indictable under title 29, United States Code, section 186 (dealing with restrictions on payments and loans to labor organizations) or section 501(c) (relating to embezzlement from union funds), (D) any offense involving fraud connected with a case under title 11, fraud in the sale of securities, or the felonious manufacture, importation, receiving, concealment, buying, selling, or otherwise dealing in a controlled substance or listed chemical (as defined in section 102 of the Controlled Substances Act), punishable under any law of the United States, or (E) any act which is indictable under the Currency and Foreign Transactions Reporting Act[.]

8. See § 11(B), *supra.*

tiple predicate acts. *See, e.g., United States v. Walgren,* 885 F.2d 1417 (9th Cir. 1989) ("'it is not proper under RICO to charge two predicate acts where one action violates two statutes,'" quoting *United States v. Kragness,* 830 F.2d 842 (8th Cir. 1987)); *Polycast Technology Corp. v. Uniroyal, Inc.,* 728 F. Supp. 926 (S.D.N.Y. 1989) (noting the Second Circuit's warning in *United States v. Indelicato,* 865 F.2d 1370 (2d Cir.) (en banc), *cert. denied,* 491 U.S. 907 (1989), that "it would 'disapprove any attempt by the government or a private plaintiff to go beyond Congress' intent and fragment an act that is plainly unitary into multiple acts in order to invoke RICO'"); *see also United States v. Biaggi,* 909 F.2d 662 (2d Cir. 1990), *cert. denied,* 499 U.S. 904 (1991) (bribery and accepting a gratuity (a lesser included offense of bribery)—both based on the same act (a promise of future employment)—constitute a single predicate act).

Whether a particular complaint improperly alleges a single act that violates two predicate offense statutes or properly alleges multiple acts that violate multiple predicate offense statutes is a matter of judgment and, to some degree, one of characterization and conclusion. *See, e.g., United States v. Hobson,* 893 F.2d 1267 (11th Cir.), *cert. denied,* 498 U.S. 957 (1990) (rejecting the defendant's contention that "he committed only one isolated act relating to the importation and possession" of controlled substances "consist[ing] of making . . . a $1.5 million advance payment for the load"; held, this "characterization of the issue misconceives the facts"—the separate importation and possession convictions "did not involve merely a single isolated act of paying money but rather a series of acts, including a demand for repayment of a large sum of money or delivery . . . which 'by its nature project[ed] into the future with a threat of repetition'").

State Law Offenses. The state law offenses set forth in section 1961(1)(A) are described generically: "any act or threat involving murder, kidnapping, gambling, arson, robbery, bribery, extortion, dealing in obscene matter, or dealing in narcotic or other dangerous drugs, which is chargeable under State law and punishable by imprisonment for more than one year." In determining whether a predicate act has been alleged within this subsection, the court looks not only at the laws so labeled in the state statutory compilation but also at the nature of the act charged and the punishment available under any state criminal statute punishing that act. *Rose v. Bartle,* 871 F.2d 331 (3d Cir. 1989) ("'[t]he test for determining whether the charged acts fit into the generic category of the predicate offense is whether indictment [or complaint] charges a type of activity generally known or categorized in the proscribed category.' . . . [A]ll that is required of the plaintiffs is to 'specify the nature of the predicate acts to a degree that will allow the defendants to comprehend the specific acts which they are required to answer'"); *United States v. Garner*, 837 F.2d 1404 (7th Cir. 1987), *cert. denied*, 486 U.S. 1035 (1988) ("The labels placed on a state statute do not determine whether that statute proscribes bribery for purposes of the RICO statute"); *United States v. Kotvas*, 941 F.2d 1141 (11th Cir. 1991), *cert. denied*, 506 U.S. 1055 (quoting and following *Garner*).

2. Selected Predicate Acts

a. Mail and Wire Fraud Mail and wire fraud are the two most frequently alleged predicate acts. The mail fraud statute, 18 U.S.C. § 1341, prohibits any person from knowingly causing the use of the mails—or, since 1994, private carrier services like Federal Express—"for the purpose of executing" any "scheme or artifice to defraud."[9] The actual violation is the mailing, which must relate to the underlying fraudulent scheme. The mailing need not, however, be an essential element of the scheme. It is sufficient if it is incidental to an essential part of the scheme. *Schmuck v. United States*, 489 U.S. 705 (1989). The mailing need not contain any misrepresentations or omissions. Even "innocent" mailings are sufficient if they are incident to an essential part of the scheme to defraud. *Id.*; *Pereira v. United States*, 347 U.S. 1 (1954).

---

9. *Florida Software Sys., Inc. v. Columbia/HCA Healthcare Corp.*, 1999 U.S. Dist. LEXIS 6178 (M.D.Fla. Apr. 19, 1999) ("[T]hird-Party Defendants claim that [third-party plaintiff's] mail fraud allegations are defective because named items were sent via private carriers, such as Federal Express and U.P.S., instead of U.S. Mail. This argument is baseless as the relevant statute, as amended in 1994, now includes mail delivered 'by the Postal Service, or . . . any private or commercial interstate carrier'").

In its entirety, 18 U.S.C. § 1341 provides the following:

> Whoever, having devised or intending to devise any scheme or artifice to defraud, or for obtaining money or property by means of false or fraudulent pretenses, representations, or promises, or to sell, dispose of, loan, exchange, alter, give away, distribute, supply, or furnish or procure for unlawful use any counterfeit or spurious coin, obligation, security, or other article, or anything represented to be or intimated or held out to be such counterfeit or spurious article, for the purpose of executing such scheme or artifice or attempting so to do, places in any post office or authorized depository for mail matter, any matter or thing whatever to be sent or delivered by the Postal Service, or deposits or causes to be deposited any matter or thing whatever to be sent or delivered by any private or commercial interstate carrier, or takes or receives therefrom, any such matter or thing, or knowingly causes to be delivered by mail according to the direction thereon, or at the place at which it is directed to be delivered by the person to whom it is addressed, any such matter or thing, shall be fined under this title or imprisoned not more than five years, or both. If the violation affects a financial institution, such person shall be fined not more than $1,000,000 or imprisoned not more than 30 years, or both.

The wire fraud statute, 18 U.S.C. § 1343,[10] was patterned after the mail fraud statute, and it is interpreted consistently with that statute. *United States v. Computer Sciences Corp.*, 689 F.2d 1181 (4th Cir. 1982), *cert. denied*, 459 U.S. 1105 (1983); *United States v. Lemire*, 720 F.2d 1327 (D.C. Cir. 1983), *cert. denied*, 467 U.S. 1226 (1984). To state a violation of the wire or mail fraud statute, it is necessary to show (1) a scheme to defraud, (2) participation by the defendant in the scheme, (3) specific intent to defraud, and (4) the use of the United States wires or mails in furtherance of the scheme. *See, e.g.*, *United States v. Burks*, 867 F.2d 795 (3d Cir. 1989); *In re Phillips Petroleum Secs. Litig.*, 881 F.2d 1236 (3d Cir. 1989). As discussed below, to state a RICO claim, a fifth element—reliance—must be added.

Scheme to Defraud. "[T]o defraud" within sections 1341 and 1343 means to use "'dishonest methods or schemes and usually signif[ies] the deprivation of something of value by trick, deceit, chicane or overreaching.'" *McNally v. United States*, 483 U.S. 350, 358 (1987), quoting *Hammerschmidt v. United States*, 265 U.S. 182, 188 (1924). In *McNally*, the Supreme Court held that the mail fraud statute was limited in scope to the protection of property rights, which did not encompass a citizen's right to honest government. In late 1988, 18 U.S.C. § 1346 was enacted to reverse the holding in *McNally*. Under section 1346, a "scheme or artifice to deprive another of the intangible right of honest services" constitutes a "scheme or artifice to defraud."[11]

The scheme to defraud must involve misrepresentations or omissions reasonably calculated to deceive persons of ordinary prudence and comprehension. *Walters v. First Nat'l Bank, N.A.*, 855 F.2d 267 (6th Cir. 1988), *cert. denied*, 489 U.S. 1067 (1989). Fraud occurs only when a person of ordinary prudence and comprehension would rely on the misrepresentations. *Associates in Adolescent Psychiatry, S.C. v. Home Life Ins. Co.*, 941 F.2d 561 (7th Cir. 1991) (finding no fraud where challenged statements were mere "puffery," could readily be checked by reference to publicly available information, and were contradicted by documents that unambiguously

10. 18 U.S.C. § 1343 provides the following:

> Whoever, having devised or intending to devise any scheme or artifice to defraud, or for obtaining money or property by means of false or fraudulent pretenses, representations, or promises, transmits or causes to be transmitted by means of wire, radio, or television communication in interstate or foreign commerce, any writings, signs, signals, pictures, or sounds for the purpose of executing such scheme or artifice, shall be fined under this title or imprisoned not more than five years, or both. If the violation affects a financial institution, such person shall be fined not more than $1,000,000 or imprisoned not more than 30 years, or both.

11. In its entirety, 18 U.S.C. § 1346 provides that "[f]or the purposes of this chapter, the term 'scheme or artifice to defraud' includes a scheme or artifice to deprive another of the intangible right of honest services."

refuted—and were controlling over—"remembered or (misremembered, or invented) oral statements").

Materiality. Under the Supreme Court's decision in *Neder v. United States,* 119 S. Ct. 1827 (1999), materiality is an element of a "scheme or artifice to defraud' under the mail and wire fraud statutes. *Neder* reasoned that, under well-settled canons of statutory construction, Congress must be deemed to have incorporated the established, common law meaning of the phrase "scheme to defraud," and "the common law could not have conceived of 'fraud' without proof of materiality." While reaffirming that "[t]he common law requirements of 'justifiable reliance' and 'damages' . . . have no place in the federal fraud statutes," *Neder* concluded that "materiality of falsehood is an element of the federal mail fraud [and] wire fraud . . . statutes."

Mens Rea. The term "scheme to defraud" connotes some degree of planning by the defendant. It is essential that the evidence show that the defendant entertained an intent to defraud. *Atlas Pile Driving Co. v. DiCon Fin. Co.,* 886 F.2d 986 (8th Cir. 1989). The specific intent to deceive can be found from a material misstatement of fact made with reckless disregard of its truth. *In re Phillips Petroleum Secs. Litig.,* 881 F.2d at 1249; *Landry v. Air Line Pilots Ass'n,* 901 F.2d 404 (5th Cir.), *cert. denied,* 498 U.S. 895 (1990). However, acts done inadvertently, mistakenly, or in good faith, without an intent to defraud, do not satisfy the mens rea requirement of the statute. *O'Malley v. New York City Transit Auth.,* 896 F.2d 704 (2d Cir. 1990).

At a minimum, the mens rea element of the offense requires that reliance be anticipated by the defendant. *Pelletier v. Zweifel,* 921 F.2d 1465 (11th Cir.), *cert. denied,* 502 U.S. 855 (1991). (*See also* the discussion of (1) the reliance requirements below; (2) proximate cause in § 6(A)(4), *supra,* and (3) mens rea in § 11(G), *infra.*)

Deception Requirement. The scope of the mail and wire fraud statutes is broader than that of common law fraud. *See, e.g., McEvoy Travel Bureau, Inc. v. Heritage Travel, Inc.,* 904 F.2d 786 (1st Cir.), *cert. denied,* 111 S. Ct. 536 (1990) ("the scope of fraud under [the mail and wire fraud] statutes is broader than common law fraud, and . . . no misrepresentation of fact is required in order to establish a scheme to defraud"); *accord Atlas Pile Driving Co.,* 886 F.2d at 991.

Nonetheless, not every use of the mails or wires in furtherance of an unlawful scheme to deprive another of property constitutes mail or wire fraud giving rise to a RICO claim. The civil RICO plaintiff must have been deceived. Misconduct not involving deception of the plaintiff—even if it involves deception of third parties, to the plaintiff's detriment—is not mail or wire fraud upon which the plaintiff can predicate a RICO claim. *See, e.g., Chisolm v. TranSouth*

Fin. Corp., 95 F.3d 331 (4th Cir. 1996) ("where the predicate act giving rise to civil liability under RICO [i]s alleged to have been mail fraud, prospective plaintiffs, must, in order to demonstrate their standing to sue, plausibly allege both that they detrimentally relied in some way on the fraudulent mailing, and that the mailing was a proximate cause of the alleged injury to their business or property") (citation omitted); *Appletree Square I, L.P. v. W. R. Grace & Co.*, 29 F.3d 1283 (8th Cir. 1994) ("Because [plaintiff] has not produced any evidence to show it detrimentally relied on any of the alleged misrepresentations in its purchase of the building, it has failed to establish the existence of a genuine issue of material fact as to whether the alleged misrepresentations proximately caused its claimed injuries and thus lacks standing to bring its civil RICO claims"); *Central Distributors of Beer, Inc. v. Conn*, 5 F.3d 181 (6th Cir. 1993), *cert. denied*, 512 U.S. 1207 (1994) (plaintiff "cannot maintain a civil RICO claim against these defendants absent evidence that the defendants made misrepresentations or omissions of material fact to [plaintiff] and evidence that [plaintiff] relied on those misrepresentations or omissions to its detriment"); *McEvoy Travel Bureau*, 904 F.2d at 792–94 (dismissing travel agency's RICO claim against competitor predicated on competitor's (1) securing a contract with a major corporate client of the plaintiff, (2) securing regulatory approval of the contract by submitting a phony substitute, and (3) providing illegal kickbacks to the client: "[w]e do not see how the alleged kickbacks, rebates and rent payments—elements one and three of the alleged scheme—could themselves be construed as a scheme to deceive [plaintiff], or anyone else, by means of false or fraudulent pretenses. . . . We do not believe that the deceptive scheme to obtain [regulatory approval—element two—] can somehow be transformed into a scheme to deceive [plaintiff] where the effective reach of the deception stopped at the two regulatory associations"); *Mylan Labs, Inc. v. Akzo, M.V.*, 770 F. Supp. 1053 (D. Md. 1991) ("there must be a convergence of the deceived and the injured. . . . This convergence of identity seems inherent in the idea of fraud as provided in the fraud statutes and defined by the Supreme Court in *McNally*").[12] As long as the mailing furthers the deception, this requirement is satisfied.

12. While the circuit-level authority supports this proposition—*see, e.g.*, United States v. Shelton, 848 F.2d 1485 (10th Cir. 1988); United States v. Lew, 875 F.2d 219 (9th Cir. 1989); *cf.* United States v. Evans, 844 F.2d 36 (2d Cir. 1988) and Corcoran v. American Plan Corp., 886 F.2d 16 (2d Cir. 1989)—not all circuits have addressed the issue, and there are district court decisions holding that a plaintiff who is injured as a proximate result of fraud should be able to recover regardless of whether the plaintiff or a third party is the one deceived. *See, e.g.*, Shaw v. Rolex Watch USA, Inc., 726 F. Supp. 969 (S.D.N.Y. 1989); Texas Air Corp. v. Air Line Pilots Ass'n, 113 Lab. Cas. (CCH) ¶ 11,776 (S.D. Fla. July 14, 1989).

Tabas v. Tabas, 47 F.3d 1280 (3d Cir.), *cert. denied*, 515 U.S. 1118 (1995) ("the mailings were incident to an essential part of the scheme. Had the defendants failed to mail [the fraudulently diminished] disbursement checks to plaintiffs, plaintiffs would immediately have been alerted to defendants' alleged scheme. . . . As long as the method of delivery was through the United States Postal Service, defendants' alleged scheme satisfied the elements of the federal offense of mail fraud"); *United HealthCare Corp. v. American Trade Ins. Co.*, 88 F.3d 563 (8th Cir. 1996) (scheme to defraud health care company by diverting its insurance premiums to defendant; the "scheme to defraud . . . require[d] at least the appearance of a legitimate insurance purchase group with supporting services. Cultivating this appearance . . . require[d] the wire transfer of premium funds and the mailing of premium checks and insurance certificates"; held, "actual use of the mails and wires in furtherance of the scheme" actionable for RICO purposes).

Because of the deception requirement, simple breach of contract, breach of fiduciary duty, anticompetitive behavior, and even violation of statute do not constitute actionable mail or wire fraud, unless the plaintiff has been deceived. *See, e.g.*, *Hilton Sea, Inc. v. DMR Yachts, Inc.*, 750 F. Supp. 35 (D. Me. 1990) ("A failure to perform [a contract] as promised does not, without more, constitute fraud"); *Morda v. Klein*, 865 F.2d 782 (6th Cir. 1989) ("a breach of fiduciary duty alone, without the 'something more' of fraudulent intent, cannot constitute mail fraud"); *Lancaster Community Hosp. v. Antelope Valley Hosp. Dist.*, 940 F.2d 397 (9th Cir. 1991) (dismissing RICO claim: "put differently, it might be said that defendants hoped to 'steal' [plaintiff's] customers. . . . The 'fraud' [plaintiff] alleges is in reality nothing more or less than unalloyed anticompetitive conduct"), *cert. denied*, 502 U.S. 1094 (1992); *Rothman v. Vedder Park Management*, 912 F.2d 315 (9th Cir. 1990) (mail fraud not established where the allegedly deceptive document was a lease negotiated by the parties that allegedly violated the state mobile home residency law: "violation of a statute does not necessarily demonstrate a scheme to defraud").[13]

---

13. *Compare* Blount Fin. Servs., Inc. v. Walter E. Heller & Co., 819 F.2d 151 (6th Cir. 1987) (where contract provided that the defendant would charge the plaintiff an interest rate equal to the prime rate, "[t]he fact that the parties take different positions under the contract as to the appropriate prime rate, or the fact that the defendant charged too high a 'prime rate' and thereby concealed or refused to disclose what the plaintiff considers the true prime rate called for under the contract, does not give rise to a valid claim for fraud") *with* Dana Corp. v. Blue Cross & Blue Shield Mut. of N. Ohio, 900 F.2d 882 (6th Cir. 1990) (sustaining mail fraud count where plaintiff "made specific allegations of fraud, including the letters alleged to contain misrepresentations," even though a contract existed between the parties).

Reliance Requirement. It is not necessary to establish detrimental reliance by the victim in order to make out a violation of the mail or wire fraud statute; the offense is complete before the targeted victim relies. The RICO plaintiff, however, must prove reliance to establish injury to business or property "by reason of" a predicate act of mail or wire fraud, within the meaning of section 1964(c). *See, e.g., Matter of EDC, Inc.*, 930 F.2d 1275 (7th Cir. 1991) ("there is more to fraud than intent to defraud. These plaintiffs . . . can complain only of misrepresentations which were made to them and on which they reasonably relied"); *accord Morley v. Cohen*, 888 F.2d 1006 (4th Cir. 1989). *See generally* Rakoff, *Is Reliance Required Under RICO?* N.Y.L.J., Mar. 14, 1991, at 3, col. 1 ("Fraud without reliance is like seduction without surrender: sinful, but with no appreciable harm. . . . [P]roof of reliance . . . is a minimally necessary condition of any concept of causation that stops short of transforming liability for fraud into a kind of investor insurance").

Postinvestment Communications. A mailing or wire communication occurring after completion of the fraudulent scheme generally cannot support an allegation under section 1341 or section 1343 because, by definition, it does not contribute to the completion of the fraud. Postinvestment letters or telephone calls ordinarily do not state viable predicates for a RICO claim for this reason. *See, e.g., Dennis v. General Imaging, Inc.*, 918 F.2d 496 (5th Cir. 1990). However, if the effect of the subsequent communications is to lull the plaintiff into leaving its money in the control of the defendant or into believing that it has received the services it bought, those communications may be deemed a part of an ongoing scheme to defraud rather than an incidental development after the scheme has reached fruition. *Morley v. Cohen*, 888 F.2d 1006 (4th Cir. 1989); *United States v. Paccione*, 949 F.2d 1183 (2d Cir. 1991).

Continuity. The raw number of mail or wire fraud violations may not reflect accurately the extent of deceptive conduct. Under sections 1341 and 1343, each mailing and interstate wire communication is a separate offense, even if each relates to the same scheme to defraud and even if the defendant did not control the number of mailings or communications. The number of statutory offenses may, therefore, be only tangentially related to the underlying fraud. *Ashland Oil, Inc. v. Arnett*, 875 F.2d 1271 (7th Cir. 1989). As a result, the existence of a multiplicity of predicate acts consisting of mail and wire fraud may be no indication of the requisite continuity of the underlying fraudulent activity. *Hartz v. Friedman*, 919 F.2d 469 (7th Cir. 1990). Consequently, in measuring the duration of the misbehavior for purposes of assessing the existence of a "pattern of racketeering activity" (specifically, the continuity prong), the courts focus on the underlying deceptive activity and not otherwise innocent mailings or wire communications. *See generally* § 11(D)(2)(b), *infra; Kehr Packages, Inc. v. Fidelcor, Inc.*, 926 F.2d 1406 (3d Cir.), *cert. denied*, 501 U.S. 1222 (1991); *Feinstein v. Resolution Trust Corp.*, 942 F.2d 34 (1st Cir. 1991).

Jurisdictional Incongruity. There is one jurisdictional disparity of note between the mail and wire fraud statutes. While either an interstate or intrastate use of the mails for the purpose of furthering the fraudulent scheme suffices under section 1341, *Landry v. Air Line Pilots Ass'n*, 901 F.2d 404 (5th Cir.), *cert. denied*, 498 U.S. 895 (1990), purely intrastate wire communications are beyond the reach of section 1343. *Smith v. Ayres*, 845 F.2d 1360 (5th Cir. 1988); *Dennis v. General Imaging, Inc.*, 918 F.2d 496 (5th Cir. 1990).

Incorporation by Reference and Preemption. An unresolved issue exists as to whether—or to what extent—mail or wire fraud may be alleged as a predicate act when the fraud essentially consists of the violation of another statute not recited in section 1961(1). Tax fraud, for example, is not a predicate offense within section 1961(1). That exclusion reflects a conscious congressional decision. But the mailing of a false tax return also constitutes mail fraud. The courts are divided as to whether a RICO charge may be predicated on a mail fraud offense that substantively consists of a tax violation not included within section 1961(1). *Compare United States v. Henderson*, 386 F. Supp. 1048 (S.D.N.Y. 1974) (holding that the mail fraud statute was not intended to apply to a scheme to evade the payment of taxes) *with United States v. Miller*, 545 F.2d 1204 (9th Cir. 1976), *cert. denied*, 430 U.S. 930 (1977) (rejecting *Henderson*). (The Second Circuit, in which *Henderson* was decided, has reserved on this issue. *United States v. Regan*, 937 F.2d 823 (2d Cir. 1991), *cert. denied*, 504 U.S 940 (1992).) The Department of Justice has issued nonbinding guidelines drafted to constrain prosecutors in the filing of RICO charges relating to the filing of false income tax returns as mail fraud predicates to a RICO offense. See 9A *Department of Justice Manual* § 9–110A.100 at 230–33 (July 3, 1989). In addition, the *Manual* recites that the Department's Organized Crime and Racketeering Section "will not approve a proposed RICO indictment that contains as predicates mail fraud charges concerning federal tax evasion or related violations, unless the use of those charges is first cleared with the Criminal Section of the Tax Division." *Id.* at 16 (1991-1 Supplement).

The question of incorporating other offenses into RICO by means of mail and wire fraud allegations is not limited to the tax fraud context but arises in many others as well. *Compare Danielsen v. Burnside-Ott Aviation Training Center, Inc.*, 941 F.2d 1220 (D.C. Cir. 1991) (RICO claim based on mail and wire fraud allegations predicated, in turn, on violations of the Service Contract Act, 41

U.S.C. § 351 (SCA), stricken on the ground that "the statutory scheme for administrative relief set forth by Congress in the SCA leaves no room for a RICO action on the present allegations") *with United States v. Paccione*, 738 F. Supp. 691 (S.D.N.Y. 1990), *aff'd*, 949 F.2d 1183 (2d Cir., 1991) (denying a motion to dismiss a RICO indictment over the defendant's objection that the mail and wire fraud allegations disguised what was essentially an environmental crime excluded from section 1961(1): "Nothing in the decisions of this Circuit suggests that mail or wire fraud, properly alleged, in the conduct of an enterprise cannot be included as racketeering activity because the enterprise is alleged to have engaged in violations of regulatory schemes which do not constitute racketeering activity on their own").

This issue arises pointedly in the labor context because of the preemption factor that is introduced. The Supreme Court has repeatedly held that the National Labor Relations Act (NLRA) "preempts state and federal court jurisdiction to remedy conduct that is arguably protected or prohibited by the Act." *Amalgamated Ass'n of St., Elec. Ry. & Motor Coach Employees v. Lockridge*, 403 U.S. 274, 276 (1971). More particularly, "[w]hen an activity is arguably subject to § 7 or § 8 of the Act, the States as well as the federal courts must defer to the exclusive competence of the National Labor Relations Board if the danger of state interference with national policy is to be averted." *San Diego Bldg. Trade Council v. Garmon*, 359 U.S. 236, 245 (1959).

Sections 7 and 8 of the NLRA[14] are not predicate acts listed in section 1961(1). However, they generically describe a wide gamut of behavior, including (in section 8) various unfair labor practices that ban behavior that may independently violate the mail and wire fraud statutes, among others.[15]

---

14. 29 U.S.C.. §§ 157, 158.

15. *See, e.g.*, § 8(a) of the National Labor Relations Act, 29 U.S.C. § 158(a), which provides, among other things, that

> [i]t shall be an unfair labor practice for an employer—
>
> (1) to interfere with, restrain or coerce employees in the exercise of the rights guaranteed in section 7;
> (2) to dominate or interfere with the formation or administration of any labor organization . . .;
> (3) by discrimination in regard to hire or tenure of employment . . . to encourage or discourage membership in any labor organization . . .;
> (4) to discharge or otherwise discriminate against an employee because he has filed charges or given testimony under this Act;
> (5) to refuse to bargain collectively with the representatives of his employees.

§ 8(b) describes, in parallel fashion, unfair labor practices by labor organizations.

The question arises whether viable RICO claims may be predicated on allegations of mail or wire fraud that are, in turn, prohibited (and preempted) unfair labor practices. There is a division of authority on this question. Some courts hold that, as long as the predicate acts exist independent of the fact that they also constitute unfair labor practices, the National Labor Relations Board's exclusive jurisdiction is not violated. If, however, the existence of the predicate acts depends wholly upon a determination that a violation of labor law occurred, jurisdiction is preempted. *See, e.g., Tamburello v. Comm-Tract Corp.,* 67 F.3d 973 (1st Cir. 1995), *cert. denied,* 116 S.Ct. 1952 (1996); *MHC v. International Union, UMWA,* 685 F. Supp. 1370 (E.D. Ky. 1988). Some courts hold that where the mail or wire fraud statute is violated solely by virtue of the violation of labor law, the predicate offense is preempted. *Butchers' Union Local No. 498 v. SDC Invt., Inc.,* 631 F. Supp. 1001 (E.D. Cal. 1986) ("but for the proscription of labor law, defendants' conduct simply would not be either mail or wire fraud. . . . Under the instant complaint . . . the only reason defendants' conduct can be alleged to be unlawful is that it is denounced by the labor law"). Another view holds that since violations of sections 7 and 8 of the National Labor Relations Act can by definition never satisfy the predicate act requirement of RICO, any conceivable jurisdictional conflict between the NLRA and RICO is "merely illusory." *Hood v. Smith's Transfer Corp.,* 762 F. Supp. 1274 (W.D. Ky. 1991).

Prior to the Supreme Court's decision in *Humana Inc. v. Forsyth,* 119 S.Ct. 710 (1999), the same issue, and a similar division of authorities, could be found in the insurance area. The question regarding insurance was whether the McCarran-Ferguson Act, 15 U.S.C. § 1011, *et seq.,* precluded the assertion of mail or wire fraud predicates arising out of insurance-related activities. *Compare American Int'l Group, Inc. v. Superior Ct.,* 234 Cal. App. 3d 749, 285 Cal. Rptr. 765 (1991), *cert. denied,* 504 U.S. 911 (1992) (RICO claim preempted), *with Brownell v. State Farm Mut. Ins. Co.,* 757 F. Supp. 526 (E.D. Pa. 1991) (RICO claim not preempted). In *Humana,* the Supreme Court ruled that RICO claims were not preempted because, on the facts before the Court, "we see no frustration of state policy in the RICO litigation. . . . RICO's private right of action and treble damages provision appear to complement [state] statutory and common-law claims for relief." *Humana,* 119 S. Ct. at 719. *Humana* strictly limits any preemption argument based on the McCarran-Ferguson Act, although it does not necessarily preclude a successful one. *See, e.g., Soranno v. New York Life. Ins. Co.,* 1999 U.S. Dist. LEXIS 1963 at *17–*18 (N.D. Ill. Feb. 22, 1999) (dicta).

Whenever confronted by the issue of incorporation by reference, with or without the preemption factor, the court is called upon to make a complicated and subtle judgment. The inclusion of mail and wire fraud in section 1961(1) was not intended to provide an avenue to circumvent the exclusive listing of predicate offenses in section 1961(1). (*See* § 11(c)(1), *supra.*) If the predicate mail or wire fraud offense is viable only upon a determination that a nonlisted criminal statute—or preempted civil statute—is also violated, as in *Butchers' Union,* the RICO claim should fail. It should also fail upon a finding that Congress has expressly decided to provide an exclusive alternative remedy, as in *Danielsen,* 941 F.2d at 1220.

At the same time, the fact that another statute may independently proscribe or otherwise regulate misbehavior that also violates section 1341 or 1343, as in *Hood,* should not shield the perpetrator from RICO liability. There is no escaping, however, that it is a sometimes knotty question whether an alleged offense is substantially a mail or wire fraud violation or a congressionally excluded offense. (*See also* the discussions in §§ 11(C)(2)(c) and 11(C)(3), *infra.*)

b. Fraud in the Sale of Securities Section 1961(1)(D) recites as an item of "racketeering activity" "any offense involving . . . fraud in the sale of securities." Section 107 of the Private Securities Litigation Reform Act of 1995 ("PSLRA"), Pub. L. 104-67, amended 18 U.S.C. § 1964(c) to preclude alleging—as a predicate act in a civil RICO action—"any conduct that would have been actionable as fraud in the purchase or sale of securities," unless the defendant has been "criminally convicted in connection with the fraud."[16] The statutory focus on "conduct that would have been actionable" has been held to mean that the PSLRA does not bar, as an alleged predicate act, aiding and abetting a securities fraud, on the theory that aiding and abetting a securities fraud is not actionable, under *Central Bank of Denver v. First Interstate Bank,* 511 U.S. 164 (1994) (*see* § 17, *infra*). *Renner v. Chase Manhattan Bank,* 1999 U.S. Dist. LEXIS 978 (S.D.N.Y. Feb. 2, 1999). The problem with this analysis is its implicit interpretation of the phrase "would have been actionable" as incorporating predicate act standing requirements, rather than as merely describing a category of claims that

---

16. The PSLRA amended § 1964(c) by appending the following to the preexisting language:

> except that no person may rely upon any conduct that would have been actionable as fraud in the purchase or sale of securities to establish a violation of section 1962. The exception contained in the preceding sentence does not apply to an action against any person that is criminally convicted in connection with the fraud, in which case the statute of limitations shall start to run on the date on which the conviction becomes final.

sound in securities fraud but are brought in another guise. (It did not matter in *Renner* since the RICO claim was dismissed on other grounds.) Among other things, this analysis problematically (1) ignores that predicate-act standing requirements are not germane to determination of RICO liability (§ 6(B), *supra*); (2) overlooks that aiding and abetting a RICO violation no longer states a civil cause of action, under the interpretative approach to aiding and abetting claims set forth in *Central Bank* or under the operation-and-management test of *Reves v. Ernst & Young*, 507 U.S. 170, 183 (1993) (*see* § 17, *infra*); and (3) arguably would expand, rather than restrict, the use of securities claims as predicate acts, provided that they are alleged under rules and statutes not giving rise to a private right of action—an expansive effect that is precisely the opposite of the congressional intent.

The phraseology of section 1961(1)(D) is noteworthy. Only "sale[s]" of securities are covered, and the fraud must occur "in the sale." Contrast this language with, for example, that of section 10(b) of the Securities Exchange Act of 1934 (the 1934 Act), 15 U.S.C. § 78j(b), which imposes liability on those committing fraud "[1] in connection with the [2] purchase or [3] sale" of securities.[17] Or compare it to section 17(a) of the Securities Act of 1933 (the 1933 Act), 15 U.S.C. § 77q(a), which outlaws fraud "in the [i] offer or [ii] sale of any securities."[18] Congress chose a different locution in drafting section 1961(1)(D), and there is some uncertainty in the

---

17. § 10(b) of the 1934 Act provides the following:

> It shall be unlawful for any person, directly or indirectly, by the use of any means or instrumentality of interstate commerce or of the mails, or of any facility of any national securities exchange—
>
> . . .
>
> (b) To use or employ, in connection with the purchase or sale of any security registered on a national securities exchange or any security not so registered, any manipulative or deceptive device or contrivance in contravention of such rules and regulations as the [Securities and Exchange] Commission may prescribe as necessary or appropriate in the public interest or for the protection of investors.

18. § 17(a) of the 1933 Act provides the following:

> It shall be unlawful for any person in the offer or sale of any securities by the use of any means or instruments of transportation or communication in interstate commerce or by the use of the mails, directly or indirectly—
>
> (1) to employ any device, scheme or artifice to defraud, or
> (2) to obtain money or property by means of any untrue statement of a material fact or any omission to state a material fact necessary in order to make the statements made, in the light of the circumstances under which they were made, not misleading, or
> (3) to engage in any transaction, practice or course of business which operates or would operate as a fraud or deceit upon the purchaser.

case law as to the extent of difference in outcome this difference in phraseology is intended to achieve.[19]

Circumscribed Scope. The absence of the "in connection with" language of section 10(b) has been held to preclude the use—as RICO predicates—of section 10(b) violations by outside professionals, such as accountants, not involved in the actual sales transaction. *See, e.g., In re MDC Holdings Sec. Litig.,* No. 89-0090-E (BTM), 1991 U.S. Dist. LEXIS 17188 (S.D. Cal. July 2, 1991).

The "fraud in the sale" formulation has also been held to mean that a section 10(b) violation that does not consist of the sale of securities cannot form a RICO predicate act. *See, e.g., In re Par Pharmaceutical, Inc. Sec. Litig.,* 733 F. Supp. 668 (S.D.N.Y. 1990) (dismissing a RICO claim where the underlying section 10(b) violation consisted of the "issuance of misleading statements [which] caused [the plaintiffs] to buy their shares on the open market at artificially inflated prices"; held, "Congress could have incorporated the broad reach of § 10(b) quite simply by using similar language ['in connection with'], but it did not do so"); *accord United States v. Deeb,* 1999 U.S. App. LEXIS 9982 (9th Cir. May 24, 1999) ("By clear and unambiguous language, the statute's coverage is limited to 'fraud in the sale of securities.' If Congress had intended to include fraud in the purchase of securities in RICO's definition of 'racketeering activity,' it would only have needed to insert the words 'or purchase' after "sale" as it did in 15 U.S.C. § 78j").

The Fourth Circuit reached a parallel result in *International Data Bank Ltd. v. Zepkin,* 812 F.2d 149 (4th Cir. 1987), when it held that the corporation that was formed by two defendants who allegedly sold its stock using a misleading offering prospectus could state no RICO claim against the defendants. The corporate injury did not result from the "sale of securities"—as did, perhaps, the injury suffered by the purchasers of those securities—so its section 10(b) and section 17(a) claims were dismissed.

General Disclosure Violations. Use of general disclosure violations as predicate offenses has proved controversial. In *First*

---

19. Although the issue has largely evaporated due to the passage of time, there was a heavily litigated issue in the mid-1990s as to whether the PSLRA's abolition of securities fraud as a predicate act was "retroactive" in effect, barring securities-based RICO claims either (1) pending on the date that the PSLRA was enacted—*see, e.g.,* Matthews v. Kidder, Peabody & Co., 161 F.3d 156 (3d Cir. 1998), *cert. denied,* 119 S.Ct. 1460 (1999) (held, not retroactive in this sense), or (2) brought subsequent to enactment of the PSLRA but premised on securities violations that occurred prior to that date—*see, e.g.,* Kolfenbach v. Mansour, 36 F. Supp. 2d 1351 (S.D. Fla. 1999) (held, such claims are barred); Scott v. Steingold, 1998 U.S. Dist. LEXIS 15810, 1998 WL 704287 (N.D. Ill. Sept. 30, 1998) (same); ABF Capital Mgmt. v. Askin Capital Mgmt., L.P., 957 F. Supp. 1308 (S.D.N.Y. 1997) (same); *but see* Gubitosi v. Zegeye, 28 F. Supp. 2d 298 (E.D. Pa. 1998) (contra).

Pac. Bancorp, Inc. v. Bro, 847 F.2d 542 (9th Cir. 1988), the Ninth Circuit held that noncompliance with sections 13(d) and 14(a) of the 1934 Act, 15 U.S.C. §§ 78m(d) and 78n(a),[20] did not constitute fraud in the sale of securities and, therefore, could not serve as predicates for a RICO claim. The Ninth Circuit ruled that RICO requires "evidence of a sale," and neither of these two disclosure provisions involved any sale by the defendant.

There are, however, some district court decisions in conflict with *Bro*, holding that general disclosure obligations arising under section 13(d) may constitute predicate acts, depending on the facts. *See, e.g.*, *Lou v. Belzberg*, 728 F. Supp. 1010 (S.D.N.Y. 1990) (distinguishing *Bro* as involving only "a technical failure to comply with [§ 13(d)] reporting requirements"; stressing that, on the facts before it, the defendant "deliberately violated" section 13(d) for the purpose of effecting a fraudulent stock sale). *Accord Spencer Cos., Inc. v. Agency Rent-A-Car, Inc.*, [1981–82] Fed. Sec. L. Rep. (CCH) ¶ 98,361 (D. Mass. 1981). This area remains unsettled. *See also* Matthews, *Shifting the Burden of Losses in the Securities Markets: The Role of Civil RICO in Securities Litigation*, 65 Notre Dame L. Rev. 896, 944–47 (1990).

Non-"Sale" Statutes. The language of section 1961(1)(D) has also been held to exclude provisions of the federal securities laws governing controlling-person liability, section 15 of the 1933 Act, and section 20 of the 1934 Act, 15 U.S.C. §§ 77o and 78t.[21] The courts reason that these sections provide merely for vicarious liability for vio-

---

20. § 13(d) imposes certain disclosure obligations on anyone who purchases more than 5 percent of the outstanding securities of an issuer. Among other things, § 13(d) provides the following:

> (1) Any person who, after acquiring directly or indirectly the beneficial ownership of any equity security of a class which is registered pursuant to section 12 of this title . . . is directly or indirectly the beneficial owner of more than 5 per centum of such class shall, within 10 days after such acquisition, . . . file with the [Securities and Exchange] Commission, a statement containing such . . . information . . . as the Commission may by rules and regulations prescribe."

§ 14(a) imposes various disclosure obligations in connection with proxy contests. Under that statute,

> [i]t shall be unlawful for any person, by the use of the mails or by any means or instrumentality of interstate commerce or of any facility of a national securities exchange or otherwise, in contravention of such rules and regulations as the [Securities and Exchange] Commission may prescribe as necessary or appropriate in the public interest or for the protection of investors, to solicit or to permit the use of his name to solicit any proxy or consent or authorization in respect of any security (other than an exempted security) registered pursuant to section 12 of this title.

21. § 15 of the 1933 Act provides that

> [e]very person who, by or through stock ownership, agency or otherwise, or who, pursuant to or in connection with an agreement or understanding with one or more other persons by or through stock ownership, agency, or otherwise, controls

lations committed by others and are not triggered by fraud in the sale of securities. *See, e.g., Dymm v. Cahill*, 730 F. Supp. 1245 (S.D.N.Y. 1990); *First Nat'l Bank of Chicago v. Shearson Lehman Bros., Inc.*, No. 85-C-4266, 1989 U.S. Dist. LEXIS 15310 (N.D. Ill. Dec. 20, 1989).

No-Standing Statutes. In addition, various provisions of the federal securities laws that do not provide a private right of action, such as section 17(a) of the 1933 Act, have been held to be unavailable to the RICO plaintiff as potential predicate acts because they afford no private right of action. *See, e.g., Dymm v. Cahill*, 730 F. Supp. at 1260. Little analysis generally appears in these decisions, and there are strong arguments for dispensing with strict adherence to predicate-act standing requirements. (*See* § 6(B), *supra*.)

"Sale." As to what is a "sale" of securities within the meaning of section 1961(1)(D), it should be noted that the term is defined in both section 2(3) of the 1933 Act[22] and in section 3(14) of

---

> any person liable under sections 11 or 12, shall also be liable jointly and severally with and to the same extent as such controlled person to any person to whom such controlled person is liable, unless the controlling person has no knowledge of or reasonable grounds to believe in the existence of the facts by reason of which the liability of the controlled person is alleged to exist.

§ 20(a) of the 1934 Act provides that

> [e]very person who, directly or indirectly, controls any person liable under any provision of this title or of any rule or regulation thereunder shall also be liable jointly and severally with and to the same extent as such controlled person to any person to whom such controlled person is liable, unless the controlling person acted in good faith and did not directly or indirectly induce the act or acts constituting the violation or cause of action.

22. § 2(3) of the 1933 Act, 15 U.S.C. § 77b(3), provides that

> [t]he term "sale" or "sell" shall include every contract of sale of disposition of a security or interest in a security, for value. . . . The terms defined in this paragraph . . . shall not include preliminary negotiations or agreements between an issuer (or any person directly or indirectly controlling or controlled by an issuer, or under direct or indirect common control with an issuer) and any underwriter or among underwriters who are to be in privity of contract with an issuer (or any person directly or indirectly controlling or controlled by an issuer, or under direct or indirect common control with an issuer). Any security given or delivered with, or as a bonus on account of, any purchase of securities or any other thing, shall be conclusively presumed to constitute a part of the subject of such purchase and to have been offered and sold for value. The issue or transfer of a right or privilege, when originally issued or transferred with a security, giving the holder of such security the right to convert such security into another security of the same issuer or of another person, or giving a right to subscribe to another security of the same issuer or of another person, which right cannot be exercised until some future date, shall not be deemed to be an offer or sale of such other security; but the issue or transfer of such other security upon the exercise of such right of conversion or subscription shall be deemed a sale of such other security.

the 1934 Act.[23] To the extent that the alleged predicate acts derive from either of these acts, the pertinent statutory definition should be heeded in determining whether a "sale" has been effected. The courts have sometimes construed these provisions rather restrictively. *See, e.g., Pinter v. Dahl,* 486 U.S. 622 (1988) (holding that one who is merely a "substantial factor" in causing a sale of securities is not a "seller" within section 12(1) of the Securities Act of 1933, 15 U.S.C. § 77l(1); examining the language of section 2(3) in reaching this conclusion).

"Securities." The term "security" is also defined both in section 2(1) of the 1933 Act, 15 U.S.C. § 77b(1),[24] and section 3(a)(10) of the 1934 Act, 15 U.S.C. § 78c(a)(10).[25] These definitions tend to be broadly construed. *See, e.g., Reves v. Ernst & Young,* 494 U.S. 56 (1990) (holding that uncollateralized, uninsured promissory notes due on demand were "securities" within section 3(a)(10) of the Securities Exchange Act of 1934, reasoning that "Congress' purpose in enacting the securities laws was to regulate *investments,* in whatever form they are made and by whatever name they are called" (court's emphasis)); *see also* Schneider, *The Elusive Definition of a Security—1990 Update,* 24 Rev. Sec. & Commodities Reg. 13 (1991).

There is a distinction to be drawn between the requirement that the plaintiff plead and prove "fraud in the sale of securities" under section 1961(1)(D) and the question of whether the plaintiff

---

23. § 3(14) of the 1934 Act, 15 U.S.C. § 78c(14), provides that "[t]he terms 'sale' and 'self' each include any contract to sell or otherwise dispose of."

24. § 2(1) of the 1933 Act provides that

> [t]he term "security" means any note, stock, treasury stock, bond, debenture, evidence of indebtedness, certificate of interest or participation in any profit-sharing agreement, collateral-trust certificate, preorganization certificate or subscription, transferable share, investment contract, voting-trust certificate, certificate of deposit for a security, fractional undivided interest in oil, gas, or other mineral rights, or, in generally, any interest or instrument commonly known as a "security" or any certificate of interest or participation in, temporary or interim certificate for, receipt for, guarantee of, or warrant or right to subscribe to or purchase, any of the foregoing.

25. § 3(a)(10) of the 1934 Act provides that

> [t]he term "security" means any note, stock, treasury stock, bond, debenture, certificate of interest or participation in any profit-sharing agreement or in any oil, gas, or other mineral royalty or lease, any collateral-trust certificate, preorganization certificate or subscription, transferable share, investment contract, voting-trust certificate, certificate of deposit for a security, or in general, any instrument commonly known as a "security"; or any certificate of interest or participation in, temporary or interim certificate for, receipt for, or warrant or right to subscribe to or purchase, any of the foregoing; but shall not include any currency or any note, draft, bill of exchange, or bank's acceptance which has a maturity at the time of issuance of not exceeding nine months, exclusive of days of grace, or any renewal thereof the maturity of which is likewise limited.

has standing to pursue a RICO claim even if it does not satisfy the technical standing requirements of all the underlying predicate acts. In *Securities Investor Protection Corp. v. Vigman*, 908 F.2d 1461 (9th Cir. 1990), *rev'd on other grounds, Holmes v. Securities Investor Protection Corp.*, 503 U.S. 258 (1992), the Ninth Circuit held that the section 10(b) purchaser/seller limitation does not apply to the RICO plaintiff "so long as the plaintiff suffered injury 'by reason of' the alleged" RICO violation. 903 F.2d at 1466. That addresses the question of predicate-act standing (discussed in § 6(B), *supra*), which is distinct from the issue discussed in this section (which is not *who* may sue but who may *be* sued—that is, not standing but liability).

c. Hobbs Act (Extortion) Under section 1961(1), extortion may form a predicate act in one of two ways. First, violation of the Hobbs Act,[26] 18 U.S.C. § 1951, is identified as "racketeering activity" in section 1961(1)(B). Second, section 1961(1)(A) encompasses "any act or threat involving . . . extortion . . . which is chargeable under State law and punishable by imprisonment for more than one year." The state statutes differ, and each must be reviewed individually to ascertain its precise parameters. Many, however, substantively parallel the Hobbs Act. *See, e.g., Rothman v. Vedder Park Management*, 912 F.2d 315, 317 (9th Cir. 1990); *American Computer Trust Leasing v. Jack Farrell Implement Co.*, 763 F. Supp. 1473, 1492–93 (D. Minn. 1991), aff'd, 967 F.2d 1208 (8th Cir), *cert. denied*, 506 U.S. 956 (1992). Therefore, the discussion in this section focuses on the Hobbs Act.

---

26. The Hobbs Act provides the following:

(a) Whoever in any way or degree obstructs, delays, or affects commerce or the movement of any article or commodity in commerce, by robbery or extortion or attempts or conspires so to do, or commits or threatens physical violence to any person or property in furtherance of a plan or a purpose to do anything in violation of this section shall be fined not more than $10,000 or imprisoned not more than twenty years, or both.

(b) As used in this section—

(1) [Robbery defined.]

(2) The term "extortion" means the obtaining of property from another, with his consent, induced by wrongful use of actual or threatened force, violence or fear, or under color of official right.

(3) The term "commerce" means commerce within the District of Columbia, or any Territory or Possession of the United States; all commerce between any point in a State, Territory, Possession, or the District of Columbia and any point outside thereof; all commerce between points within the same State through any place outside such State; and all other commerce over which the United States has jurisdiction.

(c) This section shall not be construed to repeal, modify or affect section 17 of Title XV, sections 52, 101–115, 151–166 of Title XXIX or sections 151–188 of Title 45.

The Hobbs Act is violated by any act of extortion that "in any way or degree obstructs, delays or affects commerce." For a solid discussion of the statute, *see generally* Note, *The Hobbs Act and RICO: A Remedy for Greenmail?* 66 Tex. L. Rev. 647 (1988). The statute does not entail any additional requirement that the defendant have been engaged in racketeering at the time the extortion was committed. *United States v. Culbert,* 435 U.S. 371 (1978).

Jurisdiction. The jurisdictional threshold of the statute is easily satisfied. A de minimis impact on commerce, even a purely "probable or potential" effect, is sufficient. *See, e.g., United States v. DiGregorio,* 605 F.2d 1184 (1st Cir.), *cert. denied,* 444 U.S. 937 (1979); *United States v. Phillips,* 577 F.2d 495 (9th Cir.), *cert. denied,* 439 U.S. 831 (1978); *United States v. Daley,* 564 F.2d 645 (2d Cir. 1977), *cert. denied,* 435 U.S. 933 (1978).

Wrongful Means and Ends. The statutory definition of extortion in section 1951(b)(2) includes two aspects—(1) the objective: the obtaining of property from another, and (2) the means: the wrongful use of force, fear, or color of official right to do so. "Extortion as defined in the Hobbs Act consists of the use of wrongful means to achieve a wrongful objective." *United States v. Clemente,* 640 F.2d 1069, 1076 (2d Cir.), *cert. denied,* 454 U.S. 820 (1981). A person employs "wrongful means" within the meaning of the statute not only by employing means that are inherently illegal but also by employing any of the means identified in the statute ("actual or threatened force, violence or fear") to obtain property to which "the alleged extortionist has no lawful claim." *United States v. Enmons,* 410 U.S. 396, 400 (1973). Under the *Enmons* doctrine, when the objective is to obtain property to which one "has no lawful claim" (and is, thus, "wrongful"), then the means are also wrongful. It is the wrongful use of an otherwise valid power that converts permissible action into extortion. *United States v. Hyde,* 448 F.2d 815 (5th Cir. 1971), *cert. denied,* 404 U.S. 1058 (1972). A broad spectrum of legitimate business transactions can constitute wrongful means if used to obtain property to which no lawful claim exists. *United States v. Clemente,* 640 F.2d at 1077–78.

Extortion Versus Hard Bargaining. There are at least two distinct scenarios in which a defendant may seek to obtain property to which it has no lawful claim. In the first, the victim receives something that is of no value to him or her in exchange for the property relinquished. In the second, the victim receives something that he or she does value. In the latter category, some acts will be found to constitute extortion, others merely "hard bargaining." In a hard-bargaining scenario, the victim has no preexisting right to pursue its business interest free of the fear it is quelling by transferring property to the defendant. By comparison, the victim in an extortion scenario has the preexisting right to pursue its business interest free of the fear it is quelling by relinquishing its property. *Brokerage Concepts, Inc. v. U.S. Healthcare, Inc.,* 140 F.3d 494 (3d Cir. 1998); *Viacom Int'l, Inc. v. Icahn,* 747 F. Supp. 205 (1990), *aff'd,* 946 F.2d 998 (2d Cir. 1991), *cert. denied,* 502 U.S. 1122 (1992).

The absence of a wrongful objective is no defense if property is obtained by "inherently wrongful means." In that circumstance, the Hobbs Act is violated regardless of whether the defendant has a lawful claim to the property. *United States v. Zappola,* 677 F.2d 264 (2d Cir.), *cert. denied,* 459 U.S. 866 (1982); *United States v. Sturm,* 870 F.2d 769 (1st Cir. 1989); *United States v. Agnes,* 753 F.2d 293 (3d Cir. 1985).

The Third Circuit has held that there is no requirement that the defendant harbor an economic motivation for its extortionate activities. Under this analysis, lack of economic motivation does not constitute a defense to Hobbs Act crimes. *Northeast Women's Center, Inc. v. McMonagle,* 868 F.2d 1342 (3d Cir.), *cert. denied,* 493 U.S. 901 (1989). This is presumably no longer a matter in controversy, since the Supreme Court has ruled that there is no longer an economic-motivation requirement in definitions of "enterprise." (*See generally* § 11(B)(2), *supra.*)

"Property." The range of property rights protected by the Hobbs Act is sweeping in breadth. The Hobbs Act protects intangible as well as tangible property, including rights involving the conduct of business. *See, e.g., United States v. Zemek,* 634 F.2d 1159 (9th Cir. 1980), *cert. denied,* 450 U.S. 916 (1981) (right to solicit business accounts); *United States v. Santoni,* 585 F.2d 667 (4th Cir. 1978), *cert. denied,* 440 U.S. 910 (1979) (right to make business decisions free from outside pressure wrongfully imposed); *United States v. Local 560, Int'l Bhd. of Teamsters,* 780 F.2d 267 (3d Cir. 1985), *cert. denied,* 476 U.S. 1140 (1986) (union members' "right to democratic participation" in union); *United States v. Nadaline,* 471 F.2d 340 (5th Cir.), *cert. denied,* 411 U.S. 951 (1973) (right to solicit business accounts); *United States v. Tropiano,* 418 F.2d 1069 (2d Cir. 1969), *cert. denied,* 397 U.S. 1021 (1970) (right to solicit business accounts); *Northeast Women's Center, Inc. v. McMonagle,* 868 F.2d at 1349–50 (right to conduct business). *But see Town of West Hartford v. Operation Rescue,* 915 F.2d 990 (2d Cir. 1990) (discussed immediately *infra).*

"Obtaining" Property. The Hobbs Act's requirement that property be "obtained" is also given a broad construction. There is no requirement that the person who commits the extortion receive the benefit of that act. *Town of West Hartford v. Operation Rescue,* 915 F.2d 990 (2d Cir. 1990) (antiabortion protesters, seeking relaxed police enforcement of laws, offered limitations on protests in return; also holding that, while "[t]he definition of

'property' under the Hobbs Act is admittedly expansive . . . the term 'property' cannot plausibly be construed to encompass altered official conduct").

"Fear." "'[E]xtortion by wrongful use of fear of economic harm is established by showing that the defendant preyed upon or exploited the victim's fear of economic harm.'" *United States v. Nedza,* 880 F.2d 896, 902 (7th Cir.), *cert. denied,* 493 U.S. 938 (1989); *accord United States v. Margiotta,* 688 F.2d 108 (2d Cir. 1982), *cert. denied,* 461 U.S. 913 (1983). The evidence need not demonstrate that either a direct or indirect threat was actually made. *United States v. Lasinski,* 728 F.2d 887 (7th Cir.), *cert. denied,* 469 U.S. 8 (1984). A threat "is not a state of mind in the threatener; it is an appearance to the victim, so long as the victim's conclusion is reasonable." *United States v. Nedza,* 880 F.2d at 902 (internal quotations deleted).

"Color of Official Right." Extortion under color of official right requires a public official to make a wrongful use of his or her office to obtain money not lawfully due. *United States v. O'Grady,* 742 F.2d 682 (2d Cir. 1984). De jure ability to perform the promised acts is not required. The issue is whether the victim reasonably believed, at the time of the extortionate act, that the defendant could deliver the power of his or her office for the victim's benefit. *United States v. Blackwood,* 768 F.2d 131 (7th Cir.), *cert. denied,* 474 U.S. 1020 (1985); *United States v. Mazzei,* 521 F.2d 639 (3d Cir.), *cert. denied,* 429 U.S. 1014 (1975).

Wrongful use of office does not necessarily require that the wrongdoer instill fear in the victim. The Hobbs Act is equally violated if an official accepts a favor knowing that it is motivated by a hope of benefit from the exercise of the official's influence. *United States v. Garner,* 837 F.2d 1404 (7th Cir. 1987), *cert. denied,* 486 U.S. 1035 (1988).

Nonextortionate Behavior. A party is entitled to threaten or to attempt to do any act that it has a right to do. *Rothman v. Vedder Park Management,* 912 F.2d 315 (9th Cir. 1990) ("In the words of Justice Holmes, 'As a general rule, even if subject to some exceptions, what you may do in a certain event you may threaten to do, that is, give warning of your intention to do in that event, and thus allow the other person the chance of avoiding the consequences'"). A person may even "baldly exercis[e] its economic might in threatening or attempting to do that which it is entitled to do, provided that its objective is not wrongful." *Union Nat'l Bank v. Federal Nat'l Mortgage Ass'n,* 860 F.2d 847 (8th Cir. 1988). Further, a simple request for money claimed to be due does not fulfill the requirements of the Hobbs Act. The statute requires that the request be wrongful and unlawful, not simply mistaken. *O'Malley v. New York City Transit Auth.,* 896 F.2d 704 (2d Cir. 1990).

Contract Rights. The mere threat to breach or fail to comply with a contract does not state a Hobbs Act violation. *Robert Suris Gen. Contracting Corp. v. New Metro. Fed. Savs. & Loan Ass'n,* 873 F.2d 1401 (11th Cir. 1989) (plaintiff's alleged fear of economic loss from alleged extortion held indistinguishable from the fear of economic loss accompanying any party to a contract who suspects that compliance and consideration may not be forthcoming). Where a party has a right to take acts pursuant or with respect to a contract, doing so does not violate the Hobbs Act. *American Computer Trust Leasing v. Jack Farrell Implement Co.,* 763 F. Supp. 1473, 1493 (D. Minn. 1991) ("Because [counterclaim defendant's] deactivation [of the defendants' software] was not unlawful or wrongful but merely an exercise of its rights under the software license agreement, its deactivation does not violate either [state or federal] extortion statute and thus is not a racketeering activity"), *aff'd,* 967 F.2d 1208 (8th Cir.), *cert. denied,* 506 U.S. 956 (1992).

However, scheming to place another party in a position of financial risk by negotiating a contract with no intent to perform it—but rather harboring a plan to exact financial concessions when the time comes to perform—may state a predicate Hobbs Act violation. *Battlefield Builders, Inc. v. Swango,* 743 F.2d 1060 (4th Cir. 1984) (distinguishing a situation in which the defendant enters the contract in good faith and thereafter seeks to renegotiate its contractual obligations; deemed significant that the defendants misled the plaintiff into a position of economic risk so that they could extract additional benefits as their price for not causing harm to the plaintiff); *accord Richmark Corp. v. Timber Falling Consultants, Inc.,* 730 F. Supp. 1525 (D. Or. 1990).

Success Irrelevant. It is no defense to a claim of extortion that the defendant did not succeed in its ultimate goal. Attempts to extort and conspiring to extort are offenses under section 1951(a), and any act that is indictable under the Hobbs Act is a predicate offense for RICO purposes, 18 U.S.C. § 1961(1)(B). *Northeast Women's Center, Inc. v. McMonagle,* 868 F.2d at 1350. *See also United States v. Hocking,* 860 F.2d 769 (7th Cir. 1988) (a Hobbs Act violation is complete at the time "one attempts to induce a victim engaged in interstate commerce to part with property").

Incorporation by Reference and Preemption. Paralleling the earlier discussion (§ 11(C)(2)(a), *supra*), an unresolved issue exists in connection with the Hobbs Act concerning the incorporation by reference of other, "preempted" offenses not listed in section 1961(1). In *Petrochem Insulation, Inc. v. Northern Cal. & N. Nev. Pipe Trades Council,* 119 Lab. Cas. (CCH) ¶ 10,923, 137 L.R.R.M. 2194, 1991 U.S. Dist. LEXIS 6659 (N.D. Cal. Apr. 30, 1991), the complaint alleged a Hobbs Act predicate for the RICO claim. The claim of criminal extortion, however, was wholly dependent upon a violation of the National Labor Relations Act. The plaintiff's theory was that the defendants' use of fear of economic harm was extortionate because they sought to obtain property—an agreement—to which they were not lawfully entitled only because the agreement violated section 8(e) of the NLRA, 29 U.S.C. § 158(e). The *Petrochem* court reasoned that, because the sole predicate acts were bottomed on violations of the labor laws, the RICO claims were preempted by the NLRA. To the extent that the predicate Hobbs Act offenses were viable only upon a determination that a nonlisted criminal statute, or preempted civil statute, was also violated, the RICO claim was properly dismissed. (*See generally* the discussion in § 11(C)(2)(a), *supra,* and § 11(C)(3), *infra.*)

3. Preempted Predicate Acts This subject has been discussed previously (*see* §§ 11(C)(2)(a) and (c), *supra*). The issue is whether a viable RICO claim may be predicated on a section 1961(1) offense that, in turn, incorporates by reference or is dependent upon a finding of a violation of a statute that is either, or both, (i) not listed in section 1961(1) and (ii) outside the jurisdiction of the federal courts. Whether or not "preemption" is the appropriate term,[27] the exclusive-remedy issue arises in a variety of contexts in addition to those previously discussed. *See, e.g., Hubbard v. United Airlines, Inc.,* 927 F.2d 1094 (9th Cir. 1991) (because alleged mail fraud "would not be wrongful in the absence of the obligation contained in the collective-bargaining agreement," RICO claim amounts to "an attempt to enforce a contractual right incident to the employment relationship" and is preempted by the Railway Labor Act); *Masters v. Daniel Int'1 Corp.,* No. 87-1290-C, 1991 U.S. Dist. LEXIS 7595 (D. Kan. May 3, 1991) (RICO claim barred by exclusive federal remedy provided by Energy Reorganization Act, which specifically creates a "'detailed' federal regulatory enforcement scheme complete with remedies" for retaliatory dismissals triggered by whistle-blowing).

As discussed earlier (§§ 11(C)(2)(a) and (c)), the linchpin of the decision should be whether the RICO predicate offense is viable only upon the determination that (1) a nonlisted criminal

27. *See, e.g.,* Danielsen v. Burnside-Ott Aviation Training Center, Inc., 941 F.2d 1220 (D.C. Cir. 1991) ("We have a slight semantic difficulty with the use of the word preemption. . . . [O]ur task is more accurately described as determining whether there is a statutory provision of an exclusive remedy rather than the preemption of an entire field").

statute—or preempted civil statute—is also violated or (2) Congress has expressly chosen to provide an exclusive alternate remedy. If so, the RICO claim should fail. However, the mere fact that another statute may independently proscribe or regulate misbehavior that also violates a RICO predicate should not shield the perpetrator from RICO liability. This is not always an easy line to draw. It is, however, the salutary direction in which the courts appear to be trending.

D. "Pattern of Racketeering Activity"

"[T]he heart of any RICO complaint is the allegation of a pattern of racketeering." *Agency Holding Corp. v. Malley-Duff & Assocs., Inc.*, 483 U.S. 143, 154 (1987). Section 1961(5) provides that "'pattern of racketeering activity' requires at least two acts of racketeering activity, . . . the last of which occurred within ten years (excluding any period of imprisonment) after the commission of a prior act of racketeering activity."[28] Twice the Supreme Court has attempted to elucidate what constitutes a "pattern" within this provision, yet the concept remains elusive.[29]

1. Supreme Court Precedent The Supreme Court's first foray into the area appeared in an extended footnote in *Sedima, S.P.R.L. v. Imrex Co., Inc.*, 473 U.S. 479 (1985). The Court began by pointing out a linguistic oddity about the definition of "pattern of racketeering"—namely, that it differs from several other definitions in section 1961 "in that it states that a pattern *'requires* at least two acts of racketeering activity,' . . . not that it 'means' two such acts" (Court's emphasis). From that premise, the *Sedima* Court "impli[ed]" that "while two acts are necessary, they may not be sufficient. . . . [I]n common parlance two of anything do not generally form a 'pattern.' " From the legislative history, it derived that "two isolated acts of racketeering activity do not constitute a pattern" and that the distinguishing characteristic of a pattern "is th[e] factor of *continuity plus relationship.*" 473 US. at 496 n.14 (Court's emphasis).

The continuity requirement, according to *Sedima*, consists of a "'threat of continuing activity.'" The Court defined the relationship requirement in terms of a now-repealed statute,[30] 18 U.S.C.

---

28. In full, § 1961(5) provides the following: "'pattern of racketeering activity' requires at least two acts of racketeering activity, one of which occurred after the effective date of this chapter and the last of which occurred within ten years (excluding any period of imprisonment) after the commission of a prior act of racketeering activity[.]"

29. *Cf.* Pines, *Amending the Foreign Corrupt Practices Act to Include a Private Right of Action*, 82 CALIF. L. REV. 185, 224–225 (1994) (citing **Treatise**).

30. Repealed by the Sentencing Reform Act of 1984, Pub. L. No. 98-473, tit. II, §§ 212(a)(2) and 235(a)(1), 98 Stat. 1987, 2031.

§ 3575(e) (of the Dangerous Special Offender Sentencing Act), which provided that "criminal conduct forms a pattern if it embraces criminal acts that have the same or similar purposes, results, participants, victims, methods of commission, or otherwise are interrelated by distinguishing characteristics and are not isolated events." *Id.*

While footnote 14 of *Sedima* introduced the concepts of relationship and continuity, it did little to advance a coherent vision of a RICO pattern. Following *Sedima,* the circuits articulated a wide variety of conflicting views and definitions of a "pattern of racketeering activity." *See, e.g.,* Note, *Clarifying a "Pattern" of Confusion: A Multi-Factor Approach to Civil RICO's Pattern Requirement,* 86 Mich. L. Rev. 1745, 1748 (1988) ("Since Sedima, . . . the confusion over what level of wrongful activity is required to trigger RICO liability has increased. [T]he effort to define this concept adequately . . . has bitterly divided both courts and commentators"); *see also* Comment, *RICO "Pattern" Before and after H.J. Inc.: A Proposed Definition,* 40 Am. U.L. Rev. 919, 925 (1991); Huestis, *RICO: The Meaning of "Pattern" Since Sedima,* 54 Brooklyn L. Rev. 621, 631 (1988).

These conflicting variants included (1) the multiple schemes test, which required proof of the defendant's involvement in similar schemes in the past or contemporaneously, on the theory that "[a] single fraudulent effort or scheme is insufficient" *(see, e.g., H.J. Inc. v. Northwestern Bell Tel. Co.,* 829 F.2d 648 (8th Cir. 1987), *rev'd,* 492 U.S. 229 (1989)); (2) the multiple factor approach, under which the court assessed continuity by considering such factors as (i) the number of unlawful acts, (ii) the length of time over which the acts were committed, (iii) the similarity of the acts, (iv) the number of victims, (v) the number of perpetrators, and (vi) the character of the unlawful activity (*Saporito v. Combustion Eng'g, Inc.,* 843 F.2d 666 (3d Cir. 1988), *vacated on other grounds,* 489 U.S. 1049 (1989); *compare Morgan v. Bank of Waukegan,* 804 F.2d 970 (7th Cir. 1986) (applying a somewhat different multifactor test and further requiring that the predicates constitute "separate transactions")); and (3) a relatedness test without regard to continuity *(see, e.g., California Architectural Bldg. Prods., Inc. v. Franciscan Ceramics, Inc.,* 818 F.2d 1466 (9th Cir. 1987), *cert. denied,* 484 U.S. 1006 (1988) (characterizing footnote 14 of *Sedima* as constituting only "suggestive" dicta that "without additional explication by the Supreme Court we decline to follow").

In 1989, the Supreme Court returned to the pattern question in *H.J. Inc. v. Northwestern Bell Tel. Co.,* 492 U.S. 229 (1989). The Court commenced its analysis by returning to the statutory language, remarking that section 1961(5) "does not so much define a pattern of racketeering activity as state a minimum necessary condition for the existence of such a pattern." *Id.* at 237. "It is not the number of predicates," the *H.J.* Court continued, "but the relationship that they bear to each other or to some external organizing principle that renders them 'ordered' or 'arranged'" and, thus, a pattern. *Id.* at 238. Resorting to the legislative history, the Court determined that Congress "had a fairly flexible concept of a pattern in mind." The concept encompassed the "factor of *continuity plus relationship*," which had been plucked by *Sedima* from RICO's legislative history. *Id.* at 239 (Court's emphasis).

The *H.J. Inc.* opinion, like the *Sedima* opinion, defined the relationship element (now termed "relatedness") rather summarily in terms of 18 U.S.C. § 3575(e). *H.J. Inc.* dwelt upon the continuity element, however, at some length. It rejected the Eighth Circuit's "multiple schemes" test as needlessly rigid. The *H.J. Inc.* Court stressed that "[w]hat a plaintiff or prosecutor must prove is continuity of racketeering activity, or its threat, *simpliciter*." *Id.* at 240–41 (Court's emphasis).

Under the "less inflexible approach" adopted in *H.J. Inc.*, continuity is "both a closed- and open-ended concept." *Id.* at 241. Closed-ended continuity refers "to a closed period of repeated conduct," while open-ended continuity denotes "past conduct that by its nature projects into the future with a threat of repetition." Closed-ended continuity may be demonstrated with proof of "a series of related predicates extending over a substantial period of time." *Id.* at 242 ("Predicate acts extending over a few weeks or months and threatening no future criminal conduct do not satisfy this requirement: Congress was concerned in RICO with long-term criminal conduct").

Open-ended continuity, in contrast, requires proof of "a threat of continued racketeering activity." *Id.* at 242. Under *H.J. Inc.*, open-ended continuity may be established in various ways. The Court furnished some examples. First, a small number of related predicates occurring close together in time will establish open-ended continuity if "the racketeering acts themselves include a specific threat of repetition extending indefinitely into the future, and thus supply the requisite threat of continuity." Second, the threat of continuity may be established with a "showing that the predicate acts or offenses are part of an ongoing entity's regular way of doing business." Third, continuity is proved "if the predicates can be attributed to a defendant operating as part of a long-term association that exists for criminal purposes." In any case, the entity involved may be a legitimate business and need not be one "traditionally grouped under the phrase 'organized crime.'" *Id.* at 242–43.

The Supreme Court emphasized that, whether closed- or open-ended, continuity is "centrally a temporal concept." *Id.* at 242. Further than this the Court declined to elaborate. The *H.J.* decision eschewed any effort to "fix in advance" a definition "with such clarity that it will always be apparent whether in a particular case a 'pattern of racketeering activity' exists." *Id.* at 243. Justice Scalia remarked in concurrence that, as far as the lower federal courts are concerned, this approach "seems to me about as helpful . . . as 'life is a fountain.'" *Id.* at 252.

2. Lower Court Authority The upshot of *Sedima* and *H.J. Inc.* is straightforward in at least one sense: "[t]he Supreme Court has not established any clear-cut test or specific formula for determining if the allegations [of a complaint] evince the required continuity." *J.D. Marshall Int'l, Inc. v. Redstart, Inc.,* 935 F.2d 815 (7th Cir. 1991). Unsurprisingly, the pattern element has subsequently generated voluminous litigation, and that has produced inconsistent results. A "concrete definition for precisely what activity will constitute a 'pattern' for purposes of the RICO statute has eluded the federal courts." *United States Textiles, Inc. v. Anheuser-Busch Cos., Inc.,* 911 F.2d 1261 (7th Cir. 1990). The lower court precedent displays pervasive attentiveness to the nebulous parameters staked out in *Sedima* and *H.J. Inc.,* but it exhibits no overarching coherence that would permit counsel, with any degree of assurance, to predict the judicial reaction to a great many, perhaps the overwhelming majority of, pattern allegations.

Inconsistency and unpredictability appear both on an intracircuit and intercircuit level. Among other things, many judges continue to evince hostility toward civil RICO claims while exhibiting no animosity toward criminal RICO prosecutions. Results in civil and criminal cases are, therefore, not always entirely congruent despite the recognition that, with rare exception, "[t]he elements of a RICO claim remain the same regardless of whether it is brought as a criminal prosecution or as a civil suit." *Costantino v. TRW, Inc.,* 773 F. Supp. 34, 45 (N.D. Ohio 1991). "[P]erhaps there is even a pattern of using the 'pattern' requirement to trim off the excesses in civil RICO suits." *United States v. O'Connor,* 910 F.2d 1466, 1468 (7th Cir. 1990), *cert. denied,* 111 S. Ct. 953 (1991). Add to this the uncertain standards and limitless factual diversity presented in so fact-driven an area of inquiry, and seemingly erratic outcomes are effectively foreordained.

a. Relatedness The First Circuit has aptly observed that "[t]he relatedness test is not a cumbersome one for a RICO plaintiff." *Feinstein v. Resolution Trust Corp.,* 942 F.2d 34, 44 (1st Cir. 1991). Under *Sedima* and *H.J. Inc.,* the plaintiff is required simply to show that the predicate acts "have the same or similar purposes, results, participants, victims, or methods of commission, or otherwise are interrelated by distinguishing characteristics and are not isolated events." *H.J. Inc,* 492 U.S. 229, 240 (1989) (quoting former 18 U.S.C. § 3575(e)).

These criteria are generously construed. The "same or similar purposes," for example, can be as generic as the desire to hoodwink someone out of money; the similar "results" may be no more than to have achieved just that; the cast of similar "participants" need not be entirely uniform over time; similar "victims" may be related to one another solely by virtue of having been victimized by the same enterprise (and not necessarily even all of the same defendants); similar "methods of commission" may be as non-specifically alike as defrauding—and any other similar "distinguishing characteristics" may be offered to prove that the offenses are related. *See, e.g., Banks v. Wolk,* 918 F.2d 418 (3d Cir. 1990) (fact that neither the plaintiff nor one of the defendants was a party to four of five alleged predicate offenses did "not carry much weight" where the defendants, as a whole, "were at least partially in the business of defrauding those who dealt with" their two enterprises and all "alleged victims . . . were 'similar' in the sense that they all were engaged in business dealings with [and were defrauded by] the [defendants] through [the enterprises]").

Occasional decisions are couched in terms of "vertical" and "horizontal" relatedness. This terminology is a bit facially forbidding but not difficult to grasp. "Horizontal" relatedness is nothing more than the relationship of the racketeering acts to one another. "Vertical" relatedness is simply the relationship they bear to the enterprise. *See, e.g., United States v. Polanco,* 145 F.3d 536, 541 (2d Cir. 1998), *cert. denied,* 119 S.Ct. 803 (1999).

Because the relatedness requirement is perceived as unproblematic, it has received markedly less judicial attention than the continuity requirement. *See, e.g., Medallion Television Enters., Inc. v. SelecTV of Cal. Inc.,* 833 F.2d 1360 (9th Cir. 1987), *cert. denied,* 492 U.S. 917 (1989) ("whether the predicate acts alleged or proven are sufficiently related is seldom at issue").

In addition, many courts consciously decline to apply the relatedness requirement criterion too strictly in tacit recognition of the fact that there is some tension between the relatedness and continuity concepts. Relatedness, for example, may imply some temporal proximity (as discussed in § 11(D)(2), *infra*), but continuity often requires duration. *See, e.g., J.D. Marshall Int'l, Inc. v. Redstart, Inc.,* 935 F.2d 815 (7th Cir. 1991).

By way of illustration, courts often hold that a single scheme involving a single injury to a single victim within a short period of time falls outside of RICO due to lack of continuity, even though all aspects are entirely related. *See, e.g., Marshall-Silver Constr. Co., Inc. v. Mandel,* 894 F.2d 593 (3d Cir. 1990) ("Where . . . a fraudulent scheme inflicts or threatens only a single injury, we continue to doubt that Congress intended to make the availability of treble damages and augmented criminal sanctions depend[e]nt solely on whether the fraudulent scheme is well enough conceived to enjoy prompt success or requires pursuit for an extended period of time. Given its 'natural and commonsense approach to RICO's pattern element,' we think it unlikely that Congress intended RICO to apply in the absence of a more significant societal threat"); *Terry A. Lambert Plumbing, Inc. v. Western Sec. Bank*, 934 F.2d 976 (8th Cir. 1991) ("a single transaction which involves only one victim and takes place over a short period of time does not constitute the pattern of racketeering required for long-term criminal activity under a RICO claim").

As a result, plaintiffs frequently allege multiple schemes to avoid a finding that a single scheme with a limited number of victims does not project the necessary continuity to satisfy the pattern requirement. In the multiple-scheme context, therefore, courts sometimes relax relatedness constraints to avoid insulating deserving misconduct from RICO liability. *See, e.g., Banks v. Wolk*, 918 F.2d 418, 425 (3d Cir. 1990) ("if too close a relationship among multiple schemes is required, cases within RICO's intended ambit may be improperly dismissed. In organized crime cases, where the RICO enterprise exists solely for criminal purposes, the necessary nexus between the predicate acts and the enterprise will often be enough to satisfy the relatedness requirement. In cases . . . which allege multiple fraudulent schemes conducted through an otherwise legitimate entity, the relatedness requirement should not insulate defendants who merely vary the methods by which they defraud their victims" (citations omitted)). At the same time, though, "courts must take care to ensure that the plaintiff is not artificially fragmenting a singular act into multiple acts simply to invoke RICO." *Schlaifer Nance & Co. v. Estate of Warhol*, 119 F.3d 91, 98 (2d Cir. 1997).

Even though relatedness is usually not problematic, that is not always the case. There must be some meaningful link tying the offenses together, and courts are attentive to ensure that the somewhat relaxed standards are satisfied. *See, e.g., Heller Fin., Inc. v. Grammco Computer Sales, Inc.*, 71 F.3d 518 (5th Cir. 1996) (no relatedness in pattern allegedly consisting of (i) commercial bribery to secure a contract from a third-party customer and (ii) mail and wire fraud to obtain a loan from the plaintiff financier because the purposes, results, methods of commission, participants, and victims of the predicate offenses all differed; "we interpret the relationship prong of the pattern requirement to require more than an articulable factual nexus"); *Schlaifer Nance & Co. v. Estate of Warhol*, 119 F.3d at 96–97 (no relatedness between, on the one hand, (i) alleged schemes to defraud artist's estate and transport works out of state and fraudulently to deny receipt of payment for use of one artistic work to escape liability to pay coowner of copyright, and, on the other hand, (ii) schemes to defraud plaintiff licensing company of the value of its license to artist's work).

b. Continuity In assessing continuity, the Supreme Court has repeatedly focused judicial attention on the duration of the alleged pattern, and the lower federal courts have taken this directive to heart. Because continuity is "centrally a temporal factor" (*H.J. Inc.*, 492 U.S. 229, 242 (1989)), duration has been labeled the *"sine qua non* of continuity." *Hindes v. Castle*, 937 F.2d 868 (3d Cir. 1991) ("While it is not in itself sufficient to establish a pattern, . . . no pattern can be shown without the required duration"). Perhaps the sole truism discernible in the cases is that the longer the time period during which predicate acts are committed, the more likely it is that continuity—and thus a pattern—will be found.

The *H.J. Inc.* opinion declared that closed-ended continuity requires proof of "a series of related predicates extended over a substantial period of time." 492 U.S. at 242. Considerable judicial attention has been devoted to determining just what "period of time" is "substantial." Generally, the courts consider that "[w]hat constitutes a 'substantial' duration must of course remain a matter for case-by-case determination." *Walk v. Baltimore & Ohio R.R.*, 890 F.2d 688, 690 (4th Cir. 1989). Depending on the circumstances, closed-ended periods (involving episodes of repeated misconduct not projecting any threat of repetition into the future) have been held not to be substantial even when they extend up to more than one year in duration.[31] The Third Circuit has decided as a matter of law that one year is not a "substantial period of time" for closed-ended continuity purposes. *See Hughes v. Consol–Pa. Coal*

---

31. *See generally* Vicom, Inc. v. Harbridge Merchant Servs., 20 F.3d 771, 780 & n.8 (7th Cir. 1994) (citing **Treatise**). *See, e.g.*, the following cases in which no pattern was found due to lack of continuity: Feinstein v. Resolution Trust Corp., 942 F.2d 34 (1st Cir. 1991) (two years); Midwest Grinding Co. v. Spitz, 976 F.2d 1016 (7th Cir. 1992) (nine months); Vicom, 20 F.3d at 780 ("less than nine months"); Kehr Packages, Inc. v. Fidelcor, Inc., 926 F.2d 1406 (3d Cir.), *cert. denied*, 501 U.S. 1222 (1991) (eight months); Wisdom v. First Midwest Bank, 167 F.3d 402 (8th Cir. 1999) (six months); Parcoil Corp. v. Nowsco Well Serv., Ltd., 887 F.2d 502 (4th Cir. 1989) (four months); Menasco, Inc. v. Wasserman, 886 F.2d 681 (4th Cir. 1989) (one year); Newport, Ltd. v. Sears, Roebuck & Co., 941 F.2d 302 (5th Cir. 1991), *cert. denied*, 502 U.S. 1096 (1992) (ten months); McCoy v. Hilliard, No. 90-5532, 1991 U.S. App. LEXIS 17760, 940 F.2d 660 (6th Cir. July 19, 1991) (one month; unpublished opinion); Triad Assocs., Inc. v. Chicago Housing Auth., 892 F.2d 583 (7th Cir. 1989), *cert. denied*, 111 S. Ct. 129 (1990) (two years).

Compare the following cases in which closed-ended patterns were held viable because, inter alia, they stated the requisite continued threat of wrongful conduct: Fleet Credit Corp. v. Sion, 893 F.2d 441 (1st Cir. 1990) (four and one-half years); Swistock v. Jones, 884 F.2d 755 (3d Cir. 1989) (fourteen months); Walk v. Baltimore & Ohio R.R., 890 F.2d 688 (4th Cir. 1989) (ten years); Newmyer v. Philatelic Leasing, Ltd., 888 F.2d 385 (6th Cir. 1989), *cert. denied*, 495 U.S. 930 (1990) (five years); Atlas Pile Driving Co. v. DiCon Fin. Co., 886 F.2d 986 (8th Cir. 1989) (three years).

Co., 945 F.2d 594 (3d Cir. 1991), *cert. denied*, 504 U.S. 955 (1992) ("[T]he issue . . . is whether twelve months is a substantial period of time. . . . We hold that twelve months is not a substantial period of time"). A panel of the Ninth Circuit, in contrast, declined to impose a bright line, one-year test for closed-end continuity in *Allwaste, Inc. v. Hinson*, 65 F.3d 1523 (9th Cir. 1995) ("a bright line, one-year rule undermines *H.J. Inc.'s* principle that flexibility rather than rigidity should govern the application of RICO"), although separate panels had no qualms about holding nine and six months, respectively, insufficient as a matter of law. *Neely v. Campos*, 1994 U.S. App. LEXIS 12704 (9th Cir. May 27, 1994) ("The predicate acts in this case occurred over a period of nine months. This period of time is not sufficient to establish continuity over a closed period of time") (unpublished opinion); *Religious Tech. Ctr. v. Wollersheim*, 971 F.2d 364 (9th Cir. 1992) ("[T]he alleged activity continued for six months at most. . . . We have found no case in which a court has held the [closed-end continuity] requirement to be satisfied by a pattern of activity lasting less than a year").[32]

While duration is the key to closed-ended continuity, open-ended schemes may satisfy the continuity requirement regardless of their brevity. The critical question is whether the predicate acts project a threat of continuing misconduct. A few months or days—even less—may be sufficient if the continuing threat is present. *See, e.g., United States v. Indelicato*, 865 F.2d 1370 (2d Cir.), *cert. denied*, 491 U.S. 907 (1989) (three simultaneous Mafia assassinations carry threat of continuity); *United States v. O'Connor*, 910 F.2d 1466 (7th Cir. 1990), *cert. denied*, 498 U.S. 1082 (1991) (two months); *Stahl v. Bucks Cty. Bank & Trust*, 1993 U.S. Dist. LEXIS 11075 at *14 (citing **Treatise**).

The threat of continuing misconduct may be derived from the nature of the predicate acts alleged as well as from their duration. *See, e.g., Eastern Publishing & Advertising Inc. v. Chesapeake Publishing & Advertising, Inc.*, 895 F.2d 971 (4th Cir.), *cert. denied*, 110 S. Ct. 3274 (1990) (a "scheme to defraud . . . [may] demonstrate the requisite continuity or threat of continuity . . . either by its intrinsic nature or sheer duration"); *Olive Can Co., Inc. v. Martin*, 906 F.2d 1147 (7th Cir. 1990) (mail and wire fraud need not inherently project a threat of continuing misconduct, but arson and bankruptcy

---

32. The *Allwaste* articulation, moreover, can fairly be characterized as dictum (albeit important dictum) since the plaintiff in *Allwaste* maintained "that it could show that the predicate acts occurred over a substantial period of time, as much as thirteen months," and the Ninth Circuit held that "[s]uch a showing would have demonstrated that the criminal activity spanned a 'substantial period of time' and, therefore would have satisfied the continuity requirement." 65 F.3d at 1528.

fraud plainly designed to prevent discovery of prior misconduct may project that threat).

The Second Circuit has observed that inherently unlawful acts, like murder, committed in pursuit of inherently unlawful goals, such as narcotics trafficking, are generally found to generate the requisite threat of continuity even if the time period is short, while racketeering activities furthering endeavors that are not inherently unlawful—such as frauds in the sale of property—are often found wanting despite even longer time frames. *United States v. Aulicino,* 44 F.3d 1102 (2d Cir. 1995) (citations omitted). This observation may, as a practical matter, reflect a dual standard applied in criminal and civil cases by federal judges weary of seeing, in RICO attire, yet another "run-of-the-mill fraud case that belongs in state court." *Midwest Grinding Co. v. Spitz,* 976 F.2d 1016, 1025 (7th Cir. 1992).

One way of establishing open-ended continuity is to prove that the predicate acts "are part of an ongoing entity's regular way of doing business." *H.J. Inc.,* 492 U.S. 229, 242 (1989). Note that it must be the predicate acts—not some other type of misbehavior—that form part of the entity's regular way of doing business. *Fleet Credit Corp. v. Sion,* 893 F.2d 441 (1st Cir. 1990) ("A threat of continued criminal activity for purposes of RICO is not established merely by demonstrating that the [defendants'] acts of common law fraud were a regular way of conducting their ongoing business. Rather, [plaintiff] must demonstrate that the *predicate acts* . . . were a regular way of conducting the ongoing businesses" (court's emphasis)); *compare Tabas v. Tabas,* 47 F.3d 1280 (3d Cir.), *cert. denied,* 515 U.S. 1118 (1995) ("as a regular way of doing business, defendants were fraudulently misrepresenting expenditures to benefit themselves and to deprive the Estate and its beneficiaries of their legitimate share of the profits. . . . [T]hese practices, defendants' regular way of doing business, continued even after plaintiffs' complaint was filed. As a consequence, plaintiffs have established a threat of continuing fraudulent conduct as required under an 'open-ended' continuity analysis").

The nature and frequency of the offenses may reflect that they are committed in the ordinary course of business. For example, it has been held that three acts of forgery within a thirteen-month period reflect an enterprise's regular way of doing business. *Ticor Title Ins. Co. v. Florida,* 937 F.2d 447 (9th Cir. 1991) ("The frequency of the forgeries suggests that this practice had become a regular way of conducting business at [the enterprise], satisfying the continuity prong of the pattern test"). In the same fashion, the filing of two false corporate annual reports has been held to pose an inherent threat of continued criminal activity. *Ikuno v. Yip,* 912 F.2d 306

(9th Cir. 1990) (the defendant "was filing [false] annual reports and there is no evidence that he would have stopped doing so if [the company] had not ceased to do business").

In contrast, acts that focus on a clearly defined, discrete, and finite goal often import no inherent threat of continuing misconduct. *See, e.g., Vicom, Inc. v. Harbridge Merchant Servs., Inc.*, 20 F.3d 771 (7th Cir. 1994) (quoting **Treatise**); *Phelps v. Wichita Eagle-Beacon*, 886 F.2d 1262 (10th Cir. 1989) (scheme to publish two allegedly false and defamatory articles, which appeared in the press on the same day, lack continuity: "'one discrete goal,' which [plaintiff] alleges was accomplished, . . . is insufficient to state a claim for relief under RICO").

Measuring Duration. Because the duration of the misconduct is so important when considering whether a pattern exists, the task of measuring duration assumes considerable significance. This issue arises perhaps most pointedly, but not exclusively, when the predicate acts include mail and wire fraud. Under mail and wire fraud statutes, every mail or wire communication allegedly in furtherance of the fraudulent scheme is a separate violation, even individual communications that are not themselves fraudulent.[33]

The courts have determined that, in measuring the duration of misconduct for purposes of evaluating continuity, they will look at the character of each alleged act to determine whether, in context, it is wrongful. Only wrongful acts are considered in measuring the duration of any alleged pattern. *See, e.g., Wisdom v. First Midwest Bank*, 167 F.3d 402 (8th Cir. 1999) ("Though mail fraud can be a predicate act, mailings are insufficient to establish the continuity factor unless they contain misrepresentations themselves"); *Tabas v. Tabas*, 47 F.3d at 1294 ("In the instant case, it is clear that the mailings were incident to an essential part of the scheme [to misappropriate an excessive share of partnership profits]. Had the defendants failed to mail disbursement checks to plaintiffs, plaintiffs would have immediately been alerted to defendants' alleged scheme. Consequently, by virtue of the disbursements mailed to plaintiffs, defendants were allegedly able to delay discovery of their scheme"); *Feinstein v. Resolution Trust Corp.*, 942 F.2d 34 (1st Cir. 1991) (dismissing as "mere buzznacking" plaintiffs' attempts to lengthen the period of wrongdoing by relying on routine billing notices from, and checks to, the defendant lender: "There is no assertion that these communications were in any way irregular, comprised a means by which the fraudulent scheme is perpetrated, or has served to perpetuate or conceal the fraud. Hence, they cannot be considered 'separate fraudulent actions' for the

33. For a discussion of mail and wire fraud as predicate acts, *see* § 11(C)(2)(b), *supra*.

sake of establishing a pattern."); *Kehr Packages, Inc. v. Fidelcor, Inc.*, 926 F.2d 1406 (3d Cir.), *cert. denied*, 501 U.S. 1222 (1991) (stressing "[t]he importance of focusing in the continuity analysis on deceptive activity rather than otherwise innocent mailings" because, "[a]lthough the mailing is the actual criminal act, the instances of deceit constituting the underlying fraudulent scheme are more relevant to the continuity analysis"); *United States Textiles, Inc. v. Anheuser-Busch Co., Inc.*, 911 F.2d 1261 (7th Cir. 1990) ("'Mail fraud and wire fraud are perhaps unique among the various sorts of "racketeering activity" possible under RICO in that the existence of a multiplicity of predicate acts . . . may be no indication of the requisite continuity of the underlying fraudulent activity. Thus a multiplicity of mailings does not necessarily translate into a "pattern" of racketeering activity'") (quoting *Sutherland v. O'Malley*, 882 F.2d 1196 (7th Cir. 1989)).

While this analysis has most frequently been applied in the context of mail and wire fraud allegations, it is not limited to that sphere. The courts scrupulously analyze each alleged pattern to determine when the truly wrongful conduct occurred. It is the duration of this misbehavior, including culpable cover-ups, that stakes the boundaries of the pattern—not innocent, routine, or even tortious behavior that may be attendant to the culpable conduct. *See, e.g., Midwest Grinding Co. v. Spitz*, 976 F.2d 1016 (7th Cir. 1992) (scheme to conceal underlying criminal activity by giving false deposition testimony and furnishing false discovery responses "do[es] nothing to extend the duration of the underlying . . . [RICO] scheme"); *Management Computer Servs., Inc. v. Hawkins, Ash, Baptie & Co.*, 883 F.2d 48 (7th Cir. 1989) (finding no pattern in what was essentially "a contract dispute involving one 'victim,' one transaction between the parties, and at most two predicate acts—the allegedly unauthorized copying of the contract [computer] programs and the allegedly unauthorized copying of the backup tapes. . . . [Defendant]'s subsequent use of the allegedly stolen software cannot be characterized as subsequent thefts . . . but would go only to the issue of damages"); *Lange v. Hocker*, 940 F.2d 359 (8th Cir. 1991) ("Plaintiffs attempt to extend the time frame of alleged racketeering activity by including acts of mismanagement that occurred in 1988 and 1989. At most, however, these alleged acts of mismanagement show managerial incompetency, which is not a crime, let alone a predicate act. . . . Further attempts to extend the time frame of defendants' alleged racketeering activity are equally specious. Resignation from a corporate office or directorship is not a predicate act; neither is refusal to surrender disputed stock ownership"); *Terry A. Lambert Plumbing, Inc. v. Western Sec. Bank*, 934 F.2d 976 (8th Cir. 1991) ("this case involves, at most, a plan to defraud a single company in connection with a single set of loan agreements. [A] single transaction which involves only one victim and takes place over a short period of time does not constitute the pattern of racketeering required for long-term criminal activity under a RICO claim. . . . [T]he fact that a bank has had problem loans in the past and has moved to protect its position in regard to a current problem loan is not, by itself, indicative of a pattern of racketeering. Bankers do not become racketeers by acting like bankers").[34]

Sporadic Misconduct. The *H.J. Inc.* opinion recites that "[a] pattern is not formed by 'sporadic activity,' and a person cannot 'be subjected to the sanctions of title IX simply for committing two widely separated and isolated criminal offenses.'" 492 U.S. at 239 (citations to legislative history omitted). Whether misbehavior is sporadic or continuous is a fact question. If sporadic, continuity is, by definition, lacking. *See, e.g., Feinstein v. Resolution Trust Corp.,* 942 F.2d 34 (1st Cir. 1991) ("two episodes, nearly two years apart in time, hundreds of miles apart in space, and involving two largely distinct groups of participants" held unrelated and sporadic). Sporadic behavior may be characterized by, among other things, a small number of alleged predicate acts. *Fleet Credit Corp. v. Sion,* 893 F.2d 441, 447 (1st Cir. 1990) ("Too few acts would suggest that the defendant were engaged only in 'sporadic activity'").

There is sometimes a fine line to be drawn between sporadic and nonsporadic activity. The Second Circuit ruled in *United States v. Biaggi,* 909 F.2d 662 (2d Cir. 1988), *cert. denied,* 499 U.S. 904 (1991), that commission of an offense and a later denial of the same under oath lacked the requisite continuity to establish a pattern—that, indeed, "aggregating the [offense] and its denial into a 'pattern' perverts the meaning of that word, at least as it is used in the RICO statute." *Id.* at 686 (a "bribe does not cease to be a sporadic offense simply because [the defendant] later falsely denied committing it. If the commission of an offense and its false denial could establish a 'pattern,' then *every* offense related to a criminal enterprise would be eligible for inclusion in a pattern whenever the offender falsely denied its commission. That is not what Congress intended" (court's emphasis)).

The Second Circuit had previously ruled that commission of an offense and an obstruction of justice involving an attempt to

---

34. *See also* J.D. Marshall Int'l, Inc. v. Redstart, Inc., 935 F.2d 815 (7th Cir. 1991) ("this litigation merely involved 'a highly contentious aftermath of a single transaction'"); Sil-Flo, Inc. v. SFHC, Inc., 917 F.2d 1507 (10th Cir. 1990) ("At most what has been alleged is a business deal gone sour, accompanied by the breach of fiduciary duty and various other torts by the defendants. There certainly is no open-ended threat of future illegal activity. While the plaintiffs may have alleged a closed-ended series of predicate acts, they constituted a single scheme to accomplish 'one discrete goal' directed at one individual with no potential to extend to other persons or entities").

induce false grand jury testimony did constitute a pattern for RICO purposes. *United States v. Teitler,* 802 F.2d 606 (2d Cir. 1986). In distinguishing *Teitler,* the *Biaggi* court stressed that "[i]t is one thing to build a pattem out of an offense followed by an attempt to persuade grand jury witnesses to lie; it is quite a different matter to aggregate an offense and the offender's own false denial of it." 909 F.2d at 686 ("In the former case, the offender extends his criminal conduct beyond denial of wrongdoing. . . . In the latter case, the offender simply maintains his innocence"). Whether or not this distinction is telling, it reflects a marked judicial sensitivity toward sparing sporadic offenders RICO liability.

c. Patterns and Parties In determining whether a pattern has been stated against any particular defendant, the court considers only the alleged offenses in which that defendant was purportedly involved, directly or indirectly, or for which that defendant bears some responsibility. Extraneous offenses committed by other persons attached to the enterprise may not form the basis of the pattern charged against wholly uninvolved persons. *See, e.g., Banks v. Wolk,* 918 F.2d 418 (3d Cir. 1990) (defendants "Wolk and Weiner are alleged only to have participated in the AP Building fraud, and there is no indication that either was involved, directly or indirectly, in any of the additional schemes. Consequently, we must consider only the AP Building scheme allegations in determining whether a sufficient 'pattern' has been alleged against either Wolk or Weiner. Even if the AP Building scheme were part of a pattern of acts committed by the [other defendants], the additional schemes cannot affect the liability of Wolk or Weiner, since they neither participated in those frauds nor agreed to their commission"); *Feinstein v. Resolution Trust Corp.,* 942 F.2d 34 (1st Cir. 1991) ("the facts as alleged, while arguably sufficient to show relatedness with regard to the actions of common participants [in all of the frauds], did not implicate any of the other defendants in the same way. . . . In the absence of any demonstrable imbrication [overlap], the plaintiffs' claim that these episodes were successive segments in a single scheme implicating the defendants' collective actions is nothing more than a conclusory assertion which need not be honored under Rule 12(b)(6)").

d. Multifactor Test Before the Supreme Court's decision in *H.J. Inc.,* several circuits had adopted multiple-factor tests in an effort to set a coherent analytical framework within which to decide pattern issues. The First and Seventh Circuits, for example, considered the following factors in determining whether a pattern had been stated:

1. the number of predicate acts,
2. the variety of predicate acts,

3. the length of time over which they were committed,
4. the number of victims,
5. the presence of separate schemes, and
6. the occurrence of distinct injuries.

See generally Roeder v. Alpha Indus., Inc., 814 F.2d 22 (1st Cir. 1987); *Morgan v. Bank of Waukegan*, 804 F.2d 970 (7th Cir. 1986).

The Third Circuit adopted a generally similar test but substituted the number of perpetrators for item (5) and the character of the unlawful activity for item (6). *See, e.g., Barticheck v. Fidelity Union Bank/First Nat'l State*, 832 F.2d 36 (3d Cir. 1987).

Following the Supreme Court's decision in *H.J. Inc.*, these courts divided over the status of their preexisting tests. Most courts now tend to apply them, giving due deference to *H.J.*, and focusing on *H.J.'s* expansive recognition that "[t]he limits of the relationship and continuity concepts . . . , and the precise methods by which relatedness and continuity or its threat may be proved, cannot be fixed in advance. . . . " 492 U.S. at 243. For example, even though a panel of the Third Circuit suggested shortly after *H.J.* that its multifactor test was "no longer tenable in light of *H.J. Inc.*," *Swistock v. Jones*, 884 F.2d 755 (3d Cir. 1989), other panels of that court subsequently concluded "that *H.J. Inc.* has not rendered obsolete our prior multifactor pattern inquiry" but requires only that "we must focus on these factors as they bear upon the separate questions of continuity and relatedness." *Banks v. Wolk*, 918 F.2d 418 (3d Cir. 1990); *accord Tabas v. Tabas*, 47 F.3d 1280 (3d Cir.), *cert. denied*, 515 U.S. 1118 (1995) ("Because we have found a pattern of racketeering activity in both the duration of and the on-going threat implicit in defendants' regular way of doing business, we will not go on to analyze this case under the six *Barticheck* factors. The fact that we do not employ the *Barticheck* factors in our analysis here does not, however, mean that they might not be relevant in a different case in determining if continuity exists").[35]

A similar view has been expressed by the Seventh Circuit, which still utilizes its multifactor test in determining whether a pattern exists. In the Seventh Circuit, the impact of *H.J. Inc.*, "beyond its express holding that two schemes need not be shown to prove a 'pattern,' is that we now analyze these various factors with an eye towards achieving a 'natural and commonsense' result." *United States Textiles, Inc. v. Anheuser-Busch Cos., Inc.*, 911

35. *See also* Hindes v. Castle, 937 F.2d 868, 873 (3d Cir. 1991), and Marshall-Silver Constr. Co. v. Mandel, 894 F.2d 593, 595 n.1 (3d Cir. 1990), in which the Third Circuit held that all the factors included within its pre-*H.J. Inc.* test, "except the similarity of the acts, 'remain, in greater and lesser degrees, relevant to the issue of continuity.'" *Hindes*, 937 F.2d at 873 (quoting *Marshall-Silver*, 894 F.2d at 595 n.1).

F.2d 1261 (7th Cir. 1990); *see also Management Computer Servs., Inc. v. Hawkins, Ash, Baptie & Co.*, 883 F.2d 248 (7th Cir. 1989); *accord Vicom, Inc. v. Harbridge Merchant Servs. Inc.*, 20 F.3d 771 (7th Cir. 1994) ("In order to analyze the continuity prong of the pattern requirement, our post-H.J., Inc. caselaw has continued to find helpful the factors we set out in Morgan v. Bank of Waukegan").

The Sixth Circuit is satisfied that "[n]either *Sedima* [n]or *H.J. Inc.* worked a significant change in [pre-existing Sixth Circuit] law. To the contrary, they have buttressed the validity of the multi-factor approach to the determination of whether a pattern exists." *Columbia Natural Resources, Inc. v. Tatum*, 58 F.3d 1101, 1110 (6th Cir. 1995), *cert. denied*, 516 U.S. 1158 (1996) ("to state the inquiry simply, a pattern is the sum of various factors including: the length of time the racketeering activity existed; the number of different schemes (the more the better); the number of predicate acts within each scheme (the more the better); the variety of species of predicate acts (the more the better); the distinct types of injury (the more the better); the number of victims (the more the better); and the number of perpetrators (the less the better)").

The Tenth Circuit compiled a post-*H.J.* multifactor approach to resolving continuity issues in *Resolution Trust Corp. v. Stone*, 998 F.2d 1534 (10th Cir. 1993), focusing on (1) "the duration of the related predicate acts" and (2) "the extensiveness of the RICO enterprise's scheme," with the latter prong entailing consideration of: (i) the number of victims; (ii) the number of racketeering acts; (iii) the variety of racketeering acts; (iv) whether the injuries caused were distinct; (v) the complexity and size of the scheme; and (vi) the nature or character of the enterprise or unlawful activity. *Id.* at 1543–44.

The First Circuit, in contrast, has decided that *H.J. Inc.* precludes reliance on that circuit's prior multifactor approach—which had been drawn verbatim from the Seventh Circuit precedent. *Fleet Credit Corp. v. Sion*, 893 F.2d 441 (1st Cir. 1990) ("the pre-*H.J.* approach is no longer a reliable guide").

The *H.J. Inc.* Court was aware of the circuits' various multifactor tests, 492 U.S. at 229 n.2, but did not endorse any of them. By its effective incorporation of the former 18 U.S.C. § 3575(e) into RICO, the Supreme Court has provided something of its own multifactor test for assessing the relatedness criterion: "criminal acts that [1] have the same or similar [a] purposes, [b] results, [c] participants, [d] victims, [e] methods of commission, or [2] otherwise are interrelated by distinguishing characteristics and [3] are not isolated events." *Sedima, S.P.R.L. v. Imrex Co.*, 473 U.S. 479, 496 n.14 (1985); *H.J. Inc.*, 492 U.S. at 240. It is particularly in the area of continuity that the Supreme Court has afforded precious little guidance, and a multifactor approach along the lines adopted by most circuits could conceivably help fill the gap.

Analyzed most simply, "'continuity' means that separate events occur over time and perhaps threaten to recur, while 'relatedness' means—given that different acts of racketeering activity have occurred—that there is a way in which the acts may be viewed as having a common purpose." *Procter & Gamble Co. v. Big Apple Indus. Bldgs., Inc.*, 879 F.2d 10, 17 (2d Cir. 1989), *cert. denied*, 493 U.S. 1022 (1990). Drawing on the multiple-factor tests developed by the circuits discussed above, in light of the directives issued by the Supreme Court and subsequent lower court precedent, the following nonexclusive list of factors itemizes the data necessary to determine whether the relatedness and continuity criteria have been satisfied:

1. the nature and number of (a) offenses and (b) schemes;
2. the nature and number of victims;
3. the nature, number, and identity of (a) perpetrators and (b) enterprises;
4. the involvement of each perpetrator and enterprise in each (a) offense and (b) scheme;
5. the dates and duration of (a) offenses and (b) schemes;
6. the goals of each offense and scheme;
7. the methods utilized in committing each offense and effectuating each scheme, including the presence of repetitive misbehavior; and
8. the nature, extent, and distinctiveness of resulting damages.

E. "Collection of an Unlawful Debt"

Section 1962(a), (b), and (c) each provide that the prohibited activities are barred not only if achieved through a pattern of racketeering activity but also if accomplished "through collection of an unlawful debt." Section 1961(6) defines "unlawful debt" to mean the following:

> a debt (A) incurred or contracted in gambling activity which was in violation of the law . . . or which is unenforceable under State or Federal law . . . because of the laws relating to usury, and (B) which was incurred in connection with the business of gambling in violation of the law . . ., or the business of lending money or a thing of value at a rate usurious under State or Federal law.[36]

---

36. In full, § 1961(6) provides that

> "unlawful debt" means a debt (A) incurred or contracted in gambling activity which was in violation of the law of the United States, a State or political subdivision thereof, or which is unenforceable under State or Federal law in whole or in part as to principal or interest because of the laws relating to usury, and (B) which was incurred in connection with the business of gambling in violation of the law of the United States, a State or political subdivision thereof, or the business of lending money or a thing of value at a rate usurious under State or Federal law, where the usurious rate is at least twice the enforceable rate.

Consequently, this provision defines two separate categories of unlawful debts: one generated by gambling activity and the other involving usurious lending (loan-sharking) activity. *Saglioccolo v. Eagle Ins. Co.*, 112 F.3d 226 (6th Cir. 1997) ("Under RICO, 'unlawful debt' pertains to illegal gambling debt or debt unenforceable because of usury laws"); *accord United States v. Giovanelli*, 945 F.2d 479, 491 (2d Cir. 1991).

There are two primary differences in proving liability for misconduct committed "through collection of an unlawful debt" as opposed to "through a pattern of racketeering activity." First, "collection of an unlawful debt" entails no requirement that the defendant have committed multiple predicate acts; the collection of a single unlawful debt suffices. *See, e.g., United States v. Giovanelli*, 945 F.2d at 490 ("Unlike a 'pattern of racketeering activity' which requires proof of two or more predicate acts, to satisfy RICO's 'collection of unlawful debt' definition, the Government [or plaintiff] need only demonstrate a single collection"); *accord United States v. Pepe*, 747 F.2d 632 (11th Cir. 1984). Second, there is no exhaustive list of offenses constituting the "collection of an unlawful debt" as there is (in section 1961(1)) an exclusive list defining "racketeering activity." *United States v. Vastola*, 899 F.2d 211 (3d Cir.), *vacated on other grounds*, 110 S. Ct. 3233 (1990). (*See also* § 11(C), *supra*.) Rather, section 1961(6) generically describes the type of state and federal statutes that trigger its prohibition.

"[C]ollection of an unlawful debt" is rarely alleged in civil cases, and even more rarely successfully alleged. *See, e.g., Sundance Land Corp. v. Community First Fed. Sav. & Loan Ass'n*, 840 F.2d 653 (9th Cir. 1988) ("neither the [Federal Home Loan] Bank Board regulations nor HOLA [the Home Owner's Loan Act] can be fairly characterized as 'laws relating to usury,' because they do not limit the amount of interest that a bank or other lending institution can charge. Rather, they address only the method by which they may collect interest, or the kind of credit or property they may have received in return for a loan").

On the gambling side, even a "garden variety debt" obtained as a result of illegal betting falls within the category of proscribed "gambling activity." *United States v. Angiulo*, 847 F.2d 956 (1st Cir.), *cert. denied*, 488 U.S. 928 (1988) ("The definition of 'unlawful debt' clearly contemplates the type of gambling debts involved in . . . illegal poker games"). A usurious lending claim is a bit more involved. It requires proof that

> [1] the debt was unenforceable in whole or in part because of state or federal laws relating to usury, [2] the debt was incurred in connection with "the business of lending money . . . at a [usurious] rate,". . . [3] the usurious rate was at least twice the enforceable rate. . . [and] [4] as a result of the above confluence of factors, [plaintiff] was injured in its business or property.

Sundance Land Corp., 840 F.2d at 666.

As these elements reflect, the civil RICO action is not simply an action to recover excessive interest or to enforce a penalty for an overcharge on a loan. "RICO is concerned with evils far more significant than the simple practice of usury." *Durante Bros. & Sons, Inc. v. Flushing Nat'l Bank*, 755 F.2d 239, 248–49 (2d Cir. 1985), *cert. denied*, 473 U.S. 906 (1986); *Sundance Land Corp.*, 840 F.2d at 666. In fact, there is some doubt, based on the legislative history, that RICO was ever intended to be used against banking institutions. Congress's purpose in requiring that the usurious rate be at least twice the enforceable rate was "to limit the effect of this definition to cases of clear 'loan-sharking.'" S. Rep. No. 91-617, 91st Cong., 1st Sess., 158–59 (1969); *see also Sundance Land Corp.*, 840 F.2d at 667 n.19.

F. "Affect[ing] Interstate or Foreign Commerce"

Section 1962(a), (b), and (c) are limited in scope to conduct involving enterprises "engaged in, or the activities of which affect, interstate or foreign commerce." Predictably, the impact on commerce need not be substantial. *See, e.g., United States v. Doherty*, 867 F.2d 47 (1st Cir. 1989) ("RICO requires no more than a slight effect upon interstate commerce"); *United States v. Robinson*, 763 F.2d 778 (6th Cir. 1985) ("minimal impact"); *United States v. Muskovsky*, 863 F.2d 1319 (7th Cir. 1988), *cert. denied*, 489 U.S. 1067 (1989) ("'even a minimal effect on interstate commerce satisfies this jurisdictional element'"); *United States v. Beasley*, 72 F.3d 1518 (11th Cir.), *cert. denied*, 518 U.S. 1027 (1996) ("only a slight effect on interstate commerce is required"). The Ninth Circuit has equated RICO's jurisdictional reach with that of the Sherman Act, 15 U.S.C. § 1, *et seq. Musick v. Burke*, 913 F.2d 1390 (9th Cir. 1990).

The Supreme Court elucidated on the breadth of RICO jurisdiction in *United States v. Robertson*, 514 U.S. 669 (1995). The defendant in *Robertson* had been convicted of a section 1962(a) violation for having invested the proceeds of narcotics transactions in an Alaskan gold mine. The Ninth Circuit reversed the RICO conviction on the theory that the gold mine was not an "enterprise which is engaged in, or the activities of which affect, interstate or foreign commerce." The Supreme Court reversed on the ground that the mine was "engaged in . . . interstate . . . commerce," in light of record evidence that the defendant had (1) purchased supplies and equipment for the mine in California and sent them to Alaska; (2) solicited California workers to travel to Alaska to work in the mine; and (3) taken $30,000 worth of gold, or 15 percent of the mine's output, out of state. *Robertson*, 514 U.S. at 671.

Although most of the authorities construing the commerce requirement are criminal, the standard is at least nominally just as relaxed in civil cases. *See, e.g., Jund v. Town of Hempstead,* 941 F.2d 1271 (2d Cir. 1991) ("If the defendants' conduct produces any interference with or effect upon interstate commerce, whether slight, subtle or even potential, it is sufficient to uphold a prosecution under the Hobbs Act" and, therefore, to support a RICO claim); *cf. Bunker Ramo Corp. v. United Business Forms, Inc.,* 713 F.2d 1272 (7th Cir. 1983) ("The interstate commerce nexus requirement of RICO is satisfied if an enterprise affects interstate commerce through its activities, even if it is the racketeering activities of the enterprise that affect interstate commerce").

There have been occasional civil cases in which the commerce nexus was deemed lacking—notwithstanding the fact that the same nexus would probably have been sufficient if criminal behavior were implicated. *See, e.g., Musick v. Burke,* 913 F.2d 1390 (9th Cir. 1990) (use of out-of-state supplies by a catering-truck operator is insufficient as a matter of law to create federal jurisdiction under RICO). Since *Robertson,* those cases—always rare—are of dubious precedential value.

G. Mens Rea

RICO is fundamentally a criminal statute. Although section 1964(c) creates a civil cause of action, "the racketeering activity giving rise to RICO liability must be criminal in nature." *Klein v. King,* [1990] Fed. Sec. L. Rep. (CCH) ¶ 95,002 (N.D. Cal. Mar. 26, 1990) (observing that "'racketeering activity' is defined [in section 1960(1)] as including traditional state law crimes . . ., acts 'indictable' under federal laws . . ., and other federal 'offenses' "); *cf. H.J. Inc. v. Northwestern Bell Tel. Co.,* 492 U.S. 229 (1989) (noting, among other things, that predicate acts must "pose a threat of continued *criminal* activity," that "Congress was concerned with long-term *criminal* conduct," and that "Congress drafted RICO broadly enough to encompass a wide range of *criminal* activity" (emphasis added)). *See generally Republic of Panama v. BCCI Holdings,* 119 F.3d 935 (11th Cir. 1997) ("Section 1961 requires that a RICO plaintiff establish that a defendant could be convicted for violating any of its predicate statutes. . . . Therefore, in order to survive a motion to dismiss, a plaintiff must allege facts sufficient to support each of the statutory elements for at least two of the pleaded predicate acts") (citations omitted).

To be criminal, conduct must be committed with the mens rea appropriate to the offense. In order to establish liability under RICO, the plaintiff must prove that the defendant acted with the appropriate mens rea at one or two levels, depending on the circuit. In all circuits, the defendant must possess "the specific intent associated with the various underlying predicate offenses." *Genty v. Resolution Trust Corp.*, 937 F.2d 899, 908 (3d Cir. 1991); *see also Lancaster Community Hosp. v. Antelope Valley Hosp. Dist.*, 940 F.2d 397 (9th Cir. 1991) ("A specific intent to deceive is an element of the predicate act"), *cert. denied*, 502 U.S. 1094 (1992). In some circuits, since RICO itself imposes additional criminal liability, the defendant must act "with the specific intent to participate in the overall RICO enterprise." *Zolfaghari v. Sheikholeslami*, 943 F.2d 451 (4th Cir. 1991). But that is not a universally shared view. *See, e.g., United States v. Biasucci*, 786 F.2d 504 (2d Cir.), *cert. denied*, 479 U.S. 827 (1986) ("RICO imposes no additional mens rea requirement beyond that found in the predicate crimes"); *accord United States v. Blinder*, 10 F.3d 1468 (9th Cir 1993).

Mens rea may be shown directly (as by an admission) or circumstantially, as by "the existence of a scheme which was reasonably calculated to deceive persons of ordinary prudence and comprehension [when that] intention is shown by examining this scheme itself." *Ikuno v. Yip*, 912 F.2d 306, 310–11 (9th Cir. 1990). If the necessary mens rea is not alleged or proven, the plaintiff's claim is fatally defective. *See, e.g., Blue Line Coal Co. v. Equibank*, 769 F. Supp. 891 (E.D. Pa. 1991) (summary judgment granted in the absence of any facts "permit[ting] a reasonable inference of any fraudulent intent or conspiratorial motive" on the part of the defendant).

§ 12. Section 1962(a): Elements of Claim

In order to recover under section 1962(a), a plaintiff must plead and prove that

1. a person (§ 11(A), *supra*),
2. acting with the necessary mens rea (§ 11(G), *supra*),
3. received income
4. from a pattern of racketeering activity (§ 11(D), *supra*) or through collection of an unlawful debt (§ 11(E), *supra*).
5. This income was invested in an enterprise (§ 11(B), *supra*)
6. that bears the necessary nexus to interstate or foreign commerce (§ 11(F), *supra*)
7. resulting in injury to the plaintiff's business or property (§ 6(A)(2)–(3), *supra*)
8. by reason of (§ 6(A)(4), *supra*)
9. the defendant's use or investment of the income in the enterprise (§ 7, *supra*).[37]

---

37. Under the minority view, injury from the predicate acts alone is sufficient. *See* § 7, *supra*.

Apart from the subject of "income" raised in item (3), each of the other elements has previously been discussed in the referenced sections. "Income" is not defined in the statute, and there is no reason to accord it any other than its ordinary meaning. That, however, is not necessarily as easy as it sounds because "income" has a variety of meanings.

In *Azurite Corp. v. Amster & Co.*, 730 F. Supp. 571 (S.D.N.Y. 1990), the court held that the defendants had "received . . . income derived, directly or indirectly, from a pattern of racketeering activity" when they purchased stock at deflated prices due to their fraud. The *Azurite* court reasoned that if the defendants had sold their stock and captured the value that their fraud had created, there would be no question that they had received "income." It declined to conclude that no income had been received simply because they had "used the savings they garnered to purchase more stock than they would have had if the price had been at its true market value." *Id.* at 579.

Contrast with *Azurite* the Seventh Circuit's decision in *Hemmings v. Barian*, 822 F.2d 688 (7th Cir. 1987). Chief Judge Posner concluded in *Hemmings* that even if a defendant had defrauded the plaintiff into selling him a business on an installment plan—with no intention of making future installment payments—the defendant's "savings" (from not paying the money owed) could not properly be deemed income within section 1962(a). As a purely factual matter, the *Hemmings* opinion noted, while the defendant may have used income that he owed the plaintiff (the balance of the purchase price), there was no suggestion that the funds actually spent were derived from fraud. That money was not "extracted from [the plaintiff] by fraud" but was instead "lawful income" from some other source. No section 1962(a) violation was therefore stated. *Id.* at 692.

It is difficult to draw a principled distinction between *Hemmings* and *Azurite*. In both cases, the defendant's "income," if any, consisted of the proceeds of the fraud. In both cases, the buyer paid less than was due as a result of fraudulent behavior and invested the difference in another investment. *Hemmings* "traced" the source of the physical funds expended and determined it to be of untainted origin. *Azurite* focused instead on the defendant's wherewithal to make the subsequent investment, which was a direct product of the fraud. Stated another way, *Hemmings* used a bookkeeping approach to analyze the "income" question, while *Azurite* implicitly employed a metaphysical definition (akin to the definition used for federal income tax purposes).

While the *Azurite* approach certainly fulfills the congressional injunction that RICO be liberally construed, it has its drawbacks.

The income *Azurite* posits is phantom income. Unless the funds used to make an investment are "traced," in the loose sense that *Hemmings* dictates, virtually every investment made by a defendant following the receipt of phantom income is arguably made, in whole or in part, with the phantom funds. The plaintiff can select its preferred investment—namely, one that has injured the plaintiff—to hold the defendant liable under RICO. While this may not necessarily seem an offensive result if there is only one plaintiff, there may not be only one. There may be two or 10 or 20 plaintiffs, all claiming in separate actions that the same phantom funds were invested or used to their detriment. The *Hemmings* approach has the benefit of averting this result and is preferable for that reason and because it provides an objective means of determining what, in fact, the "income" comprises.

§ 13. Section 1962(b): Elements of Claim

To recover under section 1962(b), the plaintiff must plead and prove that

1. a person (§ 11(A), *supra*),
2. acting with the necessary mens rea (§ 11(G), *supra*),
3. through a pattern of racketeering activity (§ 11(D), *supra*) or collection of an unlawful debt (§ 11(E), *supra*),
4. "acquire[d] or maintain[ed]"
5. "any interest in"
6. or control of (§ 8, *supra*)
7. an enterprise (§ 11(B), *supra*)
8. engaged in or affecting interstate or foreign commerce (§ 11(F), *supra*)
9. resulting in injury to the plaintiff's business or property (§ 6(A)(2)–(3), *supra*)
10. by reason of (§ 6(A)(4), *supra*)
11. the defendant's acquisition or maintenance of the interest in, or control over, the enterprise (§ 8, *supra*).[38]

As indicated in the parentheticals, most of these elements have previously been discussed. The courts have not found the remaining items (items (4) and (5)) to be problematic. The words are accorded their plain meaning. *See, e.g., Northeast Jet Center, Ltd. v. Lehigh-Northampton Airport Auth.*, 767 F.Supp. 672 (E.D. Pa. 1991) (dismissing a section 1962(b) claim where plaintiff alleged only "that a

38. Under the minority view, injury from the predicate acts alone is sufficient. *See* § 8, *supra*.

campaign of misrepresentation and disparagement compelled the plaintiff to sell off some of its property at an undesirable price. No acquisition of an 'ownership interest' [in the plaintiff/enterprise itself] is alleged"). Cf. *Russello v. United States,* 464 U.S. 16 (1983) (interpreting the word "interest" for purposes of section 1963(a)(1): "Every property interest, including a right to profits or proceeds, may be described as an interest in something").

§ 14. Section 1962(c): Elements of Claim

In *Sedima, S.P.R.L. v. Imrex Co.,* 473 U.S. 479 (1985), the Supreme Court articulated the elements of a section 1962(c) claim for relief:

> A violation of § 1962(c) . . . requires (1) conduct (2) of an enterprise (3) through a pattern (4) of racketeering activity. . . . In addition, the plaintiff only has standing if, and can only recover to the extent that, he has been injured in his business or property by the conduct constituting the violation.

Id. at 496.

These elements can be itemized more discretely. Under section 1962(c), a plaintiff must plead and prove that

1. a person (§ 11(A), *supra*)
2. employed by or associated with (§ 9(B), *supra*)
3. an enterprise (§§ 9(A) and 11(B), *supra*)
4. that is engaged in or affects interstate or foreign commerce (§ 11(F), *supra*)
5. conducted or participated in the conduct of the enterprise's affairs (§ 9(C), *supra*)
6. through a pattern of racketeering activity (§ 11(D), *supra*) or collection of an unlawful debt (§ 11(E), *supra*)
7. while acting with the necessary mens rea (§ 11(G), *supra*)
8. resulting in injury to the plaintiff's business or property (§ 6(A)(2)–(4), *supra*).

Each of these elements has previously been discussed in the referenced sections.

§ 15. Section 1962(d): Elements of Claim

In order to recover under section 1962(d), a plaintiff must plead and prove

1. that a person (§ 11(A), *supra*)
2. conspired to violate section 1962(a), (b), or (c) (which are discussed in §§12–14, *supra*). To plead conspiracy adequately, the plaintiff must set forth allegations addressing
   a. the period of the conspiracy,

   b. the object of the conspiracy,
   c. the overt acts taken in furtherance of the conspiracy,
   d. the agreement to commit predicate acts, and
   e. knowledge that the acts were part of a pattern of racketeering activity.[39] The plaintiff must also establish
3. injury to the plaintiff's business or property (§ 6(A)(2)–(3), *supra*)
4. by reason of (§ 6(A)(4), *supra*)
5. overt acts that, depending on the circuit, must also be predicate acts (§ 10, *supra*).

Each of these elements has previously been discussed in the sections identified in the parentheticals.

Bear in mind that the conspiracy claim is only as valid as the claim of underlying violation of section 1962(a), (b), or (c), although there is no requirement that the underlying violation necessarily have been consummated. (*See generally* § 10, *supra*.)

Nature of Conspiratorial Agreement. Prior to the Supreme Court's decision in *Salinas v. United States*, 522 U.S. 52 (1997), the circuits were split as to whether the agreement to commit the predicate acts, set forth in item 2(d), above, must be an agreement on the part of the defendant personally to commit two acts of racketeering activity.[40] In *Salinas*, the Supreme Court ruled that this was not an essential element of the culpable agreement: "A conspiracy may exist even if a conspirator does not agree to commit or facilitate each and every part of the substantive offense. . . . A conspirator must intend to further an endeavor which, if completed, would satisfy all of the elements of a substantive criminal offense. . . . He may do so in any number of ways short of agreeing to undertake all of the acts necessary for the crime's completion." *Id.*, 522 U.S. at 65. However, the complaint must allege an agreement by each defendant to the commission of two predicate acts by someone associated with the enterprise. *Goren v. New Vision Int'l, Inc.*, 156 F.3d 721 (7th Cir. 1998) ("From a conceptual standpoint a conspiracy to violate RICO can be analyzed as composed

---

39. *See generally* Shearin v. E. F. Hutton Group, Inc., 885 F.2d 1162 (3d Cir. 1989). The defendant's agreement to participate reflects the necessary mens rea (§ 11(G), *supra*).

40. Compare Miranda v. Ponce Fed. Bank, 948 F.2d 41 (1st Cir. 1991) (defendant must personally agree to commit two acts of racketeering activity) *and* United States v. Rastelli, 870 F.2d 822 (2d Cir.), *cert. denied*, 493 U.S. 892 (1989) (same) *with* United States v. Carter, 721 F.2d 1514 (11th Cir.), *cert. denied*, 469 U.S. 819 (1984) (1962(d) also renders unlawful any agreement by one person that another violate § 1962(c) by committing two acts of racketeering activity) *and* Adams v. United States, 759 F.2d 1099 (3d Cir.), *cert. denied*, 474 U.S. 971 (1985) (same). *Salinas* opted for the latter view.

of two agreements . . . : an agreement to conduct or participate in the affairs of an enterprise and an agreement to the commission of at least two predicate acts. Thus, a defendant who did not agree to the commission of crimes constituting a pattern of racketeering activity is not in violation of section 1962(d), even though he is somehow affiliated with a RICO enterprise, and neither is the defendant who agrees to the commission of two criminal acts but does not consent to the involvement of an enterprise").

Impact of Reves *on Conspiracies to Violate Section 1962(c).* There is one issue unique to alleged conspiracies to violate 1962(c). In *Reves v. Ernst & Young,* 507 U.S. 170, 183 (1993), the Supreme Court declared that there is no liability under section 1962(c) "unless one has participated in the operation or management of the enterprise itself" (*see* § 9(C), *supra*). The circuits are split as to whether the operation-and-management test applies to an alleged conspiracy to violate section 1962(c)—that is, as to whether there is a distinction to be drawn between, on the one hand, conspiring to operate or manage an enterprise, and, on the other, conspiring with someone who is operating or managing the enterprise.

The Third and Ninth Circuits draw this distinction and recognize liability only under the former scenario (conspiring to operate or manage) and not under the latter (conspiring with someone who is operating or managing). They represent the minority view, which posits that a contrary holding would effectively eviscerate *Reves. See, e.g., United States v. Antar,* 53 F.3d 568 (3d Cir. 1995); *Neibel v. Trans World Assur.,* 108 F.3d 1123 (9th Cir. 1997).

The Second, Fifth, Seventh, and Eleventh Circuits disagree, holding that *Reves'* management and control test does not apply to a RICO conspiracy claim. These courts consider that, since *Reves* did not address section 1962(d), it has no bearing on a section 1962(d) conspiracy claim, regardless of whether the alleged conspirators are plotting a section 1962(c) violation. *United States v. Quintanilla,* 2 F.3d 1469 (7th Cir. 1993); *United States v. Starrett,* 55 F.3d 1525 (11th Cir. 1995), *cert. denied,* 517 U.S. 1127 (1996); *Napoli v. United States,* 45 F.3d 680 (2d Cir.), *cert. denied,* 514 U.S. 1134 (1995).

The majority rule is consonant with the bright-line distinction drawn by the Supreme Court in *Salinas v. United States,* 522 U.S. 52 (1997), between substantive and conspiracy offenses. It also would appear—in criminal cases (like *Salinas*)—to promote the antiracketeering goals animating the statute. However, the majority rule does permit every failed section 1962(c) claim to be recast as a section 1962(d) conspiracy claim, which undermines *Reves.* It is also incompatible with the conclusion that civil aiding and abetting liability is foreclosed by *Reves* and by the statutory analysis of the Supreme Court in *Central Bank of Denver v. First Interstate Bank,* 511

U.S. 164 (1994) (*see* § 17, *infra*) because it would permit every failed aiding-and-abetting claim to be recast as a conspiracy claim.

This is a situation in which it is appropriate to distinguish between civil and criminal conspiracy claims. In the civil realm, the purpose of section 1962(d) liability is to impute liability for a specific injury, not to redress the harm to society that a conspiracy, as such, represents. *Cf. Beck v. Prupis,* 162 F.3d 1090 (11th Cir. 1998) (Tjoflat, J.) ("Agreements to engage in criminal activity are considered dangerous to society in and of themselves, because of 'the special danger incident to group activity.' . . . In a civil context, however, the purpose of a conspiracy claim is to impute liability—to make X jointly liable with D for what D did to P"), *cert. granted* 119 S. Ct. 2046 (1999). Therefore, it is sensible to confine liability to conspiring to operate or manage the enterprise, which is the substantive RICO offense. Accordingly, for civil purposes, the minority view is the more persuasive.

CHAPTER 5

Imputed and Secondary Liability

§ 16. Vicarious Liability

The cases applying the doctrine of vicarious liability under RICO are, at least on the surface, in something of a state of disarray. Radically conflicting verbal appraisals of the doctrine are not uncommon. For example, *compare First Nat'l Bank of Louisville v. Lustig*, 727 F. Supp. 276 (E.D. La. 1989) ("respondeat superior can never be the basis of liability for a civil RICO suit"), *with International Bhd. of Elec. Workers Local 340 v. Sacramento Valley Chapter of Nat'l Elec. Contractors Ass'n*, No. Civ. S-86-881 LKK, 1990 U.S. Dist. LEXIS 10634 (E.D. Cal. Aug. 9, 1990), *vacated in part on other grounds on reconsideration*, 226 Lab. Cas. (CCH) 10,488 (E.D. Cal. Dec. 20, 1990) (imposing vicarious RICO liability appears "entirely consistent with the underlying purpose" of the statute).

In part, the unsettled state of the case law appears to be due to the dual character of RICO as both a civil and criminal statute. The doctrine of vicarious liability has a different purpose and scope, and a somewhat checkered history, in the criminal sphere.[1] Under settled criminal law doctrines, vicarious liability attaches only to organizations and not to individuals (who must personally commit some criminal act or direct, encourage, or aid others to do so). Vicarious criminal liability is not imposed in search of a deep pocket, as in tort law, but only to prevent antisocial activity and deter others from engaging in it.[2]

---

1. *See* the thoughtful discussion of this topic in Lacovara & Nicoli, *Vicarious Criminal Liability of Organizations: RICO as an Example of a Flawed Principle in Practice*, 64 ST. JOHN'S L. REV. 725 (1990).

2. *See generally* LA FAVE & SCOTT, CRIMINAL LAW §§ 3.2(f), 3.9 (2d ed. 1986). *Compare* W. KEETON ET AL., PROSSER & KEETON ON LAW OF TORTS 500 (5th ed. 1984).

Civil RICO recovery is entirely dependent on proof of a criminal violation. Under section 1964(c), the right to recover damages is conditioned on the plaintiff's suffering injury "by reason of a violation of section 1962." The structure of the statute largely requires that civil and criminal liability be construed in tandem (the wrinkle is the interposition of section 1964(c) in civil cases, but that is not immediately germane). Accordingly, the only vicarious liability existing under RICO—even in civil cases—is organizational, and it is appropriate only when consistent with criminal law purposes.

Although the text of RICO does not address vicarious liability directly, there is some pertinent statutory guidance on the issue. As previously discussed, almost all courts hold that the "person" liable under section 1962(c) cannot be the same as the "enterprise" through which the misconduct is committed.[3] This mandatory dichotomy between person and enterprise provides a significant statutory limitation and the imputation of liability under section 1962(c).

Where an organization is identified as the RICO "enterprise" and an agent or employee of the organization is named as the defendant "person," the courts hold that the organization may not be held vicariously liable under section 1962(c) for the racketeering acts of the agent or employee. They reason that to impose vicarious liability in these circumstances would improperly evade the statutory requirement that the person and enterprise be distinct. *See, e.g., Petro-Tech, Inc. v. Western Co. of N. Am.*, 824 F.2d 1349 (3d Cir. 1987) ("respondeat superior . . . liability would disrupt the intended operation of § 1962(c), by making the § 1962(c) enterprise liable"); *Landry v. Air Line Pilots Ass'n*, 892 F.2d 1238 (5th Cir.), *cert. denied*, 111 S. Ct. 244 (1990) ("It would be incongruous here to find that while [defendant], as the enterprise, cannot be a RICO person, it can be held vicariously liable for the acts of [one of its agents]. If this were the rule, all legal enterprises could be found liable under RICO if their employees or agents were involved in perpetrating predicate acts through or against them. This is contrary to the rule Congress meant to impose as evidenced by the language of the statute").

Some circuits have taken liberties with this limited prohibition of vicarious liability under section 1962(c) and suggested, in sweeping statements, that vicarious liability is never appropriate under RICO. *See, e.g., D & S Auto Parts, Inc. v. Schwartz*, 838 F.2d

3. *See* §§ 9(A) and 11(B)(4), *supra*.

964 (7th Cir.), *cert. denied,* 486 U.S. 1061 (1988) ("*[r]espondeat superior's* premise is liability without fault, a concept inconsistent with the language of § 1962(c) as interpreted by this court. . . . [W]e follow the First and Eighth Circuits in rejecting the doctrine of *respondeat superior* in civil RICO cases" (court's emphasis)). *Accord Schofield v. First Commodity Corp. of Boston,* 793 F.2d 28 (1st Cir. 1986); *Luthi v. Tonka Corp.,* 815 F.2d 1229 (8th Cir. 1987).

Broad language of this sort is misleading for two reasons. First, it reflects more of a semantic than a substantive dispute. The phrase "vicarious liability" is slightly inapt when applied to organizations. Organizations invariably act through agents. The question of organizational liability, therefore, can as appropriately be labeled a question of "direct" as of "vicarious" liability. The crux of the issue is whether, in the circumstances, the organization should be held liable for the acts of persons employed by or associated with it. Purporting to dispense with "vicarious" liability does not address the nub of the issue.

Second, it is an overstatement, if taken out of context, to suggest that there can be no vicarious liability under any subsection of section 1962 other than 1962(c). Language of the sort quoted above almost invariably appears in section 1962(c) cases, like *Schwartz, Schofield,* and *Luthi,* in which imputed liability is statutorily forbidden. *See, e.g., Miranda v. Ponce Fed. Bank,* 948 F.2d 41 (1st Cir. 1991) (summarizing the holding of *Schofield* as a limitation on vicarious liability under § 1962(c)); *Cox v. Administrator,* 17 F.3d 1386 (11th Cir 1994), *cert. denied,* 513 U.S. 1110 (1995) ("Despite the inclusion of some broad language, the cases . . . stand only for the proposition that, in order to preserve the non-identity rule, vicarious liability should not be imposed under § 1962(c) where the [defendant] is also the RICO enterprise"; also noting that the Eleventh Circuit does not enforce the person/enterprise distinction under section 1962(c)). Under section 1962(a) and (b), organizational liability is regularly imposed—in all circuits—because those subsections do not distinguish between the "person" liable and the "enterprise" used. *See, e.g., Liquid Air Corp. v. Rogers,* 834 F.2d 1297 (7th Cir. 1987), *cert. denied,* 492 U.S. 917 (1989) ("vicarious liability under subsection (a) is consistent with Congressional intent, provided the corporation derived some benefit from the RICO violation"); *Brady v. Dairy Fresh Prods. Co.,* 974 F.2d 1149 (9th Cir. 1992) ("liability may arise pursuant to section 1962(a) under agency and respondeat superior principles when the individual or entity is benefitted by its employee or agent's RICO violations. The corporation or other entity will thus be forced to compensate victims when it is the beneficiary of its employees or agents' racketeering activity, but not when it is merely the victim or prize of the racketeering"); *Landry v.*

Air Line Pilots Ass'n, 901 F.2d at 425 ("the RICO person and the enterprise need not be distinct for a person to be held liable under subsection (b). A finding of vicarious liability on the part of an enterprise which derived the benefit from its representative's wrongful acts is also consistent with this view"); *accord Crowe v. Henry*, 43 F.3d 198 (5th Cir. 1995) (§ 1962(a)–(b)). Presumably, organizational liability is equally appropriate under section 1962(d) on the same rationale, at least to the extent that the substantive violations occurred under section 1962(a) or (b).

Moreover, even under section 1962(c), an organization may be liable—as a result of the acts of its agents—where it is acting to conduct the affairs of a different "enterprise" (that is, other than itself) in violation of subsection (c). *Ashland Oil, Inc. v. Arnett*, 875 F.2d 1271 (7th Cir. 1989). It is apparent, therefore, that organizational liability is sometimes appropriate under RICO. The question is under what circumstances. An organization may also be vicariously liable under section 1962(c) where it is distinct from the enterprise and imposition of such liability would not effectively constitute an impermissible end-run around the mandatory distinction between person and enterprise. *Davis v. Mutual Life Ins. Co.*, 6 F.3d 367, 380 (6th Cir. 1993) ("The rule to be drawn from these cases is that plaintiffs may not use RICO to impose liability vicariously on corporate 'enterprises,' because to do so would violate the distinctiveness requirement. No such prohibition . . . prevents the imposition of liability vicariously on corporate 'persons' on account of the acts of their agents, particularly where the corporation benefitted by those acts. Such a prohibition, if it existed, would prevent corporate persons from ever being found liable under RICO, since corporate principals may act only through their agents"); *Brady v. Dairy Fresh Prods. Co.*, 974 F.2d 1149 (9th Cir. 1992) ("an employer that is benefitted by its employee or agent's violations of section 1962(c) may be held liable under the doctrines of respondeat superior and agency when the employer is distinct from the enterprise").

Putting to one side the section 1962(c) bar, which is a statutory imperative, the courts have articulated a variety of similar but not identical standards to categorize when RICO liability should be imputed to an organization. Some courts distinguish between upper-level and lower-level employees, requiring express or implicit authorization of senior management for misconduct committed by subordinates. *See, e.g., R.E. Davis Chem. Corp. v. Nalco Chem. Co.*, 757 F. Supp. 1499 (N.D. Ill. 1990) ("vicarious liability may be imposed upon a corporate defendant under § 1962(a) only if the corporation, through its upper level employees or officers, knew of and acquiesced in the racketeering conduct of its lower level employees"); *Banque Worms v. Luis A. Duque Pena E Hijos, Ltd.*, 652 F.

Supp. 770 (S.D.N.Y. 1986) (declining to impose liability where to do so would "yield the absurd result . . . [of] holding an innocent corporation liable for the unauthorized wrongdoing of a lower level employee").

Other courts distinguish between corporations that are passive instruments of the misconduct and those that are active participants in it, imputing liability only in the latter case. *See, e.g., Collective Fed. Sav. Bank v. Creel,* 746 F. Supp. 1307 (M.D. La. 1990) ("it is necessary to distinguish between an 'enterprise' that actively violated the statutes and an 'enterprise' whose disloyal employee or partner violated the statutes on his own. Unless active participation is shown, the 'enterprise' is a 'passive instrument' and not subject to RICO damages or liability"); *Amendolare v. Shenkers Int'l Forwarders, Inc.,* 747 F. Supp. 162 (E.D.N.Y. 1990) ("many courts have indicated that vicarious liability is at least potentially available to hold the 'enterprise' liable so long as the enterprise is not the innocent 'victim' or 'conduit' of the criminal enterprise. . . . Whether an entity should be characterized as a 'passive conduit' or a 'central figure' is . . . contingent on the complicity of high level officers").

Yet other courts focus on whether the organization benefited, directly or indirectly, from the RICO violation, as the critical criterion in assessing the propriety of imputing liability. *See, e.g., Dynabest, Inc. v. Yao,* 760 F. Supp. 704 (N.D. Ill. 1991) (where president of corporation committed the violations, "the doctrine of vicarious liability or respondeat superior is 'entirely appropriate' under § 1962(a) so long as the principal/employer benefitted from the RICO violation"); *see also Liquid Air Corp. v. Rogers,* 834 F.2d at 1307, and *Landry v. Air Line Pilots Ass'n,* 901 F.2d at 425 (quoted above in connection with imputed liability under section 1962(a) and (b)).

While all of these locutions are different, all reflect an attempt to apply traditional vicarious liability principles under RICO with defined restrictions that recognize the uniqueness of the statute. The courts are looking principally at the level of the agent or employee whose conduct is at issue and ascertaining whether that person was acting within the scope of his or her authority when committing the violations. This analytical framework is consistent with the vicarious liability provisions of the Model Penal Code, which support the proposition that RICO—substantially a criminal statute—should be accorded a circumscribed application of vicarious liability.

The Model Penal Code, in text and commentary, urges rejection of the general doctrine of respondeat superior for serious crimes. Organizational liability—specifically, corporate liability—is limited to situations involving directors or officers "sufficiently high in the hierarchy to assume that their acts are reflective of the corporate body."[4] Apart from minor offenses, corporate criminal liability under the Model Penal Code is imposed for an agent or employee's wrongful conduct only when "the commission of the offense was authorized, requested, commanded, performed or recklessly tolerated by the board of directors, or by a high managerial agent acting in behalf of the corporation within the scope of his office or employment." Section 207(1)(c).[5] The 1971 Federal Criminal Code Commission proposal concerning organizational liability was substantially identical.[6]

This position is consistent with the trend of recent authority in civil RICO cases and promotes the underlying policy of the act, which seeks to cleanse the market of corrupt businesses and enterprises, not innocent ones. *See, e.g., Clark v. Security Life Ins. Co.,* 270 Ga. 165, 167, 509 S.E.2d 602 (1998) (citing **Treatise**). The American College of Trial Lawyers has endorsed the approach as well.[7] This position requires the court to draw a line between those organizations managed or directed by high-level wrongdoers and those unwittingly used or victimized by corrupt and errant lower-level employees. It is the right line to draw. *See, e.g., K & S Partnership v. Continental Bank, N.A.,* 127 F.R.D. 664 (D. Neb. 1989), *aff'd in relevant part,* 913 F.2d 1296 (8th Cir. 1990) ("before RICO liability may be imposed it must be proven that it was the corporate policy which created the scheme or senior corporate management which implemented the scheme. . . . The intent of RICO . . . is to force the corrupt business from the marketplace altogether. [I]t makes little sense to impose RICO treble damage liability upon an otherwise legitimate entity unless it is shown that the corporate policy was to violate RICO in the first place"); *Gruber v. Prudential-Bache Secs., Inc.,* 679 F. Supp. 165 (D. Conn. 1987) (distinguishing between "aggressor" corporations and "conduit" corporations and declining to subject a conduit to vicarious liability for the racketeering acts of lower-level employees); *Dakis v. Chapman,* 574 F. Supp. 757 (N.D. Cal. 1983) (declining to impute liability for securities violations by a low-level executive acting without corporate sanction;

4. Model Penal Code and Commentaries § 339 (1985).

5. "High managerial agent" is defined in Model Penal Code § 2.07(4)(c) to mean "an officer of a corporation or an unincorporated association, or, in a case of a partnership, the partner, or any other agent of a corporation or association having duties of such responsibility that his conduct may fairly be assumed to represent the policy of the corporation or association." Most states have enacted the Model Penal Code and have substantially followed its proposed limitations on organizational liability.

6. Federal Criminal Code Comm'n, Final Report of the Nat'l Comm'n on Reform of the Fed. Criminal Laws 35 (1971).

7. American College of Trial Lawyers, A Proposal for the Application of Vicarious Liability Under Civil Rico (1992).

"RICO was aimed at bands of marauding criminals, whose ongoing use of criminal behavior was part of their concerted 'business plan' to control or eliminate otherwise legitimate commerce"). Under this approach, organizational liability is imposed only when the organization can meaningfully be said to be at fault.[8]

Governmental Defendants. Additional public policy issues are raised by attempts to impose vicarious liability on governmental entities for the misconduct of their employees. If the public's trust has been breached by a faithless governmental employee, it makes little sense to impose treble-damage liability on the public as a consequence. For that reason, the Ninth Circuit has ruled that vicarious liability does not apply to governmental entities under RICO. *Lancaster Community Hosp. v. Antelope Valley Hosp. Dist.*, 940 F.2d 397 (9th Cir. 1991), *cert. denied,* 502 U.S. 1094 (1992). ("[plaintiff] cannot impose liability on the 'body politic' by appeals to the doctrine of *respondeat superior* or to principles of agency. For public policy is offended if all the citizens of a state are made liable for extraordinary damages as a result of the actions of a few dishonest officials"); *accord Nu-Life Constr. Corp. v. Board of Educ.*, No. 86 Civ. 0807 (ADS), 1991 U.S. Dist. LEXIS 17545 (E.D.N.Y. Dec. 2, 1991). *But see Genty v. Resolution Trust Corp.*, 937 F.2d 899 (3d Cir. 1991) (suggesting that municipal corporations might be subject to vicarious liability under RICO pursuant to "the prevailing view in most jurisdictions . . . [which] hold[s] that corporate entities in most cases can have imputed to them the mens rea to be civilly liable for wrongs committed with a specific intent" but nonetheless declining to apply RICO to governmental entities on the ground that they are not subject to punitive damages).

§ 17. Aider and Abettor Liability

Under 18 U.S.C. § 2, anyone who aids and abets an offense is punishable as a principal.[9] Consequently, prior to the Supreme

---

8. *See also* Note, *Judicial Efforts to Redirect an Errant Statute: Civil RICO and the Misapplication of Vicarious Corporate Liability,* 65 B.U.L. REV. 561, 606 (1985) ("Vicarious liability is intended to encourage employers to monitor their employees and to force businesses to internalize risks, to insure against them or to spread the cost of injury to the consumer. These purposes are inconsistent with RICO's goal of financially undercutting the corrupt enterprise and removing it from the marketplace. . . . Courts should require direct corporate responsibility for the RICO violation").

9. 18 U.S.C. § 2 provides the following:

a Whoever commits an offense against the United States or aids, abets, counsels, commands, induces or procures its commission, is punishable as a principal.

b. Whoever willfully causes an act to be done which if directly performed by him or another would be an offense against the United States, is punishable as a principal.

Court's decision in *Central Bank of Denver v. First Interstate Bank,* 511 U.S. 164 (1994), it was routinely held that one who aids and abets a violation of section 1962 has personally violated the statute and is a potential defendant in a civil RICO action under section 1964(c). *See, e.g., Banks v. Wolk,* 918 F.2d 418 (3d Cir. 1990) ("RICO recognizes liability for those who merely aid and abet the underlying predicate offenses"); Shapiro, *Attorney Liability under RICO § 1962(c) after Reves v. Ernst & Young,* 61 U. Chi. L. Rev. 1153, 1155 & n.17 (citing **Treatise**).

Central Bank appears to have changed the equation dramatically. In *Central Bank,* the Supreme Court ruled that no civil aiding and abetting liability exists under section 10(b) of the Securities Exchange Act of 1934, 15 USC § 78j(b), because (i) section 10(b) does not expressly provide for aiding and abetting liability; (ii) "Congress has not enacted a general aiding and abetting statute"; and (iii) "when Congress enacts a statute under which a person may sue . . . there is no general presumption that the plaintiff may also sue aiders and abettors." 511 U.S. at 181, 191. Applying this analysis to RICO, the Third Circuit has concluded that—because the RICO statute similarly does not provide for aiding and abetting liability—*Central Bank* necessarily precludes recognition of any civil claim for aiding and abetting a RICO violation. *Rolo v. City Investing Co.,* 155 F.3d 644 (3d Cir. 1998). The Third Circuit's analysis is persuasive. Indeed, there are even more reasons why the *Central Bank* analysis logically forecloses a civil aiding and abetting claim under RICO. The private right of action under section 10(b) of the Exchange Act (at issue in *Central Bank*) was judicially, not legislatively, created. In contrast, the civil RICO claim was created by Congress in section 1964(c). Congress had the opportunity to provide explicitly for a civil aiding and abetting RICO remedy not only when it enacted the statute in 1970, but also on each of the 15 occasions since that time when it has amended the statute (through December 31, 1999). Accordingly, the argument for implying aiding and abetting liability under section 10(b)—which was rejected in *Central Bank*—was far stronger than any argument for implying such liability under RICO. To the extent that this issue remains open, however, the nature of aider and abettor liability is examined in greater detail below.

In order to establish aiding and abetting liability for civil RICO purposes, the plaintiff must prove that (1) the defendant was associated with the wrongful conduct, (2) participated in it with the intent to bring it about, and (3) sought by his or her actions to make it succeed. *See, e.g., Armco Indus. Credit Corp. v. SLT Warehouse Co.,* 782 F.2d 475 (5th Cir. 1986). Proof of "mere negative acquiescence" in the act—or "planned silence"—is not enough. *Chamarac Prop., Inc. v. Pike,* 1993 U.S. Dist. LEXIS 14593 (S.D.N.Y.

Oct. 15, 1993) ("Mere acquiescence is not enough"). There must be evidence of an overt act or acts by the defendant designed to aid in the success of the venture. *See, e.g., id.* at *15 ("aider and abettor liability . . . requires evidence of an overt act designed to further the success of the venture"); *In re Sahlen & Assocs., Inc. Sec. Litig.,* 773 F. Supp. 342 (S.D. Fla. 1991) ("a defendant's failure to expose the existence of a fraudulent scheme of which he is aware does not rise to the level of aiding and abetting"); *First City Nat'l Bank v. Federal Deposit Ins. Corp.,* 730 F. Supp. 501 (E.D.N.Y. 1990) ("The amended complaint essentially implies that [the accountants] had knowledge of the [fraudulent] financing scheme . . . and had a professional relationship with [that is, prepared financial statements for] the defendants. These allegations alone, including the allegations of possible conflicts of interest, do not show that [the accountants] aided or abetted any of the alleged predicate acts"); *accord Armco Indus. Credit Corp. v. SLT Warehouse Co.,* 782 F.2d 475 (5th Cir. 1986); *Laterza v. American Broadcasting Co.,* 581 F. Supp. 408 (S.D.N.Y. 1984); *United Centrifugal Pumps v. Schotz,* No. C-89-2291, 1991 U.S. Dist. LEXIS 11347 (N.D. Cal. June 13, 1991).

An unwitting participant in a RICO enterprise is not an aider and abettor. Even recklessness does not satisfy the required criminal intent.[10] The aider and abettor must "consciously share" the wrongful intent of the principal. *Schultz v. Rhode Island Hosp. Trust Nat'l Bank, N.A.,* 94 F.3d 721, 731 (1st Cir. 1996) (affirming dismissal in the absence of any evidence that the defendant "'consciously shared' in the principal wrongdoer's . . . specific intent to defraud the plaintiffs"). Nor will courts impute knowledge to individuals by operation of law to satisfy the prerequisites of aiding and abetting liability. Knowledge is a matter of fact that must be pleaded and proved. *See, e.g., First City Nat'l Bank,* 730 F. Supp. at 508–9 (dismissing section 1962(c) claim naming bank directors as aiders and abettors on the theory that, under state banking statutes, each director "'[wa]s deemed to have such knowledge of the affairs of the corporation . . . as to enable him to determine whether any acts, proceeding or omission of its directors is a violation of [state banking law]' "; held, "[t]o be found liable of aiding and abetting mail or wire fraud—specific intent crimes—a defendant must have shared the principal's criminal intent").

Aiding and abetting liability under RICO is subject to the same statutory limitations as direct liability. The defendant must, for example, have aided and abetted at least two acts forming a pattern of racketeering activity. *See, e.g., Banks v. Wolk,* 918 F.2d 418 (3d Cir. 1990) (requiring that aider and abettor have "participated

---

10. *See generally* § 11(G), *supra,* for a discussion of mens rea.

in two or more predicate acts sufficient to constitute a pattern"). In addition, to the extent that section 1962(c) requires that the "person" and "enterprise" be different,[11] the entity that is the "enterprise" cannot also be an aider and abettor of the section 1962(c) offense. *Petro-Tech, Inc. v. Western Co. of N. Am.*, 824 F.2d 1349 (3d Cir. 1987) ("aiding and abetting liability would disrupt the intended operation of § 1962(c), by making the § 1962(c) enterprise . . . liable"); *Rodriguez v. Banco Central,* 727 F. Supp. 759 (D.P.R. 1989), *modified on other grounds,* 917 F.2d 664 (1st Cir. 1990) (affirming the vibrancy of the doctrine of "aiding and abetting liability under § 1962(c) . . . so long as the aider and abettor is not also the 'enterprise'"). However, as previously discussed in connection with vicarious liability,[12] this limitation applies only to section 1962(c) claims in which the person and enterprise are the same. It does not apply to claims brought under section 1962(a) or (b)—or even to section 1962(c) claims where the enterprise is a different entity. *See, e.g., Petro-Tech,* 824 F.2d at 1361 ("there can be . . . aiding and abetting liability under § 1962(a) when the enterprise benefits from the racketeering activity").

As the foregoing suggests, the courts apply functionally the same analysis to aiding and abetting claims as to vicarious liability claims. In addition to honoring the section 1962(c) distinction between "person" and "enterprise," the cases also require that an organization pegged as an aider and abettor must not be a "passive conduit" but rather an active participant deriving benefit from the violation. *Id.; First Nat'l Bank of Louisville v. Lustig,* 727 F. Supp. 276 (E.D. La. 1989) ("§ 1962(a) requires a RICO plaintiff to plead and prove that the defendant is liable as a principal within the meaning of 18 U.S.C. § 2 for the underlying predicate acts. A corporation that is only the passive instrumentality of an employee's wrongdoing cannot be held liable as a principal. . . . [I]t is [not] sufficient to plead and prove that defendant . . . has done nothing more than receive income from allegedly fraudulent [behavior]"). The same Model Penal Code standard urged above (in § 16, *supra*) for organizational liability generally is equally apt for resolving aiding and abetting claims.

If an aiding and abetting claim survives *Central Bank,* the question arises whether the Supreme Court's conclusion in *Reves v. Ernst & Young,* 507 U.S. 170, 183 (1993)—that the defendant must

---

11. *See* §§ 9(A) and 11(B)(4), *supra.*

12. *See* § 16, *supra.*

be involved in the operation and management of the enterprise (discussed in § 9(c), *supra*)—applies to aiders and abettors. A number of district court decisions have so held. *See, e.g., LaSalle Nat'l Bank v. Duff & Phelps Credit Rating Co.*, 951 F. Supp. 1071 (S.D.N.Y. 1996); *131 Main Street Assoc. v. Manko*, 897 F. Supp. 1507 (S.D.N.Y. 1995).

CHAPTER 6

Relief

§ 18. Damages

There is no well-developed, coherent body of law concerning damages under RICO. The guiding principle is easily stated but not always easily applied. The measure of damages is the harm caused by the predicate acts constituting the pattern of racketeering activity. *Ticor Title Ins. Co. v. Florida,* 937 F.2d 447 (9th Cir. 1991), citing *Sedima, S.P.R.L. v. Imrex Co.,* 473 U.S. 479, 497 (1985) ("the compensable injury necessarily is the harm caused by predicate acts sufficiently related to constitute a pattern, for the essence of the violation is the commission of those acts in connection with the conduct of an enterprise").

A plaintiff injured by civil RICO violations deserves a "complete recovery" for the harm caused by the predicate acts. *Carter v. Berger,* 777 F.2d 1173, 1176 (7th Cir. 1985). However, that amount—trebled—is all that the plaintiff is entitled to, not a windfall. If the RICO claim is brought in tandem with a common law claim (for example, a fraud claim) grounded on the same facts, the plaintiff is not entitled both to treble damages under RICO and to single damages at common law. *See, e.g., Faircloth v. Finesod,* 938 F.2d 513 (4th Cir. 1991) ("This court has forbidden [the] stacking of RICO damages with damages for the predicate acts"). RICO contemplates trebled, not quadrupled, damages.

To earn their damages, plaintiffs are required "to set out a reasonable and principled basis of recovery," and then to establish their entitlement "by competent proof, not . . . mere speculation and surmise." *Fleischhauer v. Feltner,* 879 F.2d 1290, 1299 (6th Cir. 1989), *cert. denied,* 110 S. Ct. 1122 (1990). Whether or not cognizable damages have been suffered is a question of fact. *Viacom Int'l Inc. v. Icahn,* 946 F.2d 998 (2d Cir. 1991), *cert. denied,* 502 U.S. 1122 (1992) (affirming summary judgment for the defense in "greenmail" case because the undisputed "facts convince us that Viacom [the target company] was not injured by the transaction it entered with Icahn [the corporate raider]. The directors themselves determined that the stock was worth more than [the price they paid Icahn] and refused to accept an offer at that price").

A. Limitations on Damages

The principal limitations on recovery are imposed by the requirements of (1) proximate causation and (2) injury to "business or property." Only damages "to business or property" occurring "by reason of" the RICO violation are compensable under section 1964(c). *See generally* § 6(A)(3)–(4), *supra,* and, *e.g., Oscar v. University Students Co-op. Ass'n,* 965 F.2d 783 (9th Cir. 1992) (en banc), *cert. denied,* 506 U.S. 1020 (1992) ("First, a showing of 'injury' requires proof of concrete financial loss, and not mere 'injury to a valuable intangible property interest.' . . . Second, it is clear that personal injuries are not compensable under RICO"); *Genty v. Resolution Trust Corp.,* 937 F.2d 899 (3d Cir. 1991) ("RICO plaintiffs may recover damages for harm to business and property only, not physical and emotional injuries" resulting from the RICO violation); *Stamp v. Brown,* No. 81-C-1475, 1990 U.S. Dist. LEXIS 6688 (N.D. Ill. June 1, 1990) ("Because RICO is a statutory tort, 'causation principles that generally apply in tort cases apply in civil RICO cases'"; where RICO defendants were not responsible for causing corporate insolvency but only for concealing it, the sole recoverable damages are those attributable to "deepened insolvency").

B. Link to Predicate Damages

A number of predicate offenses come equipped with tailor-made measures of civil damages. The various securities frauds statutes (for example, section 10(b) of the Securities Exchange Act of 1934, 15 U.S.C. § 78j(b), and SEC rule 10b-5) are obvious examples. Since, under *Sedima,* the plaintiff's "compensable injury necessarily is the harm caused by [the] predicate acts," 473 U.S. 479, 497 (1985), it might be assumed that the predicate-act measure of damages is the appropriate RICO measure of damages. In some cases, that will be correct. *See, e.g., Sowell v. Butcher & Singer, Inc.,* 926 F.2d 289 (3d Cir. 1991) (securities fraud predicate acts; applying out-of-pocket loss measure of damages as established in rule 10b-5 case law).

The goal, however, is to ensure that the plaintiff is fully compensated. That may not be achieved if the predicate-act measure of damages is employed. In that event, another appropriate measure of damages will be substituted. *See, e.g., Liquid Air Corp. v. Rogers,*

834 F.2d 1297 (7th Cir. 1987), *cert. denied,* 493 U.S. 917 (1989) (rejecting defendants' attempt to characterize the predicate offenses as sounding in "conversion"—in contrast to their earlier characterizations of "fraud"—in a transparent effort to obtain lower damages assessment: "[w]e have noted how futile it can be to employ a case-by-case approach in determining the 'underlying' cause of action" to select a fair measure of damages); Kaiser, *Extortion in the Workplace,* 61 BROOKLYN L. REV. 965, 979 (1995) (citing **Treatise**).

There may also be practical problems in implementing use of predicate measures of damages. If, for example, different types of predicate acts are implicated, each may have a different (possibly a conflicting) measure of damages attached to it. To what extent should each be used? Additionally, since the predicate offenses set forth in section 1961(1) are criminal in nature, many have no measure of damages attached to them at all. *See, e.g., City of New York v. Bower,* No. 89 Civ. 4179 (LMM), 1991 U.S. Dist. LEXIS 1204 (S.D.N.Y. Jan. 31, 1991) (Hobbs Act predicate acts—extortion committed by city official; entire salary treated as measure of damages (and trebled) under pendent breach-of-fiduciary-duty claim). Further, various conflicting measures of damage are used in conjunction with certain of the predicate acts. (*See* the securities fraud cases in § 18 (C), *infra.*)

The foregoing tends to explain why the judiciary has resorted to a general proposition that full compensation be made rather than relying on predicate measures of damages or developing any unique RICO damages theories. Indeed, the one unique RICO damages theory that was developed in the 1980s—the "racketeering injury" theory (requiring the court to quantify and award damages for "racketeering injury" only)—was roundly rebuffed by the Supreme Court in *Sedima.* (*See* § 6(A)(2), *supra.*) The result is a seemingly aleatory selection of damages measures applied by federal judges depending on the circumstances presented.

C. Benefit-of-Bargain Versus Out-of-Pocket Loss

Courts apply both the benefit-of-bargain and out-of-pocket loss measures in calculating RICO damages. The judgment turns on which is more appropriate on the facts to ensure a complete—but not an excessive—recovery. *Compare Sowell v. Butcher & Singer, Inc.,* 926 F.2d 289 (3d Cir. 1991) (securities fraud case; applying out-of-pocket loss measure) and *Fleischhauer v. Feltner,* 879 F.2d 1290 (6th Cir. 1989) (securities fraud case; "[a]lthough in some cases expectancy damages might be appropriate, clearly they are not in this case" since the fraud only caused the parties to make the investment but did not cause the investment to wither) *with Ross v. Jackie Fine Arts, Inc.,* No. 2:85-2425-1, 1991 U.S. Dist. LEXIS

13535 (D.S.C. Sept. 4, 1991) (securities fraud case; applying benefit-of-bargain rule where scam procured investment in worthless art).

1. Lost Profits Consequently, lost profits may be recovered, where appropriate, subject to proof of proximate causation. *See, e.g., Advanced Business Sys., Inc. v. Philips Information Sys. Co.*, 750 F. Supp. 774 (E.D. La. 1990); *Sound Video Unlimited, Inc. v. Video Shack, Inc.*, 700 F. Supp. 127 (S.D.N.Y. 1988), quoting *DeMent v. Abbott Capital Corp.*, 589 F. Supp. 1378 (N.D. Ill. 1984) ("[I]f the 'damages sustained' by a victim of a RICO violation include lost profits, we see no bar in the statute to recovery of those losses. Of course, recovery of lost profits should be subject to the ordinary limitations concerning remoteness (or proximate cause) and speculativeness (or certainty)").

2. Future Damages To the extent that the plaintiff can establish with reasonable certainty that future damages will occur as a result of the defendant's RICO violation, an award of future damages may be appropriate. *Bankers Trust Co. v. Rhoades*, 859 F.2d 1096 (2d Cir. 1988), *cert. denied*, 490 U.S. 1007 (1989) ("Only in instances where the plaintiff has suffered no injury or where the injury is unprovable, is an award of future damages inappropriate").[1]

D. Single-Satisfaction Rule

RICO recovery is subject to the single-satisfaction rule, which provides that a plaintiff is entitled to only one satisfaction for each injury. *See, e.g., Singer v. Olympia Brewing Co.*, 878 F.2d 596 (2d Cir. 1989), *cert. denied*, 493 U.S. 1024 (1990) ("Under this rule, when a plaintiff receives a settlement from one defendant, a nonsettling defendant is entitled to a credit of the settlement against any judgment obtained by the plaintiff against the nonsettling defendant as long as both the settlement and judgment represent common damages"). The rule has been codified in the Restatement (Second) of Torts § 885(3) (1982):

> A payment by any person made in compensation of a claim for a harm for which others are liable as tortfeasors diminishes the claim against the tortfeasors, at least to the extent of the payment made, whether or not the person making the payment is liable to the injured person and whether or not it is so agreed at the time of payment or the payment is made before or after judgment.

1. *See also* the catalog of damages decisions discussed in J. Rakoff & H. Goldstein, RICO: CIVIL AND CRIMINAL LAW AND STRATEGY § 4.01–.04 (Supp. 1998).

As a result, the amount of any settlement received by a plaintiff from one of multiple RICO defendants is generally deducted from any verdict the plaintiff subsequently wins against the remaining defendants. Importantly, the deduction is to be made from the total, trebled award and is not to be taken before trebling. *See, e.g., Morley v. Cohen,* 888 F.2d 1006 (4th Cir. 1989); *Singer v. Olympia Brewing Co.,* 878 F.2d 596 (2d Cir. 1989), *cert. denied,* 493 U.S. 1024 (1990); *In re National Mortgage Equity Corp. Mortgage Pool,* 636 F. Supp. 1138 (C.D. Cal. 1986); *Pennsylvania v. Cianfrani,* 600 F. Supp. 1364 (E.D. Pa. 1985). Other setoffs from individual defendants prior to the entry of judgment have also been deemed most appropriately to be deducted after trebling. *Liquid Air Corp. v. Rogers,* 834 F.2d at 1310 (value of returned goods).

The Second Circuit, however, has ruled that, to the extent a RICO claim has been successfully collected prior to the entry of judgment, "it is 'abated pro tanto, prior to any application of trebling.'" *Commercial Union Assur. Co. v. Milken,* 17 F.3d 608, 612 (2d Cir. 1994), *quoting Stochastic Decisions, Inc. v. DiDomenico,* 995 F.2d 1158, 1166 (2d Cir.), *cert. denied,* 513 U.S. 873 (1994). The Second Circuit reasons that, to the extent the plaintiff has been placed in the same position it would have been in but for the illegal conduct, all damages recoverable under section 1964(c) have been received.

Applying the single-satisfaction (or one-satisfaction) rule, it should be remembered that the deduction is to be made from the judgment ultimately won, not from any other figure (for example, not from the highest amount of "provable damages" that could conceivably have been recovered against the settling defendant). *Singer v. Olympia Brewing Co.,* 878 F.2d at 600–601.

§ 19. Trebled and Punitive Damages

Section 1964(c) dictates the award of treble damages for civil RICO violations. It provides that the plaintiff "shall recover threefold the damages he sustains," in addition to costs and lawyer's fees.[2] Imposition of treble damages is required by RICO. *Cullen v. Margiotta,* 811 F.2d 698 (2d Cir.), *cert. denied,* 483 U.S. 1021 (1987) ("civil RICO requires that a successful plaintiff be awarded treble damages"); *Abell v. Potomac Ins. Co.,* 858 F.2d 1104 (5th Cir. 1988) ("The court was required under 18 U.S.C.

---

2. Section 1964(c) provides in full that "[a]ny person injured in his business or property by reason of a violation of section 1962 of this chapter may sue therefor in any appropriate United States district court and shall recover threefold the damages he sustains and the cost of the suit, including a reasonable attorney's fee."

§ 1964(c) to treble the [plaintiffs'] damages"), *vacated on other grounds*, 492 U.S. 914 (1989); *accord MDO Dev. Corp. v. Kelly*, 735 F. Supp. 591 (S.D.N.Y. 1990).

The prevailing view is that the jury should not be informed about the trebling of its award. *See, e.g., HBE Leasing Corp. v. Frank*, 22 F.3d 41 (2d Cir. 1994) ("Every authority brought to this court's attention upholds excluding references [before the jury] to trebling and attorneys fees in the RICO context"); *Liquid Air Corp. v. Rogers*, 834 F.2d 1297 (7th Cir. 1987) (fact that verdict will be trebled "is irrelevant to a jury's deliberations and may confuse or prejudice the jury"), *cert. denied*, 492 U.S. 917 (1989).

Not infrequently, plaintiffs seek both trebled and punitive damages for alleged RICO violations. The law is in a state of flux as to whether punitive damages may be awarded in addition to treble damages under RICO. The better view is that punitive and treble damages are mutually exclusive remedies. Moreover, to the extent that punitive damages may be recovered on any additional tort claim predicated on the same facts as the RICO violation, punitive and treble damages overlap, and the latter (or lesser) should be deducted from the former (or greater).

A. RICO Punitive Awards

The traditional way of approaching the question whether both punitive and treble damages may be awarded under RICO is essentially to view it as a question of double recovery. The inquiry, on this analysis, is whether treble and punitive damages are awarded for the same purpose. That, in turn, raises the question of whether RICO's treble-damage remedy is punitive in nature. The answer to that question is problematic. RICO's treble-damage provision has been characterized as both punitive and remedial in varying contexts. *Compare Faircloth v. Finesod*, 938 F.2d 513 (4th Cir. 1991) (holding that RICO claims survive the plaintiff's death because "the primary purpose of the private right of action created by RICO is remedial") *with Genty v. Resolution Trust Corp.*, 937 F.2d 899 (3d Cir. 1991) (holding municipal corporations immune from RICO liability because "municipalities, even when acting in their proprietary capacity, are exempt from punitive damages, unless a statute expressly provides [for] such damage awards against" them, and RICO's "treble damages [provision] is best characterized as 'penal in nature'").

It is probably most accurate to say, as the Fourth Circuit has, that "civil RICO is a square peg, and squeeze it as we may, it will never comfortably fit in the round holes of the remedy/penalty dichotomy." *Faircloth v. Finesod*, 938 F.2d at 518. Courts are divided on the issue of the availability of punitive damages in civil RICO cases based on the divergence of views on the statute's punitive or remedial nature, although the trend appears to be distinctly negative. It should be stressed that the Supreme Court plainly assumed that punitive damages are unavailable in civil RICO actions in deciding *Humana Inc. v. Forsyth,* 119 S.Ct. 710 (1999), in which it ruled that the McCarran-Ferguson Act, 15 U.S.C. § 1011, *et seq.*, did not preempt RICO actions against insurers (*see* § 11(C)(2)(a), *supra*). Twice in the course of its preemption analysis, the *Humana* Court stressed that, among the differences between RICO and state insurance law, "RICO authorizes treble damages; Nevada law permits recovery of compensatory and punitive damages" and that, "[a]ccordingly, plaintiffs seeking relief under Nevada law may be eligible for damages exceeding the treble damages available under RICO." 119 S.Ct. at 714, 719. *Humana* did not specifically address the punitive damages issue, although the Court's assumption played an important role in its analysis. With respect to the lower courts that have addressed the issue, *compare Com-Tech Assocs. v. ComputerAssocs. Int'l, Inc.*, 753 F. Supp. 1078 (S.D.N.Y. 1990), *aff'd on other grounds,* 938 F.2d 1574 (2d Cir. 1991) ("this Court is of the view that at least at the pleading stage, a claim for punitive damages should be permitted to stand. . . . The Court makes no determination of its future course with regard to the availability of punitive damages in a civil RICO action"); *Ross v. Jackie Fine Arts, Inc.*, No. 2:85-2425-1, 1991 U.S. Dist. LEXIS 13585 (D.S.C. Sept. 4, 1991) (awarding actual damages of $440,000, trebled to $1.32 million, plus punitive damages totaling $13.625 million); and *Al-Kazemia v. General Acceptance & Inv. Corp.*, 633 F. Supp. 540 (D.D.C. 1986) (awarding both punitive and treble damages) *with Bingham v. Zolt*, 823 F.Supp. 1126 (S.D.N.Y. 1993), *aff'd on other grounds,* 66 F.3d 553 (2d Cir. 1995), *cert. denied,* 517 U.S. 1134 (1996) ("RICO's treble damages provision precludes recovery of punitive damages"); *Standard Chlorine of Del., Inc. v. Sinibaldi,* 821 F.Supp. 232 (D.Del. 1992) ("punitive damages are not proper under RICO since the Act already provides for treble damages"); *In re VMS Secs. Litig.*, 752 F. Supp. 1373 (N.D. Ill. 1990) ("as to the RICO claims, the treble damages provisions define the extent of possible recovery. . . . Hence, defendants' motion to strike plaintiffs' request for punitive damages is granted except as to the common law fraud claims"); *Southwest Marine, Inc. v. Triple A Mach. Shop, Inc.*, 720 F. Supp. 805 (N.D. Cal. 1989) ("The civil remedy provision of RICO, 18 U.S.C. § 1964, provides for treble damages which are themselves punitive in character. Punitive damages, in addition to these treble damages are not appropriate"); and *Mylan Labs, Inc. v. Akzo, N.V.*, 770 F. Supp. 1053 (D. Md. 1991) (striking claims for punitive damages under RICO).

This traditional approach requires the courts to address a policy question—the appropriateness of cumulating punitive and treble damages—by focusing on a metaphysical question: whether punitive and treble damages are in some sense the same. A legitimate question of congressional intent lurks there, although it is unlikely—given the paucity of congressional attention to civil RICO—that Congress can meaningfully be said to have any intent at all on the issue.[3] The question then becomes what Congress would have thought about this issue, had it addressed it. At this point, the analysis is entirely conjectural and effectively requires the courts to substitute their own policy judgments for those of Congress, in the necessary guise of divining unfocused congressional intent.

It is, nonetheless, necessary to resolve the question of whether punitive damages may be awarded. In some sense, treble damages are necessarily "punitive," at least in the sense that they are, by definition, more than compensatory. However one characterizes the treble damages awarded under section 1964(c), the fact that more than compensation is awarded should be taken into account in deciding whether other supercompensatory damages should also be awarded.

The Fifth Circuit may have provided as good a solution as exists, using the traditional analysis, when it concluded that the compensatory aspect of the RICO award—one-third of the total—is remedial, and the remaining two-thirds, constituting the trebled component, are penal. *Abell v. Potomac Ins. Co.*, 858 F.2d 1104 (5th Cir. 1988), *vacated on other grounds,* 492 U.S. 914 (1989) ("We hold that the portion of RICO damages in excess of actual damages is penal. Those added damages are 'not limited to the damages suffered'; they seem more designed to deter than to compensate").[4] This demarcation between the compensatory aspect of the single-damages award and the penal character of the trebled portion of the verdict is useful. Applying the traditional analysis, punitive

3. *See, e.g.*, Kaiser, *Extortion in the Workplace*, 61 BROOKLYN L. REV. 965, 981 (1995) (quoting **Treatise**).

4. The *Abell* analysis finds support in the Supreme Court's decision in Shearson/American Express, Inc. v. McMahon, 482 U.S. 220 (1987), which held that RICO claims are arbitrable. In so holding, the *Shearson* Court stressed the antitrust analogy that animates many RICO decisions and observed that it upheld the arbitrability of antitrust claims in Mitsubishi Motors Corp. v. Solar Chrysler-Plymouth, Inc., 473 U.S. 614 (1985), because, "[n]otwithstanding its important incidental policing function, the treble-damages cause of action [of the Clayton Act] . . . seeks primarily to enable an injured competitor to gain compensation for that injury." 473 U.S. at 635. The *Shearson* Court construed RICO similarly, based largely on the legislative history of § 1964(c), which, it declared, "reveals the same emphasis on the remedial role of the treble-damages provision" of RICO. 482 U.S. at 240. At the same time, the *Shearson* Court acknowledged the "policing function of § 1964(c)," but denominated it "important" yet "a secondary concern" of Congress. *Id.* at 240–41.

damages should not be recoverable under RICO because Congress has prescribed the quantum of damages in excess of compensation (that is, the trebled aspect of the award) to which the plaintiff is entitled. This is consonant with antitrust law, the distant sibling of RICO, under which treble damages are awardable to the exclusion of punitive damages. *See, e.g., Arnott v. American Oil Co.*, 609 F.2d 873 (8th Cir. 1979), *cert. denied*, 446 U.S. 918 (1989) ("Punitive and treble damages cannot both be awarded for violation of the antitrust laws"); 2 L. Schlueter & K. Redden, *Punitive Damages* § 21.1(B) (3d ed. 1995) ("a plaintiff may not be awarded both punitive and treble damages for a violation of the antitrust laws").

B. Common Law Punitive Awards

If a RICO claim is coupled with a common law claim for which punitive damages are awardable, the question arises as to whether RICO's treble-damages remedy should be read as limiting plaintiffs' rights to punitive damages under common law claims arising out of the same facts. Because the trebling component of the RICO verdict represents a punitive award (*see* § 19(A), *supra*), any award of punitive damages under pendent common law theories should be reduced by the amount awarded under RICO in excess of compensatory damages and lawyer's fees. *See Advanced Business Sys., Inc. v. Philips Information Sys. Co.*, 750 F. Supp. 774 (E.D. La. 1990) (to the extent that the Fifth Circuit has ruled the trebling component of a RICO award to be penal in nature, the district court "will not allow duplicative recoveries under *either* the compensatory or punitive theories" of pendent common law claims (court's emphasis)). This approach is consistent with the policy underlying the single-satisfaction rule (discussed in § 18(D), *supra*), which is intended to ensure full but not duplicative recovery to the plaintiff. It is also sound public policy.

§ 20. Equitable Relief

A. Private Injunctive Relief

It is uncertain whether injunctive relief is available to private litigants under RICO because the Supreme Court has never addressed the issue.[5] The trend of decisions, however, is distinctly negative,

5. Under § 1964(a)–(b), there is no doubt that the United States can obtain injunctive relief "to prevent and restrain violations of § 1962." *See, e.g.*, United States v. Local 30 United Slate, Tile & Composition Roofers, 871 F.2d 401 (3d Cir.) *cert. denied*, 493 U.S. 953 (1989) (holding that the injunction may issue against the enterprise even in a § 1962(c) case—i.e., the enterprise may properly be named as a defendant for injunctive relief purposes in such a case).

on the following analysis. Section 1964(a) confers broad equitable jurisdiction on the federal courts.[6] Section 1964(b) expressly permits the government to file RICO actions to secure this equitable relief.[7] However, the civil remedy for private litigants, set forth in section 1964(c), is silent as to the availability of injunctive or other equitable relief.[8] That silence has largely been interpreted as barring entry of injunctive relief under RICO.

The leading decision in the area was rendered by the Ninth Circuit in *Religious Technology Center v. Wollersheim,* 796 F.2d 1076 (9th Cir. 1986), *cert. denied,* 479 U.S. 1103 (1987), which held section 1964(c)'s financial remedy to be exclusive. The Ninth Circuit bottomed its analysis on three observations: (1) "the inclusion of a single statutory reference to private plaintiffs, and the identification of a damages and fee remedy . . ., logically carries the negative implication that no other remedy was intended"; (2) at the time that RICO was enacted, and again one year later, "Congress refused to enact a bill to . . . give private plaintiffs injunctive relief"; and (3) section 1964(c) is patterned after section 4 of the Clayton Act, 15 U.S.C. § 15(a), "which the Supreme Court has explicitly held . . . precludes private injunctive relief."

The Fifth Circuit followed *Religious Technology Center* in *In re Fredeman Litig.,* 843 F.2d 821 (5th Cir. 1988), and other circuits have advanced the same view in dicta. *See, e.g., Trane Co. v. O'Connor Secs.,* 718 F.2d 26 (2d Cir. 1983); *Dan River, Inc. v. Icahn,* 701 F.2d 278 (4th Cir. 1983); *Ganey v. Raffone,* 1996 U.S. App. LEXIS 19148 (6th Cir. July 5, 1996) (unpublished opinion). The Fifth Circuit, since

---

6. § 1964(a) provides the following:

> The district courts of the United States shall have jurisdiction to prevent and restrain violations of section 1962 of this chapter by issuing appropriate orders, including, but not limited to: ordering any person to divest himself of any interest, direct or indirect, in any enterprise; imposing reasonable restrictions on the future activities or investments of any person, including, but not limited to, prohibiting any person from engaging in the same type of endeavor as the enterprise engaged in, the activities of which affect interstate or foreign commerce; or ordering dissolution or reorganization of any enterprise, making due provision for the rights of innocent persons.

7. § 1964(b) provides that "[t]he Attorney General may institute proceedings under this section. Pending final determination thereof, the court may at any time enter such restraining orders or prohibitions, or take such other actions, including the acceptance of satisfactory performance bonds, as it shall deem proper."

8. 1964(c) provides that "[a]ny person injured in his business or property by reason of a violation of section 1962 of this chapter may sue therefor in any appropriate United States district court and shall recover threefold the damages he sustains and the cost of the suit, including a reasonable attorney's fee."

Fredeman, has suggested that its ruling was limited, and it has reserved ruling on whether all forms of injunctive relief and other equitable relief are foreclosed to private plaintiffs under RICO. *Price v. Pinnacle Brands, Inc.*, 138 F.3d 602, 605 (5th Cir. 1998); *Conkling v. Turner*, 18 F.3d 1285 (5th Cir. 1994). On remand from the Supreme Court, the Northern District of Illinois concluded in *Nat'l Org. for Women v. Scheidler*, 897 F.Supp. 1047, 1082 (N.D.Ill. 1995), that the court's power under RICO "encompasses the Plaintiffs' prayer for the court to 'enjoin Defendants and their co-conspirators from further racketeering activity.'"

Both the Fifth and Ninth Circuits have acknowledged a plausible, conflicting interpretation of section 1964. Section 1964(a) can be read as granting all-inclusive equitable powers to the district courts, and section 1964(b) simply as authorizing equitable actions by the government to reverse the traditional rule that only a victim may sue to enjoin a crime. *In re Fredeman Litig.*, 843 F.2d at 829; *Religious Technology Center v. Wollersheim*, 796 F.2d at 1084–85. The Eighth Circuit, in *Bennett v. Berg*, 685 F.2d 1053 (8th Cir. 1982), *cert. denied*, 464 U.S. 1008 (1983), suggested that it might find injunctive relief available to private litigants (as have some district courts).[9] Even the Eighth Circuit, however, seems to have receded a bit from the view that private injunctive relief is available under RICO, later declaring that *Bennett v. Berg* "expressly left the issue unresolved." *See Airlines Reporting Corp. v. Barry*, 825 F.2d 1220 (8th Cir. 1987).

The courts' reticence to recognize a private injunctive remedy under RICO may be as much a reflection of their disenchantment with the statute as a product of textual necessity. *See, e.g.*, Blakey & Gettings, *Racketeer Influenced and Corrupt Organizations (RICO): Basic Concepts—Criminal and Civil Remedies*, 53 TEMP. L.Q. 1009, 1038 (1980) (concluding that equitable relief is available to private plaintiffs under RICO); *accord* Comment, *In re Fredeman Litigation: The Fifth Circuit Joins the Ninth—No Injunctive Relief for Private RICO Plaintiffs*, 63 TUL. L. REV. 421 (1988). It is, however, a matter of little practical consequence.

Irrespective of whether private injunctive relief is available under RICO, injunctions may be awarded under pendent state claims or in conjunction with violations of any predicate acts that, independently, will support an award of injunctive relief. *See, e.g.*,

9. *See, e.g.*, Andersen-Myers Co. v. Roach, 660 F. Supp. 106 (D. Kan. 1987); Vietnam Veterans of Am. v. Guerdon Indus., Inc., 644 F. Supp. 951 (D. Del. 1986); Kaushal v. State Bank of India, 556 F. Supp. 576 (N.D. Ill.1983).

Duct-O-Wire Co. v. U.S. Crane, Inc., 31 F.3d 506 (7th Cir. 1994) (preliminary injunction issued on state law tortious interference claim); *Northeast Women's Center, Inc. v. McMonagle*, 868 F.2d 1342 (3d Cir.), *cert. denied*, 493 U.S. 901 (1989) (injunctive relief awarded under pendent state law claim); *Republic of Philippines v. Marcos*, 862 F.2d 1355 (9th Cir. 1988) (*en banc*), *cert. denied*, 490 U.S. 1035 (injunction available if plaintiff has "shown the probability of success on the merits of its pendent claims and the possibility of irreparable injury, or that the pendent claims raised serious questions and the balance of hardships to be clearly in favor of the [plaintiff]"); *see also* Henn & Monaco, *Civil Rights and RICO: Stopping Operation Rescue*, 13 Harv. Women's L.J. 251 (1990). The injunctive-relief question becomes primarily a matter of pleading and practice. It is crucial that injunctive relief is sought on the alternative state law or predicate act bases and not premised on RICO alone.

B. Injunction to Protect Damages Recovery

Prior to the Supreme Court's decision in *Grupo Mexicano de Dessarrollo, S.A. v. Alliance Bond Fund, Inc.*, 119 S. Ct. 1961 (1999), the circuits were split as to whether an injunctiion could enter pursuant to rule 65 to protect a potential future damages recovery. *Compare In re Fredeman Litig.*, 843 F.2d at 826 (no) *with Teradyne, Inc. v. Mostek Corp.*, 797 F.2d 43 (1st Cir. 1986) (yes); *Hoxworth v. Blinder Robinson & Co., Inc.*, 903 F.2d 186 (3d Cir. 1990) (yes). In *Grupo Mexicano*, the Supreme Court held that federal district courts lack the power, under rule 65, to issue an injunction freezing the assets of a defendant prior to the entry of judgment. The Supreme Court expressly left open, however, the possibility of an injunction entering pursuant to rule 64's incorporation of state law attachment remedies as an alternate route to the same end.

C. Noninjunctive Equitable Remedies

However the debate about injunctive relief is resolved, there exist a variety of noninjunctive equitable remedies that private RICO plaintiffs might seek to pursue (for example, rescission, restitution, reformation, specific performance, and cancellation of a contract or instrument). Even assuming the validity of the textual argument generally prevailing against private injunctive relief, section 1964(a) and (c) would not operate to preclude awards of damages predicated on equitable theories like rescission, restitution, cancellation, or specific performance (for the payment of money). *See, e.g.*, *Alcorn County v. U.S. Interstate Supplies, Inc.*, 731

F.2d 1160 (5th Cir. 1984). At the same time, equitable remedies such as imposition of a constructive trust or specific performance of executory contracts (involving more than the payment of money) might be deemed to run afoul of either (1) the general requirement that damages are the plaintiff's sole remedy under section 1964(c) or (2) the more specific directives of section 1964(a) (for example, "imposing reasonable restrictions on the future activities . . . of any person"). Equitable remedies not expressly contemplated by section 1964(a)—to the extent that they may form a basis for, or be ancillary to, calculation of damages—should remain available to the private RICO plaintiff.

§ 21. Costs and Lawyer's Fees

A. Costs

Section 1964(c) provides that, in addition to trebled damages, a plaintiff who prevails on a RICO claim "shall recover . . . the cost of the suit, including a reasonable attorney's fee." Although there is a paucity of RICO authority on the subject of costs, it is apparent from other authorities that the "cost of the suit" language of section 1964(c) encompasses only those items taxable under 28 U.S.C. § 1920 and related statutes.

In *Crawford Fitting Co. v. J.T. Gibbons, Inc.,* 482 U.S. 437 (1987), the Supreme Court held that, "absent explicit statutory or contractual authorization" to the contrary, federal courts in awarding costs "are bound by the limitations set out in 28 U.S.C. § 1821 [the witness fee statute] and § 1920." In *Crawford Fitting,* expert witness fees were the item of "cost" involved, and no statutory fee-shifting provision (like section 1964(c)) applied. Four years after *Crawford,* however, in *West Va. Univ. Hosps., Inc. v. Casey,* 499 U.S. 83 (1991), the Supreme Court ruled that fees for services rendered by experts in civil rights litigation—which does involve a fee-shifting statute, the Civil Rights Attorney's Fees Awards Act of 1976 (Civil Rights Act), 42 U.S.C. § 1988—could not be shifted to the losing party as part of "a reasonable attorney's fee" under section 1988. *Casey* interpreted *Crawford Fitting* as holding that the Supreme Court "would not lightly find an implied repeal of § 1821 or of § 1920, which [*Crawford Fitting*] held to be an express limitation upon the types of costs which, absent other authority, may be shifted by federal courts."

In light of *Casey,* a fee-shifting statute like section 1964(c) is insufficient in itself to expand the items of cost beyond those statutorily enumerated in section 1920 and attendant provisions. Express expansion of the term "cost" is required to go beyond section 1920.

B. Lawyer's Fees

The award of lawyer's fees in section 1964(c) marks an exception to the "American Rule," under which each party to a litigation is generally obliged to bear its own lawyer's fees regardless of outcome. *See, e.g., Chambers v. NASCO, Inc.*, 501 U.S. 32 (1991) (absent statutory exception, "the so-called 'American Rule' prohibits fee-shifting in most cases"); *Dee v. Sweet*, 268 Ga. 346, 489 S.E.2d 823 (1997) (citing **Treatise**). *See generally* G. Joseph, *Sanctions: The Federal Law of Litigation Abuse* § 26 (2d ed. 1994 & supp. 2000); Leubsdorf, *Toward a History of the American Rule on Attorney Fee Recovery*, 47 Law & Contemp. Probs. 9 (1984). More than 200 federal provisions, like section 1964(c), shift fees to prevailing parties. Some are mandatory, some discretionary. Some are "one-way" (for instance, allowing only a prevailing plaintiff to obtain fees), while others are two-way (reciprocal). *See generally* 1 M. Derfner & A. Wolf, *Court Awarded Attorney Fees* ¶¶ 1.01–.03 (1998).

Section 1964(c) is a mandatory, one-way fee-shifting provision. Any plaintiff who obtains a judgment on the merits is entitled automatically to its lawyer's fees under this provision. However, only plaintiffs who have obtained judgments on the merits may receive fees. Interim success on motions followed by settlement does not qualify under this criterion. *See, e.g., Aetna Casualty & Sur. Co. v. Liebowitz*, 730 F.2d 905 (2d Cir. 1984) ("No general or flexible terms permitting . . . a construction [allowing fees for interim success or settlement] are to be found. The statute says treble damages 'and' attorneys' fees, not 'or' attorneys' fees").

In analyzing lawyer's fees issues under section 1964(c), the courts are guided by precedent construing other statutory fee-shifting exceptions to the American Rule. For example, in *Northeast Women's Center v. McMonagle*, 889 F.2d 466 (3d Cir. 1989), *cert. denied*, 110 S. Ct. 1788 (1990), the Third Circuit approved an award of approximately $65,000 in lawyer's fees and costs in an action in which the damages awarded to the plaintiffs amounted to less than $2,700 as trebled. The Third Circuit declared that there was no requirement that the lawyer's fees be proportionate to the quantum of damages awarded: "[W]e see nothing in the language or the legislative history of . . . § 1964(c) to support the application of a proportionality rule." 889 F.2d at 474. The *McMonagle* Court relied on the Supreme Court's decision in *City of Riverside v. Rivera*, 477

U.S. 561 (1986), which was decided under the Civil Rights Act—a discretionary, two-way fee-shifting statute.

The Seventh Circuit followed *McMonagle* in *FMC Corp. v. Varonos*, 892 F.2d 1308 (7th Cir. 1990), in which it reversed a district judge who had applied the proportionality rule in a RICO case. The Seventh Circuit also ruled it an abuse of discretion to refuse any award of lawyer's fees on the ground that the lawyer's fee application by the prevailing plaintiff was "excessive." In reaching its decision, the *Varonos* Court cited civil rights and sanctions decisions awarding lawyer's fees. *Accord Rosario v. Livaditis*, 963 F.2d 1013 (7th Cir. 1992).

The precedent from other fee-shifting cases, predominantly the cases decided under the Civil Rights Act (42 U.S.C. § 1988), suggest that the following rules apply under section 1964(c):

1. A contingent fee contract between the plaintiff and plaintiff's counsel will not cap the fees awardable under section 1964(c). That contract is between the plaintiff and the plaintiff's lawyer. It does not affect the statutory entitlement to a "reasonable attorney's fee." *Blanchard v. Bergeron*, 489 U.S. 87 (1989) (section 1988 case).
2. A contingent fee contract that provides more than a "reasonable attorney's fee" is not invalid under section 1964(c). The statute does not address what fee the plaintiff must pay his or her own lawyer; it addresses only fee shifting. *Venegas v. Mitchell*, 495 U.S. 82 (1990) (section 1988 case).
3. In assessing what is a "reasonable attorney's fee," the court may consider the contingency of nonpayment only to the extent that it is reflected in different market treatment of contingency cases as a class—not the riskiness of any given case. *Pennsylvania v. Delaware Valley Citizens' Council for Clean Air*, 478 U.S. 546 (1986) (decided under section 304(d) of the Clean Air Act, 42 U.S.C. § 7604(d), a discretionary, two-way fee-shifting statute). There is, however, nothing that prevents the plaintiff and his or her counsel from considering this riskiness in establishing the contractual relationship between the two of them.
4. A pro se litigant who is also a lawyer may not be awarded lawyer's fees under section 1964(c). *Kay v. Ehrler*, 111 S. Ct. 1435 (1991) (section 1988 case).
5. Because section 1964(c) defines "the cost of the suit" to include attorney's fees, those fees are to be included as "costs" within the meaning of Fed. R. Civ. P. 68. *Marek v. Chesney*, 473 U.S. 1 (1985) (section 1988 case).
6. Where a plaintiff has failed to prevail upon a claim that is distinct in all respects from his or her successful claims, the hours

spent on the unsuccessful claims should be excluded in considering the amount of a reasonable lawyer's fee. Where, however, the lawsuit consists of related claims, a plaintiff who has won a verdict should not have his or her lawyer's fee award reduced simply because the judge or jury did not accept each contention raised. The fee award should be reasonable in relation to the results achieved where only limited success is obtained. *Hensley v. Eckerhart*, 461 U.S. 424 (1983) (section 1988 case).

In construing the Civil Rights Act, the Supreme Court has generally turned away from the contingent-fee model to the lodestar model of hours reasonably expended being compensated at reasonable rates. *Delaware Valley Citizens' Council*, 478 U.S. at 564. The lodestar model generally requires the court to evaluate the time and labor involved for its reasonableness and then to multiply the reasonable time expended by a reasonable lawyer's fee. The judge is at liberty to adjust the resulting fee (by applying appropriate multipliers) to take into account such factors as (1) the novelty and difficulty of the questions involved; (2) the skill requisite to perform the legal service properly; (3) time limitations imposed by the client or the circumstances; (4) the results obtained; (5) the experience, reputation, and ability of the lawyers; and (6) awards in similar cases. *See generally* Third Circuit Task Force, *Court Awarded Attorney Fees*, 108 F.R.D. 237 (1985). Applying for, resisting, and calculating lawyer's fees have formed something of a cottage industry.

§ 22. Contribution and Indemnification

Courts have rejected attempts by RICO defendants to seek contribution or indemnification from others for their exposure. This prohibition is generally deemed to follow from the fact that Congress created a comprehensive list of civil remedies available for a violation of the act, and it lacks any reference to contribution or indemnification.

There is no indication that Congress intended to permit the federal courts to expand the civil remedies beyond those expressly set forth in the statute. Contribution and indemnification actions, if permitted, would run counter to section 1964(c), which authorizes private suits only by persons injured in their business or property as a result of a violation—and does not authorize actions by violators. *See generally O & K Trojan, Inc. v. Municipal & Contractors Equip. Corp.*, 751 F. Supp. 431 (S.D.N.Y. 1990); *First Fin. Sav. Bank, Inc. v. American Bankers Ins. Co. of Fla., Inc.*, [1990] Fed. Sec. L. Rep.

(CCH) ¶ 95,696 (E.D.N.C. July 6, 1990); *Estate of Bayes v. Liberati*, No. 88-4182, 1990 U.S. Dist. LEXIS 7337 (E.D. Pa. June 15, 1990); *New Jersey Office Supply, Inc. v. Feldman*, No. 89-3990, 1990 U.S. Dist. LEXIS 6620 (D.N.J. June 4, 1990); *Department of Economic Dev. v. Arthur Andersen & Co.*, 747 F. Supp. 922 (S.D.N.Y. 1990); *Miller v. Affiliated Fin. Corp.*, 624 F. Supp. 1003 (N.D. Ill. 1985); *Seminole Elec. Coop., Inc. v. Tanner*, 635 F. Supp. 582 (M.D. Fla. 1986).

CHAPTER 7

Pleading and Practice Issues

§ 23. Pleading

The complexity of the RICO statute demands precision in pleading. *See, e.g., Connecticut Nat'l Bank v. Rytman,* 241 Conn. 24, 694 A.2d 1246, 1255 (1997) (quoting **Treatise**). RICO complaints are strictly scrutinized because "[t]he mere assertion of a RICO claim . . . has an almost inevitable stigmatizing effect on those named as defendants. In fairness to innocent parties, courts should strive to flush out frivolous RICO allegations at an early stage of the litigation." *Figueroa Ruiz v. Alegria,* 896 F.2d 645, 650 (1st Cir. 1990). Consequently, as a number of courts have observed, "[c]ivil RICO is an unusually potent weapon—the litigation equivalent of a thermonuclear device." *Katzman v. Victoria's Secret Catalogue,* 167 F.R.D. 649, 655 (S.D.N.Y. 1996), *aff'd mem.,* 113 F.3d 1229 (2d Cir. 1997) (citations omitted).

The plaintiff must specifically identify, and factually plead, each element of a viable RICO claim. A trial judge is not "obligated to construct a cause of action from allegations and a complaint filed by a party who was unwilling or unable to plead the cause of action himself." *Glenn v. First Nat'l Bank in Grand Junction,* 868 F.2d 368 (10th Cir. 1989) ("The law recognizes a significant difference between notice pleading and 'shotgun' pleading"). In the First Circuit's formulation:

> [T]he complaint must be anchored in a bed of facts, not allowed to float freely on a sea of bombast. That is to say, a court assessing a claim's sufficiency has no obligation to take matters on blind faith; "despite the highly deferential reading which we accord a litigant's complaint under Rule 12(b)(6), we need not credit bald assertions, periphrastic circumlocutions, unsubstantiated conclusions, or outright vituperation."

Miranda v. Ponce Fed. Bank, 948 F.2d 41, 44 (1st Cir. 1991) (citations omitted).

Under the Supreme Court's decision in *Sedima, S.P.R.L. v. Imrex Co.*, 473 U.S. 479 (1985), the plaintiff need not plead either (1) that the defendant has been convicted of any of the predicate offenses or (2) that the plaintiff has suffered any special "racketeering injury." Pleading a RICO claim is, therefore, as simple, and as difficult, as factually alleging each element of the cause of action. (*See generally* chapters 4–5, *supra*.)

The Second Circuit, in a frequently quoted passage, has itemized the necessary components of a section 1962(a), (b), or (c) complaint:

> (1) that the defendant (2) through the commission of two or more acts (3) constituting a "pattern" (4) of "racketeering activity" (5) directly or indirectly invests in, or maintains an interest in, or participates in (6) an "enterprise" (7) the activities of which affect interstate or foreign commerce. . . . [P]laintiff must [also] allege [(8)] that he was "injured in his business or property [(9)] by reason of [the] violation of § 1962."

Moss v. Morgan Stanley, Inc., 719 F.2d 5 (2d Cir. 1983), *cert. denied*, 465 U.S. 1025 (1984). For the requisite elements of a cause of action for each of subsection (a), (b), and (c), *see* §§ 12–14, *supra*. For the elements of a section 1962(d) claim, *see* § 15, *supra*.

Pleading is not ordinarily subject to a demanding standard under rule 8(a) of the Federal Rules of Civil Procedure. A plaintiff generally need only set forth the basis for federal jurisdiction (section 1964(c)), a short and plain statement of his or her claim, and a demand for relief.[1] A RICO complaint, however, must do substantially more. A complaint that does not set forth facts reflecting the requisite elements of a RICO claim does not satisfy the notice requirements of rule 8. *See, e.g., Richmond v. Nationwide Cassel, L.P.*, 52 F.3d 640 (7th Cir. 1995) ("This amended complaint is so scanty and its allegations so vague that it . . . fails to satisfy the notice requirement of Rule 8").

Every RICO complaint that is filed in federal court must satisfy the particularity requirements of Federal Rule of Civil Procedure 9(b) if—as is usually the case—it sounds in fraud, and in all events must factually plead each essential element of a claim

---

1. FED. R. CIV. P. 8(a) provides the following:

> Claims For Relief. A pleading which sets forth a claim for relief, whether an original claim, counterclaim, cross-claim, or third-party claim, shall contain (1) a short and plain statement of the grounds upon which the court's jurisdiction depends, unless the court already has jurisdiction and the claim needs no new grounds of jurisdiction to support it, (2) a short and plain statement of the claim showing that the pleader is entitled to relief, and (3) a demand for judgment for the relief the pleader seeks. Relief in the alternative or of several different types may be demanded.

under rule 12(b)(6). The following sections examine the requirements under these rules in greater detail.

A. Rule 9(b): Particularity Requirements

To the extent that any predicate acts sound in fraud—as, in practice, most do—the pleading of those acts must satisfy the particularity requirements of rule 9(b) of the Federal Rules of Civil Procedure.[2] *See, e.g., Farlow v. Peat, Marwick, Mitchell & Co*, 956 F.2d 982 (10th Cir. 1992) ("Under Rule 9(b), plaintiffs must sufficiently allege each element of a RICO violation and its predicate acts of racketeering with particularity, a requirement justified by the 'threat of treble damages and injury to reputation'"); *Midwest Grinding Co. v. Spitz*, 976 F.2d 1016 (7th Cir. 1992) ("the complaint must, at minimum, describe the predicate acts with some specificity and 'state the time, place, and content of the alleged communications perpetrating the fraud'"); *Picard Chem. Inc. Profit Sharing Plan v. Perrigo Co.*, 940 F. Supp. 1101 (W.D. Mich. 1996) ("[A] complaint may not lump all the defendants together, but must specify who was involved in each activity"); *Lubin v. Sybendon Corp.*, 688 F. Supp. 1425 (S.D.Cal. 1988) (excoriating "plaintiff's 'dragnet' tactic of indiscriminately grouping all of the individual defendants into one wrongdoing monolith"); *Craighead v. E.F. Hutton & Co., Inc.*, 899 F.2d 485 (6th Cir. 1990) (dismissing RICO claim for failure to plead predicate acts with particularity: "the plaintiffs' collection of conclusions and unrelated, unexplained events fails to set forth any instance of mail fraud, securities fraud, or any other fraud, with *any* particularity. As plaintiffs have failed to allege any predicate acts, there can be no pattern of racketeering"). *Accord Cayman Exploration Corp. v. United Gas Pipeline Co.*, 873 F.2d 1357 (10th Cir. 1989); *Alan Neuman Prods., Inc. v. Albright*, 862 F.2d 1388 (9th Cir. 1988), *cert. denied*, 493 U.S. 858 (1989); *Durham v. Business Management Assocs.*, 847 F.2d 1505 (11th Cir. 1988); *Saporito v. Combustion Eng'g, Inc.*, 843 F.2d 666 (3d Cir. 1988), *vacated on other grounds*, 489 U.S. 1049 (1989).

There is an obvious tension between the liberal pleading ordinarily permitted under rule 8(a) and the particularity requirements imposed by rule 9(b). Where rule 9(b) applies, the court considers the particularity requirement against the more general

---

2. FED. R. CIV. P. 9(b) provides the following:

"Fraud, Mistake, Condition of the Mind. In all averments of fraud or mistake, the circumstances constituting fraud or mistake shall be stated with particularity. Malice, intent, knowledge, and other condition of mind of a person may be averred generally."

policy stated in rule 8(a). *Michaels Bldg. Co. v. Ameritrust Co., N. A.*, 848 F.2d 674 (6th Cir. 1988). The policy of simplicity in pleadings requires the court—to the extent possible—to read rule 9(b)'s requirements in harmony with rule 8(a)'s call for a "short and plain statement of the claim" with "simple, concise, and direct" allegations. Nonetheless "the threat of treble damages and injury to reputation which attend RICO actions justif[ies] requiring [each] plaintiff to frame its pleadings in such a way that will give the defendant, and the trial court, clear notice of the factual basis for the alleged predicate acts." *Cayman Exploration*, 873 F.2d at 1362 ("We believe this is particularly important in cases where the predicate fraud allegations provide the only link to federal jurisdiction"). Rule 9(b) effectively carves out an exception to the otherwise generally liberal pleading requirements set forth in the federal rules. *Graue Mill Dev. Corp. v. Colonial Bank & Trust Co. of Chicago*, 927 F.2d 988 (7th Cir. 1991).

Purposes. The purpose of rule 9(b) is multifold. It is designed to (1) provide a defendant with fair notice of a plaintiff's claims; (2) safeguard a defendant's reputation from improvident charges of wrongdoing; (3) protect defendants against the institution of strike suits; and (4) prevent the use of groundless fraud claims to initiate, or expand the scope of, discovery. *See, e.g., O'Brien v. National Property Analysts Partners*, 936 F.2d 674 (2d Cir. 1991); *New England Data Servs., Inc. v. Becher*, 829 F.2d 286 (1st Cir. 1987).

General Requirements. Vague or conclusory allegations are insufficient to satisfy the particularity requirement of rule 9(b). *See, e.g, Graue Mill Dev. Corp.*, 927 F.2d at 992 ("Cryptic statements suggesting fraud are not enough; mere allegations of fraud . . ., averments to conditions of mind, or references to plans and schemes are too conclusional to satisfy the particularity requirements" (citations and internal quotations omitted)).

Instead, a complaint must contain specific facts supporting its conclusions. *Lally v. Crawford County Trust & Sav. Bank*, 863 F.2d 612 (8th Cir. 1988). The mere assertion that wrongful statements were made, without more, is insufficient to support a claim of fraud. *Stern v. Leucadia Nat'l Corp.*, 844 F.2d 997 (2d Cir.), *cert. denied*, 488 U.S. 852 (1988); *Browning Ave. Realty Corp. v. Rosenshein*, 774 F. Supp. 129, 138 (S.D.N.Y. 1991); *Zuckerman v. Harnischfeger Corp.*, 591 F. Supp. 112 (S.D.N.Y. 1984).

Time, Place, Contents, Parties. Generally, to pass muster under rule 9(b), the complaint must allege the time, place, speaker, and content of alleged misrepresentations. *Moore v. Kayport Package Express, Inc.*, 885 F.2d 531 (9th Cir. 1989) ("Rule 9(b) requires that the pleader state the time, place and specific content of the false representations as well as the identities of the parties to the misrepresentation"); *accord DiVittorio v. Equidyne Extractive Indus., Inc.*,

822 F.2d 1242 (2d Cir. 1987); *Bender v. Southland Corp.*, 749 F.2d 1205 (6th Cir. 1984); *Lally*, 863 F.2d at 613.

The complaint must also particularize each defendant's alleged participation in the fraud. *DiVittorio*, 822 F.2d at 1247 ("Where multiple defendants are asked to respond to allegations of fraud, the complaint should inform each defendant of the nature of his alleged participation in the fraud").

Scienter. Rule 9(b) provides that "malice, intent, knowledge and other condition of mind of a person may be averred generally." Consequently, allegations of scienter are not subjected to the more exacting consideration applied to the other components of fraud. However, a factual basis must be stated for conclusory allegations of intent. *Ouaknine v. MacFarlane*, 897 F.2d 75, 79–81 (2d Cir. 1988). Allegations of scienter are sufficient only if supported by facts giving rise to a "strong inference" of fraudulent intent. *O'Brien v. National Property Analysts Partners*, 936 F.2d 674 (2d Cir. 1991) ("while Rule 9(b) permits scienter to be demonstrated by inference, this 'must not be mistaken for license to base claims of fraud on speculation and conclusory allegation.' An ample factual basis must be supplied to support the charges" (citation omitted)); *see also Breard v. Sachnoff & Weaver, Ltd.*, 941 F.2d 142 (2d Cir. 1991).

Prolix Pleading. Prolixity in a complaint may reflect obfuscation in derogation of rule 9(b). *See, e.g., Old Time Enters., Inc. v. International Coffee Corp.*, 862 F.2d 1213 (5th Cir. 1988) (dismissing complaint that reflected "a perhaps somewhat fervid desire to cover all even remotely conceivable theories while retaining a level of generality and indefiniteness that would mask any legal deficiencies and preclude effective challenge. That . . . only leads to essentially nothing being alleged, for the needle in the haystack might as well not be there"); *J.D. Marshall Int'l, Inc. v. Redstart, Inc.*, 935 F.2d 815 (7th Cir. 1991) ("Adding more warts to the hog still does not make it a dragon"); *cf. Fraiberg v. Taplin*, [1990] Fed. Sec. L. Rep. (CCH) ¶ 95,239 (S.D.N.Y. May 9, 1990) ("while Rule 9(b) may originally have been intended to promote greater clarity in fraud complaints, today many counsel cram much irrelevant detail into their securities fraud complaints. The resulting muddled and unwieldy documents are so adorned with unnecessary surplusage and background that often neither the defendants nor the Court can identify the crux of the fraud claim. Such complaints are equally violative of Rule 9(b) as those that contain no detail at all").

Scope of Rule 9(b). As indicated above, rule 9(b) applies to the allegations of a RICO complaint only to the extent that they sound in fraud. This commonly occurs under section 1962(a), (b), and (c) because the most commonly alleged predicate acts—mail fraud and wire fraud—are subject to the pleading strictures of rule 9(b). *See, e.g., Feinstein v. Resolution Trust Corp.*, 942 F.2d 34 (1st Cir.

1991) ("a pleader is required 'to go beyond a showing of fraud and state the time, place and content of the alleged mail and wire communications perpetrating that fraud'");[3] *O'Brien v. National Property Analysts Partners, 936 F.2d 674 (2d Cir. 1991) ("because plaintiffs premise these claims . . . on defendants' alleged fraudulent conduct, plaintiffs must comply with Rule 9(b)").*

Section 1962(d) is treated a bit differently. Conspiracy is not "fraud" for pleading purposes. Hence, rule 9(b) does not apply to conspiracy allegations filed under section 1962(d). However, courts have tended to expand, in substance, the scope of rule 9(b)'s particularity requirements to encompass section 1962(d) and virtually all complaints filed under the RICO statute. Under section 1962(d), courts require that the complaint, at a minimum, (1) allege the parties' specific agreement to commit at least two predicate acts and (2) contain supportive factual allegations. Mere conclusions are not enough. *Hecht v. Commerce Clearing House, Inc.*, 897 F.2d 21 (2d Cir. 1990) ("Because the core of a RICO conspiracy is an agreement to commit predicate acts, a RICO civil conspiracy complaint, at the very least, must allege specifically such an agreement. . . . [Plaintiff's] pleading of a conspiracy, apart from the underlying acts of fraud, is properly measured under the more liberal pleading requirements of Rule 8(a). . . . Even so, the complaint must allege some factual basis for finding a conscious agreement among the defendants"); *Rose v. Bartle*, 871 F.2d 331 (3d Cir. 1989) ("A conspiracy claim must also contain supportive factual allegations. The allegations must be sufficient to describe the general composition of the conspiracy, some or all of its broad objectives, and the defendant's general role in that conspiracy" (citations and internal quotations omitted)). *See also* § 23(B), *infra*.

Similarly, extortion under the Hobbs Act, 18 U.S.C. § 1951, is a predicate act not sounding in fraud (*see generally* § 11(C)(2)(c), *supra*). Nonetheless, the complaint must describe factually how the acts alleged were extortionate in violation of the statute. *See, e.g., Old Time Enters., Inc. v. International Coffee Corp.*, 862 F.2d 1213 (5th Cir. 1988) (dismissal pursuant to rule 12(b)(6)).

Rule 9(b) Practice. In reviewing a decision to dismiss a complaint on rule 9(b) grounds, the court assumes the truth of plaintiffs' allegations. *O'Brien v. National Property Analysts Partners,*

---

3. To plead mail and wire fraud violations within the strictures of rule 9(b), the plaintiff must allege (1) the existence of a scheme to defraud, (2) the use of the mails in furtherance of the fraudulent scheme, and (3) culpable participation by the defendant. *See, e.g.*, Browning Ave. Realty Corp. v. Rosenshein, 774 F. Supp. 129 (S.D.N.Y 1991) (citations omitted). *See generally* O'Malley v. New York City Transit Auth., 896 F.2d 704 (2d Cir. 1990).

936 F.2d at 676–77. While courts have differed concerning the harshness of the penalty they should impose when rule 9(b) has not been satisfied, ordinarily they grant leave to amend at least once before entering a dismissal with prejudice. *See, e.g., Schreiber Distrib. Co. v. Serv-Well Furniture Co.*, 806 F.2d 1393 (9th Cir. 1986). It is usually only after a plaintiff has had discovery or a prior opportunity to plead that a complaint is dismissed with prejudice for failure to satisfy rule 9(b). *See, e.g., Devaney v. Chester*, 813 F.2d 566 (2d Cir. 1987); *O'Brien v. National Property Analysts Partners*, 936 F.2d at 676–77.[4]

RICO Case Statements. As will be discussed (§ 23(C), *infra*), many courts require the filing of RICO case statements to clarify pleadings that invoke the act. The Federal Judicial Center has prepared a model RICO case statement, which is contained in the MANUAL FOR COMPLEX LITIGATION 3d at § 33.81 & Sample Form § 41.54 (1995). By way of comparison, a judge in the Middle District of Florida, in dismissing a complaint pursuant to rule 9(b), set forth 20 criteria in this context that are appropriate for pleaders to use in assessing their RICO allegations. While the pleadings before that court included mail fraud–based claims arising under subsections 1962(c) and (d), and while subsequent Supreme Court cases might suggest some elaboration, almost all the criteria retain their vitality and have broader application:

1. State each alleged RICO predicate act by [the] defendant, complying with Rule 9(b), Fed. R. Civ. P., to the extent it is applicable.
2. State the specific statutory section that each alleged predicate act violates, separating alleged section violations in separate counts.
3. State how the predicate acts in combination satisfy the relatedness requirement. *See H.J. Inc. v. Northwestern Bell Telephone Co.*, [492 U.S. 229] (1989).
4. State how the predicate acts in combination satisfy the continuity requirement. *See H.J. Inc.*, [492 U.S. 229] (1989).
5. The complaint must allege either (1) a series of related acts extended over a substantial period of time, or (2) related predicate acts involving a distinct threat of long-term activity. *[H.] J. Inc.*, [492 U.S. at 240–42].
6. Include time, place, and how the pattern of acts occurred. *See Schreiber Distributing Co. v. Serv-Well Furniture Co., Inc.*, 806 F.2d 1393, 1399 (9th Cir. 1986).
7. State how the mail or wire fraud played an integral role in the scheme to bring the communicator's conduct within the ambit of the statutes. *United States v. La Ferriere*, 546 F.2d 182 (5th Cir. 1977). Include a statement describing how the mailing or use of the wires is in furtherance of the scheme. *United States v. Hagler*, 708 F.2d 354 (9th Cir. 1982). The statement should be more specific than stating "100 separate occasions" constituted a fraud.

---

4. Although one commentator has proposed carving RICO claims out of the scope of rule 9(b) (Note, *Excepting Civil RICO Claims from Rule 9(b)*, 10 CARDOZO L. REV. 359 (1988)), there has been no perceptible judicial, rule making, or legislative receptivity to this suggestion.

ENTERPRISE

8. State the name of the partnership, corporation, association, sole proprietorship, or other legal entity that allegedly constitutes the enterprise, or the names of the individuals comprising an association-in-fact that allegedly constitutes the enterprise.
9. If the alleged enterprise is a sole proprietorship, name the employees of that business. *See M[c]Cullough v. Suter*, 757 F.2d 142 (7th Cir. 1985).
10. If the alleged enterprise is an association-in-fact, establish that it has a common or shared purpose, and continuity of structure and personality. *See U.S. [United States] v. Cagina*, 697 F.2d 915 (11th Cir. 1983) [*cert. denied*, 464 U.S. 856 (1983)].
11. Describe the structure, purpose, function, and course of conduct of the enterprise.
12. State whether the defendant is an employee, officer, director, or agent of the enterprise; or state the manner in which the defendant associated with the enterprise.
13. Describe how the activities of the enterprise affect interstate commerce. *See U.S. [United States] v. Barton*, 647 F.2d 224 (2d Cir. 1981) [*cert. denied*, 454 U.S. 857 (1981)].

RIGHT TO RELIEF UNDER 18 U.S.C. SECTION 1962(c)

14. Describe how the affairs of the enterprise were conducted through the pattern of racketeering activity. *See U.S. [United States] v. Webster*, 669 F.2d 185 (4th Cir. 1982) [*cert. denied*, 456 U.S. 935 (1982)].
15. Describe how plaintiff was damaged, and how those damages were proximately caused by the RICO violation. *See O'Malley v. O'Neill*, 887 F.2d 1557 (11th Cir. 1989) [*cert. denied*, 110 S. Ct. 2620 (1990)].

RIGHT TO RELIEF UNDER 18 U.S.C. SECTION 1962([d])

16. Describe the alleged agreement to perform at least two of the predicate acts. *See Barton*, 647 F.2d 224 (2d Cir. 1981).
17. Describe how the plaintiff was damaged, and how those damages were proximately caused by the conspiracy to violate RICO. *See O'Malley*, 887 F.2d 1557 (11th Cir. 1989).

SOURCE OF FACTS

18. State the names of any witnesses relied upon for each of the preceding factual allegations.
19. Provide a list of documents relied upon for each of the preceding factual allegations.

CERTIFICATION

[20.] An attorney of record or Plaintiff pro se shall certify, pursuant to Rule 11, Fed. R. Civ. P., that "to the best of the signer's knowledge, information, and belief formed after reasonable inquiry it is well grounded in fact and is warranted by existing law."

Rentclub, Inc. v. TransAmerica Rental Fin. Corp., No. 90-1452-Civ.-T-17A, 1991 U.S. Dist. LEXIS 14915 (M.D. Fla. Oct. 3, 1991).

B. Rule 12(b)(6): Failure to State a Claim

Pursuant to rule 12(b)(6) of the Federal Rules of Civil Procedure, any person against whom a claim, including a RICO claim, is asserted has the option to move for a dismissal if the pleading "fail[s] to state a claim upon which relief can be granted."[5] On a motion to dismiss pursuant to rule 12(b)(6), the court must "read the facts alleged in the complaint in the light most favorable to the plaintiffs." *H.J. Inc. v. Northwestern Bell Tel. Co.*, 492 U.S. 229, 245 (1989).

The rule 12(b)(6) standard of review does not distinguish between RICO and non-RICO claims. *Rose v. Bartle*, 871 F.2d 331 (3d Cir. 1989). However, applying rule 12(b)(6) to RICO produces distinctive requirements. Most importantly, the RICO plaintiff must allege the substantive components of an "enterprise" and "pattern" sufficiently to withstand a dismissal motion. *See, e.g., Montesano v. Seafirst Commercial Corp.*, 818 F.2d 423 (5th Cir. 1987) (plaintiff must plead specific facts that establish an association that exists other than merely to commit the predicate acts forming the pattern); *Jennings v. Emry*, 910 F.2d 1434 (7th Cir. 1990) ("the first rule is that '[a] plaintiff must identify the enterprise'"); *Olive Can Co. v. Martin*, 906 F.2d 1147 (7th Cir. 1990) ("merely alleging two predicate acts . . . does not satisfy the pattern requirement"). The requirements of rules 12(b)(6) and 9(b) tend to merge in this area (*see* § 23(A), *supra*), and the motions are often made in tandem.

All elements of the RICO cause of action must be set forth factually and with sufficient specificity to permit the court to ascertain whether a viable claim exists and whether the plaintiff has standing to pursue it. *See, e.g., Republic of Panama v. BCCI Holdings*, 119 F.3d 935 (11th Cir. 1997) ("Section 1961 requires that a RICO plaintiff establish that a defendant could be convicted for violating any of its predicate statutes. Therefore, in order to survive a motion to dismiss, a plaintiff must allege facts sufficient to support each of the statutory elements for at least two of the pleaded predicate acts. . . . A RICO plaintiff's allegations of scienter cannot be 'merely conclusory and unsupported by any factual allegations'") (citations omitted); *Seidl v. Greentree Mortg. Co.*, 30 F. Supp.2d 1292

---

5. FED. R. CIV. P. 12(b) provides the following:

Every defense, in law or fact, to a claim for relief in any pleading, whether a claim, counterclaim, cross-claim, or third-party claim, shall be asserted in the responsive pleading thereto if one is required, except that the following defenses may at the option of the pleader be made by motion: . . . (6) failure to state a claim upon which relief can be granted. . . . A motion making any of these defenses shall be made before pleading if a further pleading is permitted. No defense or objection is waived by being joined with one or more other defenses or objections in a responsive pleading or motion. . . . If, on a motion asserting the defense numbered (6) to dismiss for failure of the pleading to state a claim upon which relief can be granted, matters outside the pleading are presented to and not excluded by the court, the motion shall be treated as one for summary judgment and disposed of as provided in Rule 56, and all parties shall be given reasonable opportunity to present all material made pertinent to such a motion by Rule 56.

(D.Colo. 1998) (complaint "fail[s] to state a claim with sufficient particularity because it lumps together the defendants and also lumps together the alleged enterprises and makes vague and conclusory allegations"; rejecting "conclusory allegations of [defendant's] participation in the alleged enterprise," in the absence of "specific allegations to show that [defendant] in any way participated in the direction or management of a RICO enterprise"); *Schmidt v. Fleet Bank,* 16 F.Supp.2d 340 (S.D.N.Y. 1998) ("Bare and conclusory allegations are insufficient to withstand a motion to dismiss and a plaintiff must plead facts sufficient to show that each defendant knowingly agreed to participate in the conspiracy") Federal Judicial Center, MANUAL FOR COMPLEX LITIGATION 3d at § 33.81–82 (1995) (discussing "[t]he strict pleading requirements peculiar to [civil] RICO," including, inter alia, allegations of pattern; enterprise; injury; proximate cause; investment injury under section 1962(a); acquisition injury under section 1962(b); operation and management, and distinct person and enterprise, under section 1962(c); and agreement to conspire under section 1962(d)).

C. RICO Case Statements

Many federal courts require parties articulating RICO claims to file RICO case statements. The statements are designed to amplify and clarify the allegations of the pleading, to require precision in the statement of the RICO claim, and in that fashion, to assist in identifying and narrowing factual and legal issues. Standing orders entered in many federal district courts mandate the filing of RICO case statements by all parties pleading RICO claims.[6] In the absence of standing orders, numerous judges have required filing of RICO case statements in individual actions, often in response to or in conjunction with defense motions to dismiss pursuant to rule 9(b) or 12(b)(6) or motions for a more definite statement pursuant to rule 12(e).[7] As discussed in § 23(A), *supra,* the Federal Judicial

6. *See, e.g.,* Miranda v. Ponce Fed. Bank, 948 F.2d 41 (1st Cir. 1991) (District of Puerto Rico requirement); Ifert v. Miller, No. 90-0758 MISC, 1991 U.S. Dist. Lexis 4813 (E.D. Pa. Apr. 12, 1991), *aff'd,* 981 F.2d 1297 (3d Cir. 1992); Jurisich v. Louisiana Dep't of Wildlife & Fisheries, No. 90-4228, 1991 U.S. Dist. LEXIS 5243 (E.D. La. Apr. 16, 1991); Collective Fed. Sav. v. Creel, 746 F. Supp. 1307 (M.D. La. 1990); Lyman Steel Co. v. Shearson Lehman Bros., Inc., No. C-86-355 (N.D. Ohio Feb. 13, 1986).

7. *See, e.g.,* Glessner v. Kenny, 952 F.2d 702 (3d Cir. 1991) (case arising out of District of New Jersey); Homico Constr. & Dev. Co. v. Ti-Bert Sys., Inc., 939 F.2d 392 (6th Cir. 1991) (Northern District of Ohio); Old Time Enters., Inc. v. International Coffee Corp., 862 F.2d 1213 (5th Cir. 1989) (E. D. La.); Hunt v. Gouverneur Townhouse Partners-1988 L.P., No. 90 Civ. 4900 (MGC), 1991 U.S. Dist. LEXIS 16749 (S.D.N.Y. Nov. 18, 1991); VSA v. Von Weise Gear Co., 769 F. Supp. 1080 (E.D. Mo. 1991); Bennett v. Centerpoint Bank, 761 F. Supp. 908 (D. N.H. 1991); Silverman v. Niswonger, 761 F. Supp. 464 (E. D. Mich. 1991); *In re* Pioneer Lumber Treating, Inc., 127 Bankr. 248 (Bankr. D. Haw. 1991).

Center has prepared a model RICO case statement, which is contained in the MANUAL FOR COMPLEX LITIGATION 3d at § 33.81 & Sample Form § 41.54 (1995).

The authority on which judges order parties to file RICO case statements is generally viewed as deriving from Fed. R. Civ. P. 11, 12(e), 16, and 83. The substance of RICO case statements may be considered on motions to dismiss because they are viewed as elaborations of pleadings. *See, e.g., Glessner v. Kenny*, 952 F.2d 702 (3d Cir. 1991) ("Courts may consider the RICO case statement in assessing whether plaintiffs' RICO claims should be dismissed"); *Dennis v. General Imaging, Inc.*, 918 F.2d 496 (5th Cir. 1990) (considering complaint, amended complaint, and RICO case statement on motion to dismiss); *Sil-Flo, Inc. v. SFHC, Inc.*, 917 F.2d 1507 (10th Cir. 1990) (same).

Model RICO Case Statement. The New York State Bar Association Commercial and Federal Litigation section has drafted a model civil RICO case statement order. It is drawn from case statements found in reported opinions and tailored to satisfy Supreme Court requirements. This model case statement provides as follows:

> This order has been designed to establish a uniform and efficient procedure for deciding civil actions containing claims made pursuant to 18 U.S.C. §§ 1961–1968 ("civil RICO").
>
> The proponent of the civil RICO claim shall file and serve [within _ days of _] a case statement that shall include the facts relied upon to initiate the RICO claim. In particular, the statement shall be in a form which uses the numbers and letters set forth below, unless filed as part of an amended and restated pleading (in which latter case, the allegations of the amended and restated pleading shall reasonably follow the organization set out below), and shall state in detail and with specificity the following information:
>
> 1. State whether the alleged unlawful conduct is in violation of 18 U.S.C. sections 1962(a), (b), (c), and/or (d). If you allege violations of more than one section 1962 subsection, treat each as a separate RICO claim.
> 2. List each defendant and state the alleged misconduct and basis of alleged liability of each defendant.
> 3. List the alleged wrongdoers, other than the defendants listed above, and state the alleged misconduct of each wrongdoer.
> 4. List the alleged victims and state how each victim allegedly was injured.
> 5. Describe in detail the pattern of racketeering activity or collection of an unlawful debt alleged for each RICO claim. A description of the pattern of racketeering activity shall include the following information:
>   (a) List the alleged predicate acts and the specific statutes allegedly violated by each predicate act;
>   (b) Provide the dates of the predicate acts, the participants in the predicate acts, and a description of the facts surrounding each predicate act;
>   (c) If the RICO claim is based upon the predicate offenses of wire fraud, mail fraud, fraud in the sale of securities, or fraud in connection with a case under U.S.C. Title 11, the "circumstances constituting fraud or mistake shall be stated with particularity," Fed. R. Civ. P. 9(b). Identify the time, place, and contents of the alleged misrepresentation or omissions, and the

identity of persons to whom and by whom the alleged misrepresentations or omissions were made;

(d) Describe in detail the perceived relationship that the predicate acts bear to each other or to some external organizing principle that renders them "ordered" or "arranged" or "part of a common plan[;]" and

(e) Explain how the predicate acts amount to or pose a threat of continued criminal activity.

6. Describe in detail the alleged enterprise for each RICO claim. A description of the enterprise shall include the following information:

   (a) State the names of the individuals, partnerships, corporations, associations, or other entities allegedly constituting the enterprise;

   (b) Describe the structure, purpose, roles, function, and course of conduct of the enterprise;

   (c) State whether any defendants are employees, officers, or directors of the alleged enterprise;

   (d) State whether any defendants are associated with the alleged enterprise, and if so, how;

   (e) Explain how each defendant participated in the direction of the affairs of the enterprise;

   (f) State whether you allege [(i)] that the defendants are individuals or entities separate from the alleged enterprise, or [(ii)] that the defendants are the enterprise itself, or [(iii) that the defendants are] members of the enterprise;

   (g) If you allege any defendants to be the enterprise itself, or members of the enterprise, explain whether such defendants are perpetrators, passive instruments, or victims of the alleged racketeering activity.

7. State whether you allege and describe in detail how the pattern of racketeering activity and the enterprise are separate or have merged into one entity.

8. Describe the alleged relationship between the activities and the pattern of racketeering activity. Discuss how the racketeering activity differs from the usual and daily activities of the enterprise, if at all.

9. Describe what benefits, if any, the alleged enterprise and each defendant received from the alleged pattern of racketeering activity.

10. Describe the effect of the activities of the enterprise on interstate or foreign commerce.

11. If the complaint alleges a violation of 18 U.S.C. section 1962(a), provide the following information:

    (a) State who received the income derived from the pattern of racketeering activity or through the collection of an unlawful debt; and,

    (b) Describe the use or investment of such income.

12. If the complaint alleges a violation of 18 U.S.C. section 1962(b), provide the following information:

    (a) Describe in detail the acquisition or maintenance of any interest in or control of the alleged enterprise; and

    (b) State whether the same entity is both the liable "person" and the "enterprise" under section 1962(b).

13. If the complaint alleges a violation of 18 U.S.C. section 1962(c), provide the following information:

    (a) State who is employed by or associated with the enterprise; [and]

    (b) State whether the same entity is both the liable "person" and the "enterprise" under section 1962(c).

14. If the complaint alleges a violation of 18 U.S.C. section 1962(d), describe in detail the alleged conspiracy.

15. Describe the alleged injury to business or property.

16. Describe the relationship between the alleged injury and violation of the RICO statute.

17. List the damages sustained by reason of the violation of section 1962, indicating the amount for which each defendant allegedly is liable.
18. Provide any additional information you feel would be helpful to the Court in processing your RICO claim.

N.Y. State Bar Ass'n Commercial & Fed. Litig. Sec., *The Civil RICO Case Statement* 21–24 (1989), *reprinted in* [1990] RICO Bus. Disputes Guide (CCH) ¶ 7453 at 10,280–81 (May 1990).

§ 24. Summary Judgment

Under rule 56 of the Federal Rules of Civil Procedure, any party may move for summary judgment prior to trial if "the pleadings, depositions, answers to interrogatories, and admissions on file, together with the affidavits, if any, show that there is no genuine issue as to any material fact and that the moving party is entitled to judgment as a matter of law." Fed. R. Civ. P. 56(c).[8]

In three important decisions in 1986, the Supreme Court clarified the law of summary judgment in a manner designed to encourage the use of this procedure. In *Matsushita Elec. Indus. Co., Ltd. v. Zenith Radio Corp.*, 475 U.S. 574 (1986), the Court declared that when a moving party has come forward with evidence that no genuine issue of material fact exists, it is inadequate for the opponent "simply [to] show that there is some metaphysical doubt as to the material facts." Rather, the nonmoving party must come forward with specific facts demonstrating the existence of a genuine issue for trial. "Where the record taken as a whole could not lead a rational trier of fact to find for the nonmoving party, there is no 'genuine issue for trial.'" *Id.* at 587.

Under *Anderson v. Liberty Lobby, Inc.*, 477 U.S. 242 (1986), the second of the Supreme Court's 1986 trilogy, the burden on the

---

8. Fed. R. Civ. P. 56 provides, in part, the following:

(a) **For Claimant.** A party seeking to recover upon a claim, counterclaim, or cross-claim or to obtain a declaratory judgment may, at any time after the expiration of 20 days from the commencement of the action or after service of a motion for summary judgment by the adverse party, move with or without supporting affidavits for a summary judgment in the party's favor upon all or any part thereof.

(b) **For Defending Party.** A party against whom a claim, counterclaim, or cross-claim is asserted or a declaratory judgment is sought may, at any time, move with or without supporting affidavits for a summary judgment in the party's favor as to all or any part thereof.

(c) **Motion and Proceedings Thereon.** The motion shall be served at least 10 days before the time fixed for the hearing. The adverse party prior to the day of hearing may serve opposing affidavits. The judgment shall be rendered forthwith if the pleadings, depositions, answers to interrogatories, and admissions on file, together with the affidavits, if any, show that there is no genuine issue as to any material fact and that the moving party is entitled to a judgment as a matter of law.

party seeking summary judgment, can be discharged merely by "'showing'—that is pointing out to the District Court—that there is an absence of evidence to support the non-moving party's case." The standard for determining the existence of a genuine issue of fact on summary judgment "mirrors the standard for a directed verdict under Federal Rule of Civil Procedure 50(a) . . . whether the evidence presents a sufficient disagreement to require submission to a jury or whether it is so one-sided that one party must prevail as a matter of law." Id. at 250–251. In *Celotex Corp. v. Catrett,* 477 U.S. 317 (1986), the Supreme Court ruled that there is "no express or implicit requirement in Rule 56 that the moving party support its motion with affidavits or other similar materials negating the opponent's claim."

Since the Supreme Court's 1986 trilogy, the courts of appeals and district courts have taken to heart the admonition that "[s]ummary judgment procedure is properly regarded not as a disfavored procedural shortcut, but rather as an integral part of the Federal Rules as a whole, which are designed to 'secure the just, speedy and inexpensive determination of every action.'" *Id* at 327. Focusing commonly but not exclusively on the enterprise and pattern requirements, federal judges have not hesitated to enter summary judgment on RICO claims in the absence of genuine issues of material fact. *See, e.g., Isaak v. Trumbull S&L Co.* 169 F.3d 390 (6th Cir. 1999) (affirming summary judgment on statute of limitations grounds); *Associates in Adolescent Psychiatry, S.C. v. Home Life Ins. Co.,* 941 F.2d 561 (7th Cir. 1991), *cert. denied,* 502 U.S. 1099 (1992) (affirming grant of summary judgment where "no reasonable investor would be misled by [challenged oral] statements . . . when the truth was under his nose in black and white many times over"); *Lou v. Belzberg,* 728 F. Supp. 1010 (S.D.N.Y. 1990) (granting combined summary judgment and dismissal motion because RICO allegations failed to state pattern of racketeering activity); *Trundy v. Strumsky,* 729 F. Supp. 178 (D. Mass.), *aff'd in part and vacated in part,* 915 F.2d 1557, 1990 U.S. App. LEXIS 17612 (1st Cir. 1990) (summary judgment affirmed as to one defendant who moved for summary judgment but vacated as to others who had not, since the plaintiff was not on notice that he had to bring forward all his evidence concerning his claims against the nonmoving defendants). Conversely, if a genuine issue of material fact exists as to any material RICO element, summary judgment is inappropriate. *See, e.g., Federal Ins. Co. v. Ayers,* 772 F. Supp. 1503 (E.D. Pa. 1991) (denying summary judgment "because there are genuine issues of material fact regarding the commission of the alleged predicate acts"). The Second Circuit has ruled that, if a complaint contains sufficient allegations of fact to survive dismissal and discovery both (1) confirms that the defendant stands within the enterprise and (2) unearths actual commission of crime by that defendant, it is for the factfinder "to determine whether or not his criminal activity, assessed in the context of all the relevant circumstances, constitutes participation in the operation or management of the enterprise's affairs," within the holding of *Reves v. Ernst & Young*, 507 U.S. 170 (1993). *United States v. Allen*, 155 F.3d 35, 42 (2d Cir. 1998).

§ 25. Burden of Proof

A simple preponderance of the evidence is all that is required to prove a predicate act and, therefore, the RICO violation. In *Sedima, S.P.R.L. v. Imrex Co., Inc.*, 473 U.S. 479 (1985), the Supreme Court rejected a higher standard, observing that there was no indication that Congress sought to depart from the general principle that "conduct [which] can be punished as criminal only upon proof beyond a reasonable doubt will support civil sanctions under a preponderance standard." *Id.* at 491 ("That the offending conduct is described by reference to criminal statutes does not mean that its occurrence must be established by criminal standards or that the consequences of a finding of liability in a private civil action are identical to the consequences of criminal conviction").

Although the Supreme Court nominally disclaimed "decid[ing] the standard of proof issue" in *Sedima*, 473 U.S. at 491, the lower courts have properly read the opinion as calling for an application of a preponderance standard. *See, e.g., Matter of EDC, Inc.*, 930 F.2d 1275 (7th Cir. 1991); *Liquid Air Corp. v. Rogers*, 834 F.2d 1297 (7th Cir. 1987), *cert. denied*, 492 U.S. 917 (1989); *Wilcox v. First Interstate Bank of Or.*, 815 F.2d 522 (9th Cir. 1987); *Cullen v. Margiotta*, 811 F.2d 698 (2d Cir.), *cert. denied*, 483 U.S. 1021 (1987); *Armco Indus. Credit Corp. v. SLT Warehouse Co.*, 782 F.2d 475 (5th Cir. 1986); *United States v. Local 560, Int'l Bhd. of Teamsters*, 780 F.2d 287 (3d Cir. 1985), *cert. denied*, 476 U.S. 1140 (1986). *Cf. Grogan v. Garner*, 498 U.S. 279 (1991) (reading *Sedima* as "suggesting that the preponderance standard applies to civil RICO actions" in concluding that a mere preponderance is the standard of proof for dischargeability exceptions under Chapter 11 of the Bankruptcy Code, even in cases of fraud).

It has been suggested that the burden of proof should be raised at least to a clear and convincing standard in civil RICO cases. *See, e.g.*, Note, *The Standard of Proof in Civil RICO Actions for Treble Damages: Why the Clear and Convincing Standard Should Apply*, 22 Ind. L. Rev. 881 (1989). If, however, the reason for raising the standard is the perceived overapplication of the statute, it is highly dubious that a heightened burden of proof will have any impact at all. If reform is needed, it is substantive reform—not incremental adjustments to the burden of proof.

§ 26. Sanctions

RICO litigants in federal court are subject to the same sanction provisions governing all civil actions. Principally, these are rule 11 of the Federal Rules of Civil Procedure, 28 U.S.C. § 1927, the inherent power of the court, and rule 38 of the Federal Rules of Appellate Procedure. *See generally* G. Joseph, SANCTIONS: THE FEDERAL LAW OF LITIGATION ABUSE (2d ed. 1994 & supp. 2000). State court litigants are subject to a wide array of state court rules and statutes, many of them analogous to Fed. R. Civ. P. 11.[9] There are no codified distinctions in any of the federal provisions for disparate treatment of RICO litigants. However, the complexity and uncertainty of many aspects of RICO law, and the strained and vituperative quality of much RICO litigation, has witnessed two unique developments: (1) the inauguration of RICO case statements (*see* § 23(c), *supra*) which, inter alia, subject pleaders to additional rule 11 exposure and (2) the growth of two parallel strands of RICO-specific decision making worthy of note.

To begin with, because the RICO case law is ambiguous or unsettled in so many areas (*see, e.g.*, §§ 7, 9(C), 10, 11(B), 11(D), and 19(A), *supra*), some courts have expressed reticence to impose sanctions for unfounded legal theories except in the clearest of circumstances. *See, e.g., Beeman v. Fiester,* 852 F.2d 206 (7th Cir. 1988) (affirming denial of sanctions because, inter alia, "[t]he pattern of racketeering requirement, as well as most of the other issues raised by [plaintiff's RICO] complaint, involve areas of law that were sufficiently hazy at the time the complaint was filed that it was difficult to determine the exact boundary of the rules"); *Ris v. Bedell,* 699 F. Supp. 429 (S.D.N.Y. 1988) ("Plaintiff . . . filed this suit at a time when this Circuit's RICO jurisprudence was uncertain. Despite the passage of time . . . that uncertainty continues. . . . In light of the still-coalescing RICO case law, and an absence of apparent bad faith on plaintiff's part, the motion for sanctions is denied").

At the same time, many judges are concerned that the availability of treble damages leads to the filing of baseless RICO claims and aggressively impose sanctions for meritless theories or

9. More than 225 pages full of state rules and statutes are collected in J. SOLOVY, L. KASTER, N. HIRSCH & J. THOMPSON, SANCTIONS IN FEDERAL LITIGATION app. A (1991).

groundless assertions. *See, e.g., Katzman v. Victoria's Secret Catalogue,* 167 F.R.D. 649 (S.D.N.Y. 1996), *aff'd mem.,* 113 F.3d 1229 (2d Cir. 1997) ("Rule 11's deterrence value is particularly important in the RICO context, as the commencement of a civil RICO action has 'an almost inevitable stigmatizing effect' on those named as defendants"); *O'Malley v. New York City Transit Auth.,* 896 F.2d 704 (2d Cir. 1990) ("Mere lack of clarity and the general state of some areas of RICO law cannot shield every baseless RICO claim from Rule 11 sanctions"); *Chapman & Cole v. Itel Container Int'l, B.V.,* 865 F.2d 676 (5th Cir.), *cert. denied,* 493 U.S. 872 (1989) ("'Given the resulting proliferation of civil RICO claims and the potential for frivolous suits in search of treble damages, greater responsibility will be placed on the bar to inquire into the factual and legal bases of potential claims or defenses prior to bringing such suit or risk sanctions for failing to do so'").

These two threads of decision are not necessarily inconsistent. Courts can and should take into account the ambiguity of RICO jurisprudence while simultaneously insisting on thorough prefiling investigation of both fact and law as a means of discouraging frivolous or bad-faith RICO lawsuits. *See, e.g., Hartz v. Friedman,* 919 F.2d 469 (7th Cir. 1990) ("Although [Appellate] Rule 38 sanctions may often not be appropriate in RICO cases because there is no clear definition of key terms like 'enterprise' and 'pattern,' in this case the plaintiffs could have had no reasonable expectation of altering the district court's judgment in light of the arguments they made"). Any other rule "would encourage bringing all sorts of groundless RICO claims, in direct contravention of both the language and purpose of amended Rule 11." *O'Malley v. New York City Transit Auth.,* 896 F.2d at 709. It is noteworthy that some of the largest sanctions awards ever rendered have been issued in RICO cases. *See, e.g., Avirgan v. Hull,* 932 F.2d 1572 (11th Cir.), *cert. denied,* 502 U.S. 1048 (1992) (affirming award in excess of $1.1 million); *Brandt v. Schal Assocs., Inc.,* 131 F.R.D. 485 (N.D. Ill. 1990), *aff'd,* 960 F.2d 640 (7th Cir. 1992) (in excess of $350,000).

CHAPTER 8

Statutes of Limitation

§ 27. Duration

Civil RICO actions are subject to a four-year statute of limitations. In *Agency Holding Corp. v. Malley-Duff & Assocs., Inc.*, 483 U.S. 143 (1987), the Supreme Court decided to apply this uniform four-year limitations period primarily because RICO was largely modeled on the Clayton Act, 15 U.S.C. § 15, and a four-year statute is applicable to that statute. The *Agency Holding* Court reasoned that "[t]ogether with the similarities in purpose and structure between RICO and the Clayton Act, the clear legislative intent to pattern RICO's civil enforcement provision on the Clayton Act strongly counsels in favor of application of the 4-year statute of limitations used for Clayton Act claims." *Id.* at 152 ("This is especially true given the lack of any satisfactory state law analogue to RICO").[1]

§ 28. Accrual and Equitable Tolling

Although the Supreme Court has rendered two statute-of-limitations opinions in RICO cases, it has declined to enunciate precisely when a civil RICO claim accrues. In *Agency Holding Corp. v. Malley-Duff & Assocs., Inc.*, 483 U.S. 143 (1987), the Court explicitly did not address any aspect of the accrual issue. 483 U.S. at

1. *Agency Holding Corp.*'s four-year statute of limitations has been applied retroactively. *See, e.g.*, Lund v. Shearson/Lehman/Am. Express, Inc., 852 F.2d 182 (6th Cir. 1988); Jackson v. Bank of Haw., 902 F.2d 1385 (9th Cir. 1990). This result appears dictated by the Supreme Court's subsequent decision in James B. Beam Distilling Co. v. Georgia, 501 U.S. 29 (1991) ("when the Court has applied a rule of law to the litigants in one case it must do so with respect to all others not barred by procedural requirements or res judicata").

156–57. In *Klehr v. A.O. Smith Corp.,* 521 U.S. 179 (1997), the Court rejected the Third Circuit's unique "last predicate act rule" (discussed below) but did not choose between the two competing alternatives in use; nor did it supply an accrual rule of its own. (On March 8, 1999, the Supreme Court granted certiorari in *Rotella v. Wood,* 147 F.3d 438 (5th Cir. 1998), *cert. granted,* 119 S.Ct. 1139 (1999), for the purpose of deciding when a RICO claim accrues.)

In *Klehr v. A.O. Smith Corp.,* 521 U.S. 179 (1997), the Supreme Court did clarify that the doctrine of fraudulent concealment equitably tolls the running of the limitations period in RICO actions (whenever the claim may accrue) if the plaintiff has exercised reasonable diligence in respect of its RICO claim—that is, the period is tolled if and to the extent that the plaintiff shows that it neither knew nor, in the exercise of due diligence, reasonably could have known of the RICO violation.

A. Injury Discovery Rule

The Second Circuit articulated what is, with perhaps some emendation, the majority rule in *Bankers Trust Co. v. Rhoades,* 859 F.2d 1096 (2d Cir. 1988), *cert. denied,* 490 U.S. 1007 (1989). Under the injury discovery rule adumbrated by *Bankers Trust,* "each time a plaintiff suffers an injury caused by a violation of 18 U.S.C. § 1962, a cause of action to recover damages based on that injury accrues to plaintiff at the time he discovered or should have discovered the injury." 859 F.2d at 1102. If at any later date, a new and independent injury is incurred from the same violation, the plaintiff is again "injured in his business or property" within section 1964(c), and the plaintiff's right to sue for damages from that latter injury "accrues at the time he discovered or should have discovered that [later] injury." *Id.* at 1103. A plaintiff "may sue for any injury he discovers or should have discovered within four years of the commencement of his suit, regardless [of] when the RICO violation causing such injury occurred." *Id.,* quoting *State Farm Mut. Auto. Ins. Co. v. Ammann,* 828 F.2d 4 (9th Cir. 1987) ("as to each injury civil RICO limitations period 'begins to run when the plaintiff knows or has reason to know of the injury which is the basis of the action'" (citation omitted)).

The injury discovery rule (sometimes labeled the "simple discovery rule") is also utilized by the First Circuit (*Rodriguez v. Banco Central,* 917 F.2d 664 (1st Cir. 1990)); the Fourth Circuit (*Pocahontas Supreme Coal Co., Inc. v. Bethlehem Steel Corp.,* 828 F.2d 211 (4th Cir. 1987)); the Fifth Circuit (*Rotella v. Wood,* 147 F.3d 438 (5th Cir. 1998), *cert. granted,* 119 S.Ct. 1139 (1999)); the Seventh Circuit (*McCool v. Strata Oil Co.,* 972 F.2d 1452, 1464–1465 (7th Cir.

1992)); and the Ninth Circuit (*Beneficial Standard Life Ins. Co. v. Madariaga*, 851 F.2d 271 (9th Cir. 1988)).

B. Injury/Pattern Discovery Rule

Some courts have identified a perceived, potential problem with the injury discovery rule due to its focus on the injury resulting from each predicate act. At least theoretically, if the second predicate act forming the RICO pattern occurs more than four years after the first, the RICO statute of limitations commencing with the initial injury will have expired prior to the time that the claim ever matured. The Eleventh Circuit addressed this perceived problem in *Bivens Gardens Office Bldg., Inc. v. Barnett Bank of Fla., Inc.*, 906 F.2d 1546 (11th Cir. 1990), by developing the injury/pattern discovery rule. *Bivens Gardens* held that with respect to each independent injury to the plaintiff, "a civil RICO cause of action begins to accrue as soon as the plaintiff discovers, or reasonably should have discovered, both the existence and source of his injury *and* that the injury is part of a pattern." *Id.* at 1554–55 (emphasis added). The Sixth, Eighth, and Tenth Circuits have adopted the *Bivens Gardens* formulation. *See Caproni v. Prudential Secs., Inc.*, 15 F.3d 614 (6th Cir. 1994); *Granite Falls Bank v. Henrikson*, 924 F.2d 150 (8th Cir. 1991); *Bath v. Bushkin, Gaims, Gaines & Jonas*, 913 F.2d 817 (10th Cir. 1990).

C. Last Predicate Act Rule

The Third Circuit had adopted a unique view as to the limitations period, and it was this view that was rejected by the Supreme Court in *Klehr v. A.O. Smith Corp.*, 521 U.S. 179 (1997). Under the Third Circuit's last predicate act rule, the limitations period ordinarily ran from the date on which the plaintiff knew or should have known that the elements of a civil RICO cause of action existed (essentially the injury/pattern discovery rule). However, if (1) the plaintiff later suffered further injury or (2) a further predicate act occurred, "the accrual period [ran] from the time when the plaintiff knew or should have known of the *last injury or the last predicate act* which [wa]s part of the same pattern of racketeering activity." *Keystone Ins. Co. v. Houghton*, 863 F.2d 1125, 1130 (3d Cir. 1988) (emphasis added). Under *Keystone*, if the complaint was filed within four years of the last injury or last predicate act, "the plaintiff may recover for injuries caused by other predicate acts which occurred outside an earlier limitations period but which are part of the same 'pattern.'" *Id.* at 1130–31. Although the Third Circuit's last predicate act rule was not adopted by any other circuit, it was the motivation for the Eleventh Circuit's development of the injury/

pattern discovery rule in *Bivens Gardens,* which has attracted a following in the Sixth, Eighth, and Tenth Circuits, as discussed above.

D. Analysis

There are a number of practical problems with the Eleventh Circuit's injury/pattern discovery rule, all of which parallel problems that existed under the Third Circuit rule rejected in *Klehr.* There is no objective fact—such as injury—that necessarily serves as a benchmark for determining when a plaintiff should reasonably have discovered that its "injury is part of a pattern." *Bivens Gardens,* 906 F.2d at 1555. Accrual runs from the time that the plaintiff knew or should have known "that the injury is part of a pattern." That may be a product of a predicate act that was not directed at, and did not injure, the plaintiff (*see* § 6(B), *supra*). When a plaintiff should have known of the existence of a "pattern" is potentially a difficult question to answer—certainly more difficult than when the plaintiff should have realized that it was injured. Further, the plaintiff's delay in discovering the existence of the pattern may be due to no fault of the defendant, yet the defendant's exposure is extended as a result. Moreover, if the RICO action is commenced within four years of this pattern discovery by the plaintiff, the actionable misconduct may have occurred long before the outer perimeter of the four-year limitations period enunciated in *Agency Holding Corp.*

The Eleventh Circuit (and later the Sixth, Eighth, and Tenth) believed the injury/pattern discovery rule formulated in *Bivens Gardens* to be an improvement over the Second Circuit's simple injury discovery rule because the former avoids the perceived, potential problem that a RICO claim could expire before it matures. However, that problem is likely more apparent than real. If a second predicate act occurs more than four years after the first, there will be a serious question—due to the time lapse alone—whether it is sufficiently "related" to the first to form a pattern (*see* § 11(D)(2)(a), *supra*). In addition, if relatedness and the other elements of a viable RICO claim can be established, the limitations period can be extended even under the simple injury discovery rule by application of the general federal equitable tolling doctrine—which was specifically upheld by the Supreme Court in *Klehr*—provided that the defendant engaged in "fraudulent concealment" and the plaintiff exercised "reasonable diligence" in respect of its claim. *Klehr,* 521 U.S. at 194–95.

The injury discovery rule is the preferred accrual rule for three reasons. First, it is the simplest to apply because it focuses on the plaintiff's actual or constructive discovery of its injury, which is keyed to the objective fact of injury and is readily determinable by a trier of fact. Second, commencement of the limitations period upon occurrence of the first injury does not leave a plaintiff without remedy—just without treble damages until the second predicate act occurs. That is not an unfair result because the defendant has by hypothesis not yet done anything to warrant trebling. (Furthermore, the plaintiff may commence an action for its initial injury, and the discovery afforded in that action may disclose whether the defendant has done something more meriting RICO attention. The liberal amendment of pleadings contemplated by the Federal Rules of Civil Procedure[2] will, in that event, supply the plaintiff with an opportunity to append a RICO claim if one is appropriate.) Third, if the second predicate act in the pattern occurs more than four years after the first, a RICO claim may be stated upon occurrence of the second predicate act, and the plaintiff may recover for all injury it has sustained within the four years preceding the occurrence of the second predicate act, as well as for future damages that are reasonably certain to occur. *See Bankers Trust Co. v. Rhoades,* 859 F.2d at 1103. If the four-year limitations period enunciated in *Agency Holding Corp.* is to be meaningful, it must foreclose recovery for damages occurring more than four years prior to the commencement of the RICO action.[3]

Securities Fraud as Predicate Act: Limitations Impact. As discussed in § 11(C)(2)(b), *supra,* the Private Securities Litigation Reform Act of 1995, Pub. L. 104-67, § 107, amended 18 U.S.C. § 1964(c) to preclude the use of securities fraud as a predicate RICO act unless the defendant has been "criminally convicted in connection with the fraud." Introduction of the criminal-conviction prerequisite to suit raises statute of limitations issues. Because the conviction must, by definition, postdate the occurrence of the RICO offense, the lapse of time preceding conviction will generally eat into—and could conceivably consume all of—the period within which a civil RICO action would otherwise have to be commenced. Congress addressed this issue by amending section 1964(c) to provide further that "the statute of limitations shall start

---

2. Under FED. R. CIV. P. 15, a party ordinarily is granted leave to amend its pleadings unless there is a showing of bad faith, undue delay, prejudice to the opposing party, or futility of amendment. Foman v. Davis, 371 U.S. 178 (1962); California Architectural Bldg. Prods., Inc. v. Franciscan Ceramics, Inc., 818 F.2d 1466 (9th Cir. 1987), *cert. denied,* 484 U.S. 1006 (1988).

3. *But see* Note, *Completing Klehr v. A.O. Smith Corp., and Resolving the Oddity and Lingering Questions of Civil RICO Statute of Limitations Accrual,* 1998 B.Y.U. L.REV. 1273 (advocating injury/pattern discovery rule); Humes, *RICO and a Uniform Rule of Accrual,* 99 YALE L.J. 1399 (1990) (advocating the now-discredited Third Circuit's last predicate act rule as the "optimal rule for accrual of a RICO action").

to run on the date on which the conviction becomes final."[4] That date presumably is no earlier than the date of the court of appeals' mandate (that is, if no petition for certiorari is filed),[5] which will be long after the offense occurred. If a securities fraud represents just one of multiple predicate acts, the statutory language would appear to dictate that the statute of limitations reaccrues on the date the conviction becomes final—even if, considering only the other predicate acts, the period would have accrued at an earlier time (and may even have expired), provided that at least one other predicate act occurred within 10 years of the conviction's having become final. Nothing in the amendment to section 1964(c), however, is directed at, or should affect, the 10-year period contained in the definition of "pattern of racketeering activity" in section 1961(5).

§ 29. Expired Predicate Act Statutes

The statute of limitations for any or all of the predicate offenses constituting the pattern of racketeering activity may be shorter than the four-year statute of limitations that applies to civil RICO claims under the Supreme Court's decision in *Agency Holding Corp. v. Malley-Duff & Assocs., Inc.*, 483 U.S. 143 (1987). If the limitations period for one or all of the predicate acts has expired but four years have not elapsed since the violation, the question arises whether the untimeliness of the predicate acts renders the RICO claim itself untimely. This issue arose with some frequency in rule 10b-5-based RICO cases[6] following the Supreme Court's holding in *Lampf, Pleva, Lipkind, Prupis & Petigrow v. Gilbertson*, 501

4. In full, the PSLRA amended § 1964(c) by appending to the preexisting text:

> except that no person may rely upon any conduct that would have been actionable as fraud in the purchase or sale of securities to establish a violation of section 1962. The exception contained in the preceding sentence does not apply to an action against any person that is criminally convicted in connection with the fraud, in which case the statute of limitations shall start to run on the date on which the conviction becomes final.

5. Using, *e.g.*, habeas precedent as a guide, *compare* Kapral v. United States, 166 F.3d 565 (3d Cir. 1999) (holding that a "judgment of conviction becomes final" for purposes of § 2255 either when the Supreme Court acts by affirming a conviction on its merits or denying certiorari or when the 90-day period for applying for certiorari expires) *with* Gendron v. United States, 154 F.3d 672 (7th Cir. 1998) (holding that § 2255 statute of limitations begins to run when appeals court issues its mandate in the direct appeal if prisoner does not file a certiorari petition).

6. *I.e.*, RICO cases involving as predicates alleged violations of § 10(b) of the Securities Exchange Act of 1934, 15 U.S.C. § 78j(b), and SEC rule 10b-5 promulgated thereunder (collectively "rule 10b-5"). *See generally* § 11(C)(2)(b), *supra*.

U.S. 350 (1991) and prior to enactment of the Private Securities Litigation Reform Act in 1995.[7] The Court decided in *Lampf* that the statute of limitations for civil litigation commenced pursuant to rule 10b-5 expires one year after the discovery of the facts constituting the violation and, in all events, within three years after the violation.

The four-year limitations period governing civil RICO actions is independent of the limitations periods applicable to any or all of the predicate acts. Therefore, expiration of the limitations period for one or more of the predicate acts does not render untimely a RICO claim commenced within four years from the date of the last injury. This rule is not only compelled by *Agency Holding Corp.* but is also dictated by the fact that the predicate acts are criminal violations, not their civil counterparts with whatever attendant procedural baggage they import (*see also* §§ 6(B) and 11(G), *supra*). *Phelps v. Wichita Eagle-Beacon*, 886 F.2d 1262 (10th Cir. 1989) (defendants' contention below that plaintiff's RICO claim was barred by the two-year statute of limitations for fraud rendered "moot" by the Supreme Court's intervening decision in *Agency Holding Corp.* because "the appropriate statute of limitations for civil RICO claims is four years"); *Jensen v. Snellings*, 841 F.2d 600 (5th Cir. 1988) (RICO claim timely even though civil action alleging predicate securities fraud offenses untimely); *Davis v. A.G. Edwards & Sons, Inc.*, 823 F.2d 105 (5th Cir. 1987) (same); *Landy v. Mitchell Petroleum Technology Corp.*, 734 F. Supp. 608 (S.D.N.Y. 1990) (timeliness of RICO claim not inconsistent with untimeliness of predicate securities fraud offenses because RICO accrues at time of actual injury: "The statute of limitations for a securities law violation focuses on the plaintiffs' knowledge of defendants' actions, while the RICO statute of limitations focuses on plaintiffs' knowledge of when they were actually harmed by those actions"); *Helman v. Murry's Steaks, Inc.*, 742 F. Supp. 860 (D. Del. 1990) ("the 10b-5 statute of limitations is not applicable to the securities fraud claim as a predicate act in the context of the RICO claim"). *See also Lundy v. Morgan Stanley & Co.*, 794 F. Supp. 346 (N.D. Cal. 1991).

7. *See* § 11(C)(2)(b), *supra*.

CHAPTER 9

Res Judicata and Collateral Estoppel

§ 30. Generally

Doctrines of claim preclusion and issue preclusion, familiarly known as res judicata and collateral estoppel, apply in RICO actions as in all other cases. RICO litigation raises distinctive issues in light of (1) the two-tiered structure of the statute, under which the RICO violation consists of a pattern of racketeering activity composed of other statutory violations, and (2) the concurrent jurisdiction over RICO claims that exists both in state and federal court (as a result of the Supreme Court's decision in *Tafflin v. Levitt,* 493 U.S. 455 (1990)) and in arbitral as well as judicial fora (*Shearson/American Express, Inc. v. McMahon,* 482 U.S. 220 (1987)).

A. Splitting

If the parties to a RICO action have previously litigated over the facts giving rise to the RICO claim, the prior litigation bars the subsequent RICO claim even if RICO was not invoked in the earlier action. It is the facts surrounding the transaction or occurrence that operate to constitute the "cause of action" for claim-preclusion purposes. New legal theories do not amount to a new cause of action so as to defeat application of the principle of res judicata. *See, e.g., Saud v. Bank of New York,* 929 F.2d 916 (2d Cir. 1991) (RICO plaintiff's assertion of affirmative defense of fraud in a prior contract action brought by the RICO defendant precludes the plaintiff's RICO claim: "it is 'the *factual* predicate of the several claims asserted' that determines whether *res judicata* will apply, not a litigant's ability to devise a new legal theory" (citations omitted; court's emphasis)). *See also* Restatement (Second) of Judgments, §§ 24–25 (1982).[1]

B. Concurrent Jurisdiction

In *Saud,* the prior litigation occurred in federal court. However, the RICO plaintiff is no better off if the prior action has been litigated in state court. Under 28 U.S.C. § 1738, federal courts must give a state court decision the same preclusive effect that decision would have in the state in which it was rendered;[2] *see generally Marrese v. American Academy of Orthopaedic Surgeons,* 470 U.S. 373 (1985) ("§ 1738 requires a federal court to look first to the state preclusion law in determining the preclusive effects of a state court judgment"). Under *Tafflin v. Levitt,* 493 U.S. 455 (1990), RICO claims can be asserted in state court (*see generally* § 4(B), *supra*). Combining these authorities, litigation in state court concerning the operative facts giving rise to the RICO claim precludes subsequent RICO litigation in federal court on those facts, regardless of whether a RICO claim was actually asserted in the original state court action. *See, e.g., Fox v. Maulding,* 112 F.3d 453 (10th Cir 1997) (plaintiffs' "failure to raise the present [RICO] claims as compulsory counterclaims in the [state court] foreclosure action bars their subsequent assertion against . . . [defendant], which was a party to

---

1. Restatement (Second) Of Judgments § 24 provides the following:

(1) When a valid and final judgment rendered in an action extinguishes the plaintiff's claim pursuant to the rules of merger or bar . . . the claim extinguished includes all rights of the plaintiff to remedies against the defendant with respect to all or any part of the transaction, or series of connected transactions, out of which the action arose.

(2) What factual grouping constitutes a "transaction," and what groupings constitute a "series," are to be determined pragmatically, giving weight to such considerations as whether the facts are related in time, space, origin, or motivation, whether they form a convenient trial unit, and whether their treatment as a unit conforms to the parties' expectations or business understanding or usage.

Restatement (Second) Of Judgments § 25 provides that [t]he Rule of § 24 applies to extinguish a claim by the plaintiff against the defendant even though the plaintiff is prepared in a second action (1) to present evidence or grounds or theories of the case not presented in the first action, or (2) to seek remedies or forms of relief not demanded in the first action."

2. 28 U.S.C. § 1738 provides, in part, the following:

The records and judicial proceedings of any court of any . . . State . . . shall be proved and admitted in other courts within the United States . . . by the attestation of the clerk and seal of the Court annexed, if a seal exists, together with a certificate of a judge of the court that the said attestation is in proper form.
Such . . . records and judicial proceedings or copies thereof, so authenticated, shall have the same full faith and credit in every court within the United States . . . as they have by law or usage in the courts of such State . . . from which they are taken.

that action, and against those in privity with [defendant]"); *Evans v. Dale*, 896 F.2d 975 (5th Cir. 1990) (res judicata); *Aries Realty, Inc. v. AGS Columbia Assocs.*, 751 F. Supp. 444 (S.D.N.Y. 1990) (collateral estoppel); *Resource N.E. of L.I., Inc. v. Verifacts Group, Inc.*, 28 F. Supp. 2d 786 (E.D.N.Y. 1998) (recognizing applicability of res judicata doctrine but finding no claim preclusion on the facts).

If a RICO claim is premised on certain facts or legal conclusions that have been adjudicated adversely to the RICO plaintiff in state court, collateral estoppel bars the plaintiff from relitigating those issues "by recasting his allegations as a federal RICO claim." *Polur v. Raffe*, 912 F.2d 52, 56 (2d Cir. 1990), *cert. denied*, 499 U.S. 37 1389 (1991). This result emphatically obtains when the predicate acts themselves were the subject of litigation in the prior state court actions. *See, e.g., Original Brass Rail Restaurants, Inc v. Firman*, 919 F.2d 136, 1990 U.S. App. LEXIS 19546 (3d Cir. Oct. 24, 1990) (unpublished opinion). *See generally* Restatement (Second) of Judgments §§ 27, 29 (1982).

C. Arbitration

Arbitration between the same parties over the same facts similarly precludes subsequent RICO litigation (1) where the arbitrators were empowered by the parties to entertain the RICO claims, since RICO claims are arbitrable under *Shearson/American Express, Inc. v. McMahon*, 482 U.S. 220 (1987) (*see generally* § 4(E), (*supra*)), and (2) even where the arbitrators are not so empowered if the factual predicates of the RICO claim have been "fully litigated and necessarily determined" in the arbitration. *Central Transp., Inc. v. Four Phase Sys., Inc.*, 936 F.2d 256 (6th Cir. 1991) (collateral estoppel applied where, "[w]hile the arbitration panel did not resolve the legal claims of misrepresentation, interference and civil RICO, the panel decided essential, underlying facts of these claims"); *accord Greenblatt v. Drexel Burnham Lambert, Inc.*, 763 F.2d 1352 (11th Cir. 1985); *see generally United States v. Stauffer Chem. Co.*, 464 U.S. 165 (1984), and *Parklane Hosiery Co. v. Shore*, 439 U.S. 322 (1979).

D. Bankruptcy Court

Unique questions are raised when the prior adjudication has occurred in bankruptcy court, since that tribunal is an Article I rather than an Article III court. The Fifth and Seventh Circuits have declined to bar subsequent RICO claims on jurisdictional grounds despite prior bankruptcy court litigation. Specifically, they have held that the bankruptcy court has no jurisdiction over the RICO claims because they are not "core proceedings" within the meaning of 28 U.S.C. § 157. *See Howell Hydrocarbons, Inc. v.*

Adams, 897 F.2d 183 (5th Cir. 1990) (no res judicata effect barring a creditor seeking to assert RICO claim against certain principals of the debtor's parent corporation); *Barnett v. Stern*, 909 F.2d 973 (7th Cir. 1990) (no res judicata effect barring bankruptcy trustee from bringing a RICO action against debtor). These decisions are dependent upon the courts' views concerning the proper scope of "core proceedings" within the meaning of section 157, and that issue is unresolved by the Supreme Court. *See In re Ben Cooper, Inc.*, 896 F.2d 1394 (2d Cir.), *cert. granted*, 497 U.S. 1023, *cert. vacated*, 498 U.S. 964 (1990) (involving review of a Second Circuit decision that generally espouses a broad interpretation of court proceedings, in conflict with the *Howell* and *Barnett* opinions). Independent of the jurisdictional issue, query exists whether the Fifth and Seventh Circuit approach should apply to the extent that the bankruptcy court adjudicates the factual predicates of the RICO claim in disputes over which it clearly has jurisdiction.

Chapter 10

Constitutionality

§ 31. Overview

In *H.J. Inc. v. Northwestern Bell Tel. Co.*, 492 U.S. 229 (1989), Justice Scalia filed a concurrence strongly suggesting that the pattern element of the RICO statute is unconstitutionally void for vagueness:

> Four terms ago, in *Sedima, S.P.R.L. v. Imrex Co.*, 473 U.S. 479 (1985), we gave the lower courts . . . four clues concerning the meaning of the enigmatic term "pattern of racketeering activity." . . . Today, four years and countless millions in damages and attorney's fees later (not to mention prison sentences under the criminal provisions of RICO), the Court does little more than repromulgate those hints as to what RICO means, though with the caveat that Congress intended that they be applied using a "flexible approach." . . .
>
> Today's opinion has added nothing to improve our prior guidance, which has created a kaleidoscope of circuit positions, except to clarify that RICO may in addition be violated when there is a "thread of continuity." It seems to me this increases rather than removes the vagueness.

492 U.S. at 251, 255–56 ("No constitutional challenge to this law has been raised in the present case. . . . That the highest Court in the land has been unable to derive from the statute anything more than today's meager guidance bodes ill for the day when that challenge is presented").

Justice Scalia's concurrence was joined by Chief Justice Rehnquist and Justices O'Connor and Kennedy. Since *H.J. Inc.* was decided, four of the five members of the *H.J.* majority (Justices Blackmun, Brennan, Marshall, and White) have retired, and it is possible that some of their replacements (Justices Breyer, Ginsburg, Souter, and Thomas) might share the Scalia concurrence's viewpoint.

Since *H.J. Inc.* was decided, however, every court of appeals to be confronted with the issue has determined that RICO is not impermissibly void for vagueness. These holdings have been rendered in both civil and criminal contexts and have focused not only on the pattern element but on the enterprise requirement as well. *See, e.g., United States v. Keltner*, 147 F.3d 662 (8th Cir.), *cert. denied*, 119 S.Ct. 574 (1998) (enterprise and pattern); *Columbia Natural Resources, Inc. v. Tatum*, 58 F.3d 1101 (6th Cir. 1995), *cert. denied*,

516 U.S. 1158 (1996) (pattern, as applied); *Cox v. Administrator,* 17 F.3d 1386 (11th Cir. 1994), *cert. denied,* 513 U.S. 1110 (1995) (undefined vagueness challenge); *United States v. Freeman,* 6 F.3d 586 (9th Cir. 1993), *cert. denied,* 511 U.S. 1147 (1994) (enterprise, as applied); *Abell v. Potomac Ins. Co. of Ill.,* 946 F.2d 1160 (5th Cir. 1991), *cert. denied,* 504 U.S. 911 (1992) (pattern); *United States v. Coonan,* 938 F.2d 1553 (2d Cir. 1991), *cert. denied,* 503 U.S. 941 (1992) (enterprise); *United States v. Masters,* 924 F.2d 1362 (7th Cir.), *cert. denied,* 500 U.S. 919 (1991) (pattern and enterprise); *United States v. Glecier,* 923 F.2d 496 (7th Cir.), *cert. denied,* 502 U.S. 810 (1991) (undefined challenge; evidently to pattern); *United States v. Coiro,* 922 F.2d 1008 (2d Cir.), *cert. denied,* 501 U.S. 1217 (1991) (pattern); *United States v. Woods,* 915 F.2d 854 (3d Cir. 1990), *cert. denied,* 499 U.S. 947 (1991) (pattern); *United States v. Pungitore,* 910 F.2d 1084 (3d Cir. 1990), *cert. denied,* 500 U.S. 915 (1991) (pattern); *United States v. Angiulo,* 897 F.2d 1169 (1st Cir.), *cert. denied,* 111 S. Ct. 130 (1990) (pattern); *United States v. Van Dorn,* 925 F.2d 1331 (11th Cir. 1991) (unspecified challenge; summarily dismissed as "completely lacking in merit").

A few district judges have proved, in varying degrees, receptive to the constitutional challenge invited by Justice Scalia. *See Firestone v. Galbreath,* 747 F. Supp. 1556 (S.D. Ohio 1990), *aff'd on other grounds,* 976 F.2d 279 (6th Cir. 1992) (pattern requirement unconstitutionally vague on its face and as applied); *Levin-Richmond Terminal Corp. v. International Longshoremen's & Warehousemen's Union Local 10,* 751 F. Supp. 1373 (N.D. Cal. 1990) (denying motion to strike unconstitutionality defense on grounds it raised "a substantial legal question"). The trend of district court decisions, however, has been overwhelmingly to the contrary. Commentators have similarly been disposed to conclude that the statute is not unconstitutionally void for vagueness. *See, e.g.,* Note, *RICO's "Pattern" Requirement: Void for Vagueness?,* 90 Colum. L. Rev. 489 (1989); Note, *"Mother of Mercy—Is This the End of RICO?"—Justice Scalia Invites Constitutional Void-for-Vagueness Challenge to RICO "Pattern" Again,* 65 Notre Dame L. Rev. 1106 (1990). *But see* Freman & McSlarrow, *RICO and the Due Process "Void for Vagueness" Test,* 45 Bus. Law. 1003 (1990).

The view that the statute is constitutional accords with the Supreme Court's validation of an Indiana state RICO statute in *Fort Wayne Books, Inc. v. Indiana,* 489 U.S. 46 (1989), which was decided four months before *H.J. Inc.* In *Fort Wayne Books,* the Supreme Court rejected a constitutional challenge to a statutory definition of "pattern of racketeering activity" substantially similar to section 1961(5). The court held that the statutory requirement of a "pattern" rendered the state "RICO statute . . . inherently *less* vague" than the underlying state obscenity laws.

489 U.S. at 58–59 n.7. On one reading, *Fort Wayne Books* requires a preliminary finding that the statutes criminalizing the predicate acts are unconstitutionally vague before a challenge can successfully be mounted to the pattern requirement. *See United States v. Masters,* 924 F.2d at 1367; Barsoomian, *RICO "Pattern" Before and After H.J. Inc.: A Proposed Definition,* 40 Am. U.L. Rev. 919, 936–37 (1991). Only two Justices (Brennan and Stevens) took any issue with the RICO holding, and their concerns related to the obscenity predicate acts. *See* 489 U.S. at 70–86 (opinion of Stevens, J.). Both of those Justices voted in the majority (not with Justice Scalia's concurrence) in *H.J. Inc.*

Notwithstanding *Fort Wayne Books*[1] and the trend of lower court decisions, one or more elements of the RICO statute may be unconstitutional as applied. Outside the First Amendment context, a party has standing to raise a vagueness challenge only insofar as the statute is vague as applied to his or her specific conduct. *New York v. Ferber,* 458 U.S. 747 (1982). Various aspects of the RICO Act, including but not limited to the pattern element, are the subject of imprecise or conflicting interpretations by the courts. These include, inter alia, (i) what it means to "conduct or participate . . . in the conduct" of (*that is,* operate or manage) an enterprise within section 1962(c) (*see* § 9(C), *supra*) and (ii) what constitutes a RICO "enterprise" within section 1961(4) (*see* § 11(A), *supra*). *See also* Reed, *The Defense Case for RICO Reform,* 43 Vand. L. Rev. 691 (1990).

For a number of reasons, it may be more likely that the statute will be found unconstitutional, as applied, in a civil rather than in a criminal case. First, the criminal cases in which constitutionality has been adjudicated have frequently been organized crime or public corruption prosecutions. There is no serious doubt that the participants were on notice that their behavior was criminal. The vast preponderance of civil cases has nothing to do with organized crime or glaring criminality. Second, prosecutors are required to prove the predicate acts, and the RICO offense as a whole, beyond a reasonable doubt. That tends to produce records on appeal inhospitable to a successful constitutional challenge—and provokes a substantial amount of prefiling scrutiny and culling, that is lacking in civil cases. Third, the imaginativeness of plaintiffs' counsel—in characterizing conduct as violative of predicate-offense statutes, in fashioning novel enterprises, and in conceiving creative patterns—may lead to situations in which defendants are

1. Fairly read, *Fort Wayne Books* is essentially an obscenity decision (obscenity offenses served as the predicate acts), and attention was directed primarily to First Amendment issues.

literally without a clue that their behavior might have violated the RICO statute (except in the general sense that everyone is aware of the extreme litigiousness of our society). Finally, specific civil applications of RICO may run afoul of particular constitutional guarantees (e.g., the First Amendment). *See also* Rakoff, *The Unconstitutionality of RICO,* N.Y.L.J., Jan. 11, 1990, at 3, col. 1.

Appendix

Racketeer Influenced and Corrupt Organizations Act, 18 U.S.C. §§ 1961–68

§ 1961. Definitions

As used in this chapter—

(1) "Racketeering activity" means (A) any act or threat involving murder, kidnapping, gambling, arson, robbery, bribery, extortion, dealing in obscene matter, or dealing in a controlled substance or listed chemical (as defined in section 102 of the Controlled Substances Act), which is chargeable under state law and punishable by imprisonment for more than one year; (B) any act that is indictable under any of the following provisions of title 18, United States Code: Section 201 (relating to bribery), section 224 (relating to sports bribery), sections 471, 472, and 473 (relating to counterfeiting), section 659 (relating to theft from interstate shipment) if the act indictable under section 659 is felonious, section 664 (relating to embezzlement from pension and welfare funds), sections 891–894 (relating to extortionate credit transactions), section 1029 (relating to fraud and related activity in connection with access devices), section 1084 (relating to the transmission of gambling information), section 1341 (relating to mail fraud), section 1343 (relating to wire fraud), section 1344 (relating to financial institution fraud), section 1425 (relating to the procurement of citizenship or nationalization unlawfully), section 1426 (relating to the reproduction of naturalization or citizenship papers), section 1427 (relating to the sale of naturalization or citizenship papers), sections 1461–1465 (relating to obscene matter), section 1503 (relating to obstruction of justice), section 1510 (relating to obstruction of criminal investigations), section 1511 (relating to the obstruction of state or local law enforcement), section 1512 (relating to tampering with a witness, victim, or an informant), section 1513 (relating

to retaliating against a witness, victim, or an informant), section 1542 (relating to false statement in application and use of passport), section 1543 (relating to forgery or false use of passport), section 1544 (relating to misuse of passport), section 1546 (relating to fraud and misuse of visas, permits, and other documents), sections 1581–88 (relating to peonage and slavery), section 1951 (relating to interference with commerce, robbery, or extortion), section 1952 (relating to racketeering), section 1953 (relating to interstate transportation of wagering paraphernalia), section 1954 (relating to unlawful welfare fund payments), section 1955 (relating to the prohibition of illegal gambling businesses), section 1956 (relating to the laundering of monetary instruments), section 1957 (relating to engaging in monetary transactions in property derived from specified unlawful activity), section 1958 (relating to use of interstate commerce facilities in the commission of murder-for-hire), sections 2251, 2251A, 2252, and 2260 (relating to sexual exploitation of children), sections 2312 and 2313 (relating to interstate transportation of stolen motor vehicles), sections 2314 and 2315 (relating to interstate transportation of stolen property), section 2318 (relating to trafficking in counterfeit labels for phonorecords, computer programs, or computer program documentation or packaging and copies of motion pictures or other audiovisual works), section 2319 (relating to criminal infringement of a copyright), section 2319A (relating to unauthorized fixation of and trafficking in sound recordings and music videos of live musical performances), section 2320 (relating to trafficking in goods or services bearing counterfeit marks), section 2321 (relating to trafficking in certain motor vehicles or motor vehicle parts), sections 2341–2346 (relating to trafficking in contraband cigarettes), sections 2421–24 (relating to white slave traffic); (C) any act that is indictable under title 29, United States Code, section 186 (dealing with restrictions on payments and loans to labor organizations) or section 501(c) (relating to embezzlement from union funds); (D) any offense involving fraud connected with a case under title 11, fraud in the sale of securities, or the felonious manufacture, importation, receiving, concealment, buying, selling, or otherwise dealing in a controlled substance or listed chemical (as defined in section 102 of the Controlled Substances Act), punishable under any law of the United States; or (E) any act that is indictable under the Currency and Foreign Transactions Reporting Act;

(2) "state" means any State of the United States, the District of Columbia, the Commonwealth of Puerto Rico, any territory or possession of the United States, any political subdivision, or any department, agency, or instrumentality thereof;

(3) "person" includes any individual or entity capable of holding a legal or beneficial interest in property;

(4) "enterprise" includes any individual, partnership, corporation, association, or other legal entity, and any union or group of individuals associated in fact although not a legal entity;

(5) "pattern of racketeering activity" requires at least two acts of racketeering activity, one of which occurred after the effective date of this chapter and the last of which occurred within ten years (excluding any period of imprisonment) after the commission of a prior act of racketeering activity;

(6) "unlawful debt" means a debt (A) incurred or contracted in gambling activity which was in violation of the law of the United States, a State, or political subdivision thereof, or which is unenforceable under State or Federal law in whole or in part as to principal or interest because of the laws relating to usury, and (B) which was incurred in connection with the business of gambling in violation of the law of the United States, a state, or political subdivision thereof or the business of lending money or a thing of value at a rate usurious under State or Federal law, where the usurious rate is at least twice the enforceable rate;

(7) "racketeering investigator" means any lawyer or investigator so designated by the Attorney General and charged with the duty of enforcing or carrying into effect this chapter;

(8) "racketeering investigation" means any inquiry conducted by any racketeering investigator for the purpose of ascertaining whether any person has been involved in any violation of this chapter or of any final order, judgment, or decree of any court of the United States, duly entered in any case or proceeding arising under this chapter;

(9) "documentary material" includes any book, paper, document, record, recording, or other material; and

(10) "Attorney General" includes the Attorney General of the United States, the Deputy Attorney General of the United States, the Associate Attorney General of the United States, any Assistant Attorney General of the United States, or any employee of the Department of Justice, or any employee of any department or agency of the United States so designated by the Attorney General to carry out the powers conferred on the Attorney General by this chapter. Any department or agency so designated may use in investigations authorized by this chapter either the investigative provisions of this chapter or the investigative power of such department or agency otherwise conferred by law.

§ 1962. Prohibited Activities

(a) It shall be unlawful for any person who has received any income derived, directly or indirectly, from a pattern of racketeering activity or through collection of an unlawful debt in which such person has participated as a principal within the meaning of section 2, title 18, United States Code, to use or invest, directly or indirectly, any part of such income, or the proceeds of such income, in acquisition of any interest in, or the establishment or operation of, any enterprise that is engaged in, or the activities of which affect, interstate or foreign commerce. A purchase of securities on the open market for purposes of investment, and without the intention of controlling or participating in the control of the issuer, or of assisting another to do so, shall not be unlawful under this subsection if the securities of the issuer held by the purchaser, the members of his immediate family, and his or their accomplices in any pattern or [of] racketeering activity or the collection of an unlawful debt after such purchase do not amount in the aggregate to 1 percent of the outstanding securities of any one class, and do not confer, either in law or in fact, the power to elect one or more directors of the issuer.

(b) It shall be unlawful for any person through a pattern of racketeering activity or through collection of an unlawful debt to acquire or maintain, directly or indirectly, any interest in or control of any enterprise that is engaged in, or the activities of which affect, interstate or foreign commerce.

(c) It shall be unlawful for any person employed by or associated with any enterprise engaged in, or the activities of which affect, interstate or foreign commerce, to conduct or participate, directly or indirectly, in the conduct of such enterprise's affairs through a pattern of racketeering activity or collection of unlawful debt.

(d) It shall be unlawful for any person to conspire to violate any of the provisions of subsection (a), (b), or (c) of this section.

§ 1963. Criminal Penalties

(a) Whoever violates any provision of section 1962 of this chapter shall be fined under this title or imprisoned not more than 20 years (or for life if the violation is based on a racketeering activity for which the maximum penalty includes life imprisonment), or both, and shall forfeit to the United States, irrespective of any provision of State law—

(1) any interest the person has acquired or maintained in violation of section 1962;

(2) any—

(A) interest in;

(B) security of;

(C) claim against; or

(D) property or contractual right of any kind affording a source of influence over;

any enterprise that the person has established, operated, controlled, conducted, or participated in the conduct of, in violation of section 1962; and

(3) any property constituting, or derived from, any proceeds that the person obtained, directly or indirectly, from racketeering activity or unlawful debt collection in violation of section 1962.

The court, in imposing sentence on such person shall order, in addition to any other sentence imposed pursuant to this section, that the person forfeit to the United States all property described in this subsection. In lieu of a fine otherwise authorized by this section, a defendant who derives profits or other proceeds from an offense may be fined not more than twice the gross profits or other proceeds.

(b) Property subject to criminal forfeiture under this section includes—

(1) real property including things growing on, affixed to, and found in land; and

(2) tangible and intangible personal property, including rights, privileges, interests, claims, and securities.

(c) All right, title, and interest in property described in subsection (a) vests in the United States upon the commission of the act giving rise to forfeiture under this section. Any such property that is subsequently transferred to a person other than the defendant may be the subject of a special verdict of forfeiture and thereafter shall be ordered forfeited to the United States, unless the transferee establishes in a hearing pursuant to subsection (l) that he is a bona fide purchaser for value of such property who at the time of purchase was reasonably without cause to believe that the property was subject to forfeiture under this section.

(d)(1) Upon application of the United States, the court may enter a restraining order or injunction, require the execution of a satisfactory performance bond, or take any other action to preserve the availability of property described in subsection (a) for forfeiture under this section—

(A) upon the filing of an indictment or information charging a violation of section 1962 of this chapter and alleging that the property with respect to which the order is sought would, in the event of conviction, be subject to forfeiture under this section; or

(B) prior to the filing of such an indictment or information, if, after notice to persons appearing to have an interest in the property and opportunity for a hearing, the court determines that—

(i) there is a substantial probability that the United States will prevail on the issue of forfeiture and that failure to enter the order will result in the property being destroyed, removed from the jurisdiction of the court, or otherwise made unavailable for forfeiture; and

(ii) the need to preserve the availability of the property through the entry of the requested order outweighs the hardship on any party against whom the order is to be entered:

Provided, however, that an order entered pursuant to subparagraph (B) shall be effective for not more than ninety days, unless extended by the court for good cause shown or unless an indictment or information described in subparagraph (A) has been filed.

(2) A temporary restraining order under this subsection may be entered upon application of the United States without notice or opportunity for a hearing when an information or indictment has not yet been filed with respect to the property, if the United States demonstrates that there is probable cause to believe that the property with respect to which the order is sought would, in the event of conviction, be subject to forfeiture under this section and that provision of notice will jeopardize the availability of the property for forfeiture. Such a temporary order shall expire not more than ten days after the date on which it is entered, unless extended for good cause shown or unless the party against whom it is entered consents to an extension for a longer period. A hearing requested concerning an order entered under this paragraph shall be held at the earliest possible time, and prior to the expiration of the temporary order.

(3) The court may receive and consider, at a hearing held pursuant to this subsection, evidence and information that would be inadmissible under the Federal Rules of Evidence.

(e) Upon conviction of a person under this section, the court shall enter a judgment of forfeiture of the property to the United States and shall also authorize the Attorney General to seize all property ordered forfeited upon such terms and conditions as the court shall deem proper. Following the entry of an order declaring the property forfeited, the court may, upon application of the United States, enter such appropriate restraining orders or injunctions, require the execution of satisfactory performance bonds, appoint receivers, conservators, appraisers, accountants, or trustees, or take any other action to protect the interest of the United States in the property ordered forfeited. Any income accruing to, or derived from, an enterprise or an interest in an enterprise which has been ordered forfeited under this section may be used to offset ordinary and necessary expenses to the enterprise which are required by law, or which are necessary to protect the interests of the United States or third parties.

(f) Following the seizure of property ordered forfeited under this section, the Attorney General shall direct the disposition of the property by sale or any other commercially feasible means, making due provision for the rights of any innocent persons. Any property right or interest not exercisable by, or transferable for value to, the United States shall expire and shall not revert to the defendant, nor shall the defendant or any person acting in concert with or on behalf of the defendant be eligible to purchase forfeited property at any sale held by the United States. Upon application of a person, other than the defendant or a person acting in concert with or on behalf of the defendant, the court may restrain or stay the sale or disposition of the property pending the conclusion of any appeal of the criminal case giving rise to the forfeiture, if the applicant demonstrates that proceeding with the sale or disposition of the property will result in irreparable injury, harm, or loss to him. Notwithstanding 31 U.S.C. 3302(b), the proceeds of any sale or other disposition of property forfeited under this section and any moneys forfeited shall be used to pay all proper expenses for the forfeiture and the sale, including expenses of seizure, maintenance, and custody of the property pending its disposition, advertising, and court costs. The Attorney General shall deposit in the Treasury any amounts of such proceeds or moneys remaining after the payment of such expenses.

(g) With respect to property ordered forfeited under this section, the Attorney General is authorized to—

(1) grant petitions for mitigation or remission of forfeiture, restore forfeited property to victims of a violation of this chapter, or take any other action to protect the rights of innocent persons which is in the interest of justice and which is not inconsistent with the provisions of this chapter;

(2) compromise claims arising under this section;

(3) award compensation to persons providing information resulting in a forfeiture under this section;

(4) direct the disposition by the United States of all property ordered forfeited under this section by public sale or any other commercially feasible means, making due provision for the rights of innocent persons; and

(5) take appropriate measures necessary to safeguard and maintain property ordered forfeited under this section pending its disposition.

(h) The Attorney General may promulgate regulations with respect to—

(1) making reasonable efforts to provide notice to persons who may have an interest in property ordered forfeited under this section;

(2) granting petitions for remission or mitigation of forfeiture;

(3) the restitution of property to victims of an offense petitioning for remission or mitigation of forfeiture under this chapter;

(4) the disposition by the United States of forfeited property by public sale or other commercially feasible means;

(5) the maintenance and safekeeping of any property forfeited under this section pending its disposition; and

(6) the compromise of claims arising under this chapter.

Pending the promulgation of such regulations, all provisions of law relating to the disposition of property, or the proceeds from the sale thereof, or the remission or mitigation of forfeitures for violation of the customs laws, and the compromise of claims and the award of compensation to informers in respect of such forfeitures shall apply to forfeitures incurred, or alleged to have been incurred, under the provisions of this section, insofar as applicable and not inconsistent with the provisions hereof. Such duties as are imposed upon the Customs Service or any person with respect to the disposition of property under the customs law shall be performed under this chapter by the Attorney General.

(i) Except as provided in subsection (l), no party claiming an interest in property subject to forfeiture under this section may—

(1) intervene in a trial or appeal of a criminal case involving the forfeiture of such property under this section; or

(2) commence an action at law or equity against the United States concerning the validity of his alleged interest in the property subsequent to the filing of an indictment or infor-

mation alleging that the property is subject to forfeiture under this section.

(j) The district courts of the United States shall have jurisdiction to enter orders as provided in this section without regard to the location of any property that may be subject to forfeiture under this section or that has been ordered forfeited under this section.

(k) In order to facilitate the identification or location of property declared forfeited and to facilitate the disposition of petitions for remission or mitigation of forfeiture, after the entry of an order declaring property forfeited to the United States the court may, upon application of the United States, order that the testimony of any witness relating to the property forfeited be taken by deposition and that any designated book, paper, document, record, recording, or other material not privileged be produced at the same time and place, in the same manner as provided for the taking of depositions under Rule 15 of the Federal Rules of Criminal Procedure.

(l) (1) Following the entry of an order of forfeiture under this section, the United States shall publish notice of the order and of its intent to dispose of the property in such manner as the Attorney General may direct. The Government may also, to the extent practicable, provide direct written notice to any person known to have alleged an interest in the property that is the subject of the order of forfeiture as a substitute for published notice as to those persons so notified.

(2) Any person, other than the defendant, asserting a legal interest in property that has been ordered forfeited to the United States pursuant to this section may, within thirty days of the final publication of notice or his receipt of notice under paragraph (1), whichever is earlier, petition the court for a hearing to adjudicate the validity of his alleged interest in the property. The hearing shall be held before the court alone, without a jury.

(3) The petition shall be signed by the petitioner under penalty of perjury and shall set forth the nature and extent of the petitioner's right, title, or interest in the property, the time and circumstances of the petitioner's acquisition of the right, title, or interest in the property, any additional facts supporting the petitioner's claim, and the relief sought.

(4) The hearing on the petition shall, to the extent practicable and consistent with the interests of justice, be held within thirty days of the filing of the petition. The court may consolidate the hearing on the petition with a hearing on any other

petition filed by a person other than the defendant under this subsection.

(5) At the hearing, the petitioner may testify and present evidence and witnesses on his own behalf, and cross-examine witnesses who appear at the hearing. The United States may present evidence and witnesses in rebuttal and in defense of its claim to the property and cross-examine witnesses who appear at the hearing. In addition to testimony and evidence presented at the hearing, the court shall consider the relevant portions of the record of the criminal case that resulted in the order of forfeiture.

(6) If, after the hearing, the court determines that the petitioner has established by a preponderance of the evidence that—

(A) the petitioner has a legal right, title, or interest in the property, and such right, title, or interest renders the order of forfeiture invalid in whole or in part because the right, title, or interest was vested in the petitioner rather than the defendant or was superior to any right, title, or interest of the defendant at the time of the commission of the acts that gave rise to the forfeiture of the property under this section; or

(B) the petitioner is a bona fide purchaser for value of the right, title, or interest in the property and was at the time of purchase reasonably without cause to believe that the property was subject to forfeiture under this section; the court shall amend the order of forfeiture in accordance with its determination.

(7) Following the court's disposition of all petitions filed under this subsection, or if no such petitions are filed following the expiration of the period provided in paragraph (2) for the filing of such petitions, the United States shall have clear title to property that is the subject of the order of forfeiture and may warrant good title to any subsequent purchaser or transferee.

(m) If any of the property described in subsection (a), as a result of any act or omission of the defendant—

(1) cannot be located upon the exercise of due diligence;

(2) has been transferred or sold to, or deposited with, a third party;

(3) has been placed beyond the jurisdiction of the court;

(4) has been substantially diminished in value; or

(5) has been commingled with other property which cannot be divided without difficulty;

the court shall order the forfeiture of any other property of the defendant up to the value of any property described in paragraphs (1) through (5).

§ 1964. Civil Remedies

(a) The district courts of the United States shall have jurisdiction to prevent and restrain violations of section 1962 of this chapter by issuing appropriate orders, including, but not limited to: ordering any person to divest himself of any interest, direct or indirect, in any enterprise; imposing reasonable restrictions on the future activities or investments of any person, including, but not limited to, prohibiting any person from engaging in the same type of endeavor as the enterprise engaged in, the activities of which affect interstate or foreign commerce; or ordering dissolution or reorganization of any enterprise, making due provision for the rights of innocent persons.

(b) The Attorney General may institute proceedings under this section. Pending final determination thereof, the court may at any time enter such restraining orders or prohibitions, or take such other actions, including the acceptance of satisfactory performance bonds, as it shall deem proper.

(c) Any person injured in his business or property by reason of a violation of section 1962 of this chapter may sue therefor in any appropriate United States district court and shall recover threefold the damages he sustains and the cost of the suit, including a reasonable attorney's fee, except that no person may rely upon any conduct that would have been actionable as fraud in the purchase or sale of securities to establish a violation of section 1962. The exception contained in the preceding sentence does not apply to an action against any person that is criminally convicted in connection with the fraud, in which case the statute of limitations shall start to run on the date on which the conviction becomes final.

(d) A final judgment or decree rendered in favor of the United States in any criminal proceeding brought by the United States under this chapter shall estop the defendant from denying the essential allegations of the criminal offense in any subsequent civil proceeding brought by the United States.

§1965. Venue and Process

(a) Any civil action or proceeding under this chapter against any person may be instituted in the district court of the United

States for any district in which such person resides, is found, has an agent, or transacts his affairs.

(b) In any action under section 1964 of this chapter in any district court of the United States in which it is shown that the ends of justice require that other parties residing in any other district be brought before the court, the court may cause such parties to be summoned, and process for that purpose may be served in any judicial district of the United States by the marshal thereof.

(c) In any civil or criminal action or proceeding instituted by the United States under this chapter in the district court of the United States for any judicial district, subpoenas issued by such court to compel the attendance of witnesses may be served in any other judicial district, except that in any civil action or proceeding no such subpoena shall be issued for service upon any individual who resides in another district at a place more than one hundred miles from the place at which such court is held without approval given by a judge of such court upon a showing of good cause.

(d) All other process in any action or proceeding under this chapter may be served on any person in any judicial district in which such person resides, is found, has an agent, or transacts his affairs.

§ 1966. Expedition of Actions

In any civil action instituted under this chapter by the United States in any district court of the United States, the Attorney General may file with the clerk of such court a certificate stating that in his opinion the case is of general public importance. A copy of that certificate shall be furnished immediately by such clerk to the chief judge or in his absence to the presiding district judge of the district in which such action is pending. Upon receipt of such copy, such judge shall designate immediately a judge of that district to hear and determine action.

§ 1967. Evidence

In any proceeding ancillary to or in any civil action instituted by the United States under this chapter the proceedings may be open or closed to the public at the discretion of the court after consideration of the rights of affected persons.

§ 1968. Civil Investigative Demand

(a) Whenever the Attorney General has reason to believe that any person or enterprise may be in possession, custody, or control of any documentary materials relevant to a racketeering investigation, he may, prior to the institution of a civil or criminal proceeding thereon, issue in writing, and cause to be served upon such person, a civil investigative demand requiring such person to produce such material for examination.

(b) Each such demand shall—

(1) state the nature of the conduct constituting the alleged racketeering violation which is under investigation and the provision of law applicable thereto;

(2) describe the class or classes of documentary material produced thereunder with such definiteness and certainty as to permit such material to be fairly identified;

(3) state that the demand is returnable forthwith or prescribe a return date that will provide a reasonable period of time within which the material so demanded may be assembled and made available for inspection and copying or reproduction; and

(4) identify the custodian to whom such material shall be made available.

(c) No such demand shall—

(1) contain any requirement that would be held to be unreasonable if contained in a subpoena *duces tecum* issued by a court of the United States in aid of a grand jury investigation of such alleged racketeering violation; or

(2) require the production of any documentary evidence that would be privileged from disclosure if demanded by a subpoena *duces tecum* issued by a court of the United States in aid of a grand jury investigation of such alleged racketeering violation.

(d) Service of any such demand or any petition filed under this section may be made upon a person by—

(1) delivering a duly executed copy thereof to any partner, executive officer, managing agent, or general agent thereof, or to any agent thereof authorized by appointment or by law to receive service of process on behalf of such person, or upon any individual person;

(2) delivering a duly executed copy thereof to the principal office or place of business of the person to be served; or

(3) depositing such copy in the United States mail, by registered or certified mail duly addressed to such person at its principal office or place of business.

(e) A verified return by the individual serving any such demand or petition setting forth the manner of such service shall be prima facie proof of such service. In the case of service by registered or certified mail, such return shall be accompanied by the return post office receipt of delivery of such demand.

(f) (1) The Attorney General shall designate a racketeering investigator to serve as racketeer document custodian, and such additional racketeering investigators as he shall determine from time to time to be necessary to serve as deputies to such officer.

(2) Any person upon whom any demand issued under this section has been duly served shall make such material available for inspection and copying or reproduction to the custodian designated therein at the principal place of business of such person, or at such other place as such custodian and such person thereafter may agree and prescribe in writing or as the court may direct pursuant to this section on the return date specified in such demand, or on such later date as such custodian may prescribe in writing. Such person may upon written agreement between such person and the custodian substitute for copies of all or any part of such material originals thereof.

(3) The custodian to whom any documentary material is so delivered shall take physical possession thereof, and shall be responsible for the use made thereof and for the return thereof pursuant to this chapter. The custodian may cause the preparation of such copies of such documentary material as may be required for official use under regulations which shall be promulgated by the Attorney General. While in the possession of the custodian, no material so produced shall be available for examination, without the consent of the person who produced such material, by any individual other than the Attorney General. Under such reasonable terms and conditions as the Attorney General shall prescribe, documentary material while in the possession of the custodian shall be available for examination by the person who produced such material or any duly authorized representatives of such person.

(4) Whenever any attorney has been designated to appear on behalf of the United States before any court or grand jury in any case or proceeding involving any alleged violation of this chapter, the custodian may deliver to such attorney such documentary material in the possession of the custodian as such attorney determines to be required for use in the presentation of such case or proceeding on behalf of the United States. Upon the conclusion of any such case or proceeding, such attorney shall return to the custodian any documentary material so withdrawn which has not passed into the control of

such court or grand jury through the introduction thereof into the record of such case or proceeding.

(5) Upon the completion of—

(i) the racketeering investigation for which any documentary material was produced under this chapter, and

(ii) any case or proceeding arising from such investigation,

the custodian shall return to the person who produced such material all such material other than copies thereof made by the Attorney General pursuant to this subsection which has not passed into the control of any court or grand jury through the introduction thereof into the record of such case or proceeding.

(6) When any documentary material has been produced by any person under this section for use in any racketeering investigation, and no such case or proceeding arising therefrom has been instituted within a reasonable time after completion of the examination and analysis of all evidence assembled in the course of such investigation, such person shall be entitled, upon written demand made upon the Attorney General, to the return of all documentary material other than copies thereof made pursuant to this subsection so produced by such person.

(7) In the event of the death, disability, or separation from service of the custodian of any documentary material produced under any demand issued under this section or the official relief of such custodian from responsibility for the custody and control of such material, the Attorney General shall promptly—

(i) designate another racketeering investigator to serve as custodian thereof, and

(ii) transmit notice in writing to the person who produced such material as to the identity and address of the successor so designated.

Any successor so designated shall have with regard to such materials all duties and responsibilities imposed by this section upon his predecessor in office with regard thereto, except that he shall not be held responsible for any default or dereliction that occurred before his designation as custodian.

(g) Whenever any person fails to comply with any civil investigative demand duly served upon him under this section or whenever satisfactory copying or reproduction of any such material cannot be done and such person refuses to surrender such material, the Attorney General may file, in the district court of the United States for any judicial district in which such person resides, is found, or transacts business, and serve upon such person a petition for an order of such court for the enforcement of this section, except that if such person transacts business in more than one such district such petition shall be filed in the district in which such person maintains his principal place of business, or in such other district in which such person transacts business as may be agreed upon by the parties to such petition.

(h) Within twenty days after the service of any such demand upon any person, or at any time before the return date specified in the demand, whichever period is shorter, such person may file, in the district court of the United States for the judicial district within which such person resides, is found, or transacts business, and serve upon such custodian a petition for an order of such court modifying or setting aside such demand. The time allowed for compliance with the demand in whole or in part as deemed proper and ordered by the court shall not run during the pendency of such petition in the court. Such petition shall specify each ground upon which the petitioner relies in seeking such relief, and may be based upon any failure of such demand to comply with the provisions of this section or upon any constitutional or other legal right or privilege of such person.

(i) At any time during which any custodian is in custody or control of any documentary material delivered by any person in compliance with any such demand, such person may file, in the district court of the United States for the judicial district within which the office of such custodian is situated, and serve upon such custodian a petition for an order of such court requiring the performance by such custodian of any duty imposed upon him by this section.

(j) Whenever any petition is filed in any district court of the United States under this section, such court shall have jurisdiction to hear and determine the matter so presented, and to enter such order or orders as may be required to carry into effect the provisions of this section.

Table of Cases

All references are to page numbers in the book. All cases are listed by plaintiffs' names as well as by defendants'. However, full citations are given only for the by-plaintiff listings.

Topical Index

About the Author

Gregory P. Joseph is a litigation partner of Fried, Frank, Harris, Shriver & Jacobson in New York. He is a former Chair of the 60,000-member Section of Litigation of the American Bar Association and is a Fellow of the American College of Trial Lawyers. He served for six years on the Advisory Committee on the Federal Rules of Evidence of the United States Judicial Conference, and is a member of the American Law Institute.

Mr. Joseph practices complex commercial litigation. In a world survey conducted by London-based *International Commercial Litigation,* Mr. Joseph was rated one of the ten best commercial litigators in the United States ("The Best in the World," May 1996, p. 9).

He is the author of several books, including *Modern Visual Evidence,* which has been described as "the authoritative text" on that subject (*Communication Arts,* Sept./Oct. 1995 at p. 45), and *Sanctions: The Federal Law of Litigation Abuse* (3d ed. 2000), which is cited in the Advisory Committee Notes to the Federal Rules of Civil Procedure. He is also a member of the Editorial Board of *Moore's Federal Practice* (3d ed. 1997). He served as Chair of the Committee on Professional Responsibility, and is a member of the Executive Committee, of the Association of the Bar of the City of New York. He is also a member of the Board of the Stein Center of Law & Ethics.